THE
PARALLEL
ELECTION

THE
PARALLEL
ELECTION

A BLUEPRINT
FOR DECEPTION

Evidence of Massive Election Fraud in Delaware County,

Pennsylvania in the November 2020 Election

Leah Hoopes   Gregory Stenstrom

THE PARALLEL ELECTION

Title: The Parallel Election

Subtitle: A Blueprint for Deception and Evidence of Massive Election Fraud in Delaware County, Pennsylvania in the November 2020 Election

Library of Congress Cataloging-in-Publishing Data

Authors:

Stenstrom, Gregory

Hoopes, Leah

Publisher: Interrita Publishing

Short Description:

The parallel election, a blueprint for deception and evidence of massive election fraud in Delaware County, Pennsylvania in the November 2020 election.

Long Description:

This book documents, in great detail and with irrefutable evidence, the massive election fraud that was perpetrated against the citizenry in the November 2020 United States general election, which resulted in the installation of an illegitimate government. We show you, up close, how it was done, and by whom. We call it a "parallel election," because obtaining the fraudulent results they manufactured required the wholesale substitution of fake ballots for authentic ones.

Genre: History, United States, 21st Century

ISBN: 978-1-958682-29-6 Paperback

ISBN: 978-1-958682-28-9 Hardcover

ISBN: 978-1-958682-27-2 Ebook

www.parallelelection.com

Gregory Stenstrom is Co-Founder of Www.Patriot.Online, a digital privacy ecosystem and social media platform. He has extensive experience in computer sciences, security, and fraud investigations, and a reputation as a formidable problem solver who distills complexity into actionable simplicity. A former US Naval Officer, he served as a Surface Warfare Officer, and in Commanding and Executive Officer roles for Special Warfare and Special Operations. He holds a Bachelor of Science degree from the United States Naval Academy, Annapolis, MD.

Leah Hoopes is a business owner, and Republican Committeewoman for Bethel Township in Delaware County, Pennsylvania. As a Krav Maga instructor and practitioner, she trains women in self-defense both physically, and emotionally. She is a highly effective political activist, who develops strategic plans, and recruits experts and advocates to execute them. She holds an Associate of Arts degree in Criminal Justice from Delaware Community College and an Associates of Science degree in Physical Therapy from Harcum College.

They are plaintiffs in the only remaining election fraud cases in Pennsylvania from the November 2020 general election. Viciously quashed, sued and sanctioned for challenging the "most secure election in history," they fought back, and overcame overwhelming odds to successfully expose the massive election fraud they witnessed.

FORWARD

Conveying the true events and proof of massive election fraud described in this book came at a steep price to our family, friends, finances, and personal lives. We didn't want to do this, derived no pleasure from it, and only did so because our law enforcement agencies, justice departments, courts, and elected officials failed to do their duty from local to national levels. We hope this book will motivate them to reconsider their oaths, and encourage citizens to exert their rights, and take a greater part in their own governance.

In 1841, Thomas Carlyle wrote, *"(Edmund) Burke said there were Three Estates in Parliament; but, in the Reporters' Gallery yonder, there sat a Fourth Estate more important far than they all"* (On Heroes and Hero Worship). Carlyle, who had used the expression four years earlier, during the French Revolution saw the press as instrumental in cultivating democracy, providing the fertilizer and oxygen for people to rise against tyranny.

Long ago, the New York Times was a beacon of honest journalism. When they were lions, they set the standard for holding our government accountable, with the landmark case *New York Times Co. v. Sullivan, 376 U.S. 254, 270 (1964).* It cemented their reputation as our nation's "newspaper of record." That illustrious history has faded to be replaced with reporting and opinions so biased and venomous, that it is now mere propaganda. In *Sullivan,* the US Supreme Court ruled that:

"The government may not silence speech because it criticizes government officials or employees, or their favorite ideas or initiatives, even if that speech does so in ways that many people may find unpleasant. Allegations of hurt feelings, real or spurious, do not justify censorship of public speech.

The First Amendment of the US Constitution embodies "a profound national commitment to the principle that debate on public issues should be uninhibited, robust, and wide-open, and that it may well include vehement, caustic, and sometimes unpleasantly sharp attacks on government and public officials."

Building on *New York Times v Sullivan*, another precedent setting case on free speech stated: "Viewpoint discrimination is anathema to free expression and is impermissible in both public and nonpublic fora. So, if the government allows speech on a certain subject, it must accept all viewpoints on the subject, even those that it disfavors or that are unpopular." *Pittsburgh League of Young Voters Educ. Fund v. Port Auth.*, 653 F.3d 290, 296 (3d Cir. 2011)

The notion that the November 2020 election was "the safest and most secure election in history" is a viewpoint that has been foisted upon the citizenry by corrupt components of government, and propagandized by a Fourth Estate that has forgotten it's duty.

It has been left to the disenfranchised and forgotten citizenry to remember the words of Benjamin Franklin, who warned that it was up to us to keep the Republic our nation's founders had bestowed.

They left us the tools to do so in the US Constitution, the first being our right to document our experience and findings in this book, and redress our grievances directly to our representatives.

We hope this book will spur those whom we have (actually) elected to govern us, in our State legislatures and the US Congress, to also remember our Constitution – and act on it.

ACKNOWLEDGMENTS

All things are brought to us by the grace of God and the choices we make. All glory and honor to God.

I would like to thank my fiancée, Lilliana, who loves the United States of America, her new country, for her support during the writing of this book. Her journey to citizenship, to bring her children -- now my son and daughter-- a better life is the story of our nation. She has been my inspiration for writing this book. My Mom and Dad have been, and still are my forever guides, and my true north. My four older sons and my grandchildren will all live in the world we leave to them, and they are why I keep going. All things considered, I would have preferred to have spent the time with all of them, and my aunts, uncles, cousins, and extended family, than on the tasks herein. We will do that starting now. This is my opportunity to express my love and gratitude that they continue to forgive and love me anyway.

To the Brigade, of the US Naval Academy, those that came before, those I served with, and those who followed - stay the course. Of all the duties we must honor, the first is a duty to know, and the second is to speak the truth, no matter the cost.

So many friends to thank. I will start with my brothers Stephen and William; then, Thomas, Brian, Patrick, Sean, Eva, Dmitri, David, Scott, Phil & Kay, Todd Beringer, the Michaels, Dan, Ken & Vicki, Bill, George, John, Elmo, Kevin C., Peggy & Joe, Cheryl, MK Justice, Kim W, Mary Ann, Jan V., Rick, Dr. Michael, Dr. Elizabeth, Gloria, Jodi, Richard, Val, Marea, Danielle, Tabitha, Toni, Kevin, Joe, Ian, Barron, Vince, Robert, Matt, Dave H, Bruce, Sandra, Sofia, Michelle, Karen, Andre, Susan, Joe, Tom, Donna, Nicole, FreePA, Audit the Vote PA, True the Vote, Project Amistad, The Thomas More Society, Richard P, Nik H, Your Content, Karen, Crack'd Egg, and JEXIT. Leah and I share many friends, and my thanks to everyone and every organization she has also listed below.

I am a product of our public schools, and would be remiss not to thank my teachers and friends from Stoughton Public Schools, Stoughton, Massachusetts, with special mention of my journalism teacher Mr. Tapper, my coach Mr. Charles Green, and guidance counselor Mr. Murphy.

My deepest thanks to Deborah Frankel Silver, Bruce Castor, and all the attorneys who answered the call when no one else would, who risked their livelihoods to represent us, we owe our eternal gratitude. They have honored the law and bar.

No acknowledgements would be complete without thanking our publishing mentor Gray, a patriot committed to sharing the evidence. We asked Gray to find the best editor and biggest skeptic he could, to make us prove our case. Lisa Schiffren, our editor and now my friend, and confidante, delivered.

And of course, I must thank Leah Hoopes, my friend and fellow patriot. Look where you have brought us Spartacus.

— Gregory Stenstrom, May 19th, 2022

First and foremost, all glory to God . Romans 8:28. And we know that all things work together for good to them that love God, to them who are the called according to his purpose. In every chapter of my life, my faith in God has kept me grounded, and placed me into a position I was meant to be in, always.

To my parents John and Kathy, without my upbringing, the values, and morals you instilled in me, I would not be where I am today. Your love, support, advice, and convictions are what molded me. I would not be where I am without you. Thank you for teaching me to be grateful, and to cherish my Country, and most importantly to fight for her.

My husband Zach and my son Chase, I am forever grateful for your support and understanding of the sacrifices that were made so that I could pursue the truth. Zach you are my rock, and have stuck by me through all the craziness. God brought us together for his purpose and I am blessed to call you my partner in life. To my son Chase, you are the reason I fight – your mama bear will always protect you. You gave me purpose 16 years ago, and made me a better human. Be a simple man with conviction, morals, and fight for what is right. My hope is to leave you a better Country, and freedom. I love you both beyond words.

My sister, nieces, dear friends, and family, I am beyond thankful for your love and support and sticking by me through this entire endeavor. Thank you for knowing my heart, and believing in me. Without all of you I could not have gotten through this incredibly stressful, challenging, and tumultuous journey.

To our lawyers who took us on when nobody else would, we are forever grateful. Deborah Silver, Bruce Castor, and those who supported us.

Some names I would like to acknowledge who are also fighting the good fight on the frontlines, who seek no applause or the limelight:

Kim W of Crack'd Egg, Matthew F, Vicki C, Michael M, Nik Hatziefstathiou, Sandi, Cheryl and Ron F, Ken and Vicki, Herb K, Jim, Michael K, Doug, Sam, Bill, Scott and Dina, Helene, Bevin, Alex D, Nichole M, Stephen M, Donna V, Mary Ann Y, MK Justice, Diana C, Peggy and Joe, Cheryl G, Jenn D, Anita, Maria, Val H, Alfe, Joe D, Diane, Sandra, Mike, Lia, Susan S, Becky F, Kim W, Nancy G, Donna E, Steve L, Ben J, Theresa, Brenda, Cynthia, Gail, Carlos and Susan, Jolene B, Danielle L, Dotty, John C, George, Keith, Jaime, Mike A, Lynn R, Wendy, Jason, Kellie, Ebony, Heather, and Bill Lawrence.

Organizations: Delco Watchdogs, Moms For Liberty, No Left Turn In Education, Lehigh Valley Tea Party, Patriots of PA - all chapters, AAPS, Lions For Liberty, Rush Echo Notes, Frontline Doctors, America First Patriots Club, Garnet Valley School Board Parents Group, True the Vote, Project Veritas, Project Amistad, JEXIT, Nick Moseder, and Your Content News.

To Greg, thank you for standing with me Spock.

— Leah Hoopes, May 19th, 2022

TABLE OF CONTENTS

INTRODUCTION

This book documents, in great detail and with irrefutable evidence, the massive election fraud that was perpetrated against the citizenry in the November 2020 United States general election, which resulted in the installation of an illegitimate government.

We will show you, up close, how it was done, and by whom. We call it a *"parallel election,"* because obtaining the fraudulent results they manufactured required the wholesale substitution of fake ballots for authentic ones.

If you are going to bother paying hundreds of millions of dollars to install "transformative" election reforms in 28 States allowing millions of "no excuse" mail-in ballots; then install centralized counting centers, and remove chain of custody, in 8 swing states and 32 pivot counties that would make it easy to swap out "real" mail-in ballots and USB vDrives vote records for fake ones - then why wouldn't you?

A "sting" like that would be irresistible, with the only downside being you would have to disavow and destroy all evidence after the election – unless someone was lying in wait and caught you red-handed.

Ours is a bottom-up perspective. Our focus is Delaware County, Pennsylvania, directly south of Philadelphia, where, while serving as certified poll watchers, we experienced and documented first-hand, the events that follow; and where 327,000 votes were fraudulently certified that were not the authentic votes of the citizens. The race in Pennsylvania, a critical swing state, was decided by a far smaller margin.

The methods of fraud we investigated and documented were repeated in multiple other states, as were the subsequent cover-ups, and the attacks and derision aimed at those working to expose them. Our proof consists of not only what we have in hand, but also what we know they wantonly destroyed to hide their crimes.

What will be most painful to the pundits who would otherwise be quick to disavow and exclaim "debunkment" of our evidence, is that our litigative opponents have begrudgingly confirmed in their own legal responses that what we allege is, in fact, true, but that for a myriad of reasons, it should be "inadmissible." As if by legal double-speak, the fact that hundreds of thousands of fraudulent ("fake") mail in ballots, and tens of thousands of fraudulent digital votes, that we both witnessed and have confirmed with hard physical evidence, that stole our Republic, should be ignored for technicalities usually reserved as fodder for traffic court, rather than a nation in turmoil.

Beyond our demonstration of election fraud, we report what happens to ordinary citizens when they try to expose that fraud. We – Leah Hoopes and Greg Stenstrom – have now spent a year and a half battling with both the media and the judicial system, as well as political forces close to home, and others in Washington D.C, to get a fair hearing for our evidence. So far that has not happened.

Among the most difficult obstacles we have faced in exposing the outrageous cheating that occurred in November of 2020 is a media establishment that has long since, and very openly, abandoned its historical role as an independent watchdog and Fourth Estate. Indeed, so fully do adversaries of our US Republic control the mainstream narrative, routinely dismissing the very premise of the stolen election as a "lie" and dismissing those of us who know otherwise as delusional, that they have effectively promoted a fatalism and sense of helplessness even among those who know better.

It is now May of 2022, yet major newspapers and other media outlets persist in intoning, when the topic comes up, usually with regards to former President Trump, that 'there was no election fraud.' 'The cheating, which did not happen....' "Election fraud – which has been debunked..." as if these quasi-religious incantations actually make their contentions true. It remains to be seen what effect the precedent of having to acknowledge that Hunter Biden's infamous laptop was real, will have on other reporting. In any case, polls show that among Republicans, the overwhelming majority believe the election was stolen, and a healthy minority of Democrats share that view.

At the same time, progressives and those who are part of the 'Uniparty' political machine within the judiciary and law enforcement, have blocked serious questioning of the 2020 results by effectively defanging the civil and criminal statutes specifically designed to stop fraud.

Little wonder that, at least in the establishment media, the obvious first question never gets asked: Given his adversaries' behavior throughout the Trump presidency – from the endless touting of the Russia hoax even after it was exposed as a fraud, to the multiple failed impeachments, to the shameless pursuit of Trump associates by the FBI and intelligence agencies – how could anyone doubt that they were beyond fixing an election to remove him from office?

For the record: Our efforts to reveal the truth have nothing to do with our party affiliations, though we are both registered Republicans. We will show that the notion that the "DNC Services Corporation PAC" otherwise known as the "Democratic National Committee" (DNC) represents "Democrats," and that the "Republican National Committee Inc" (RNC) represents "Republicans" is highly dubious, in many meaningful ways. In many places, including Delaware County, they are two corporate heads on a single body – a "Uniparty."

We do not take them on lightly. During our investigation, we have been viciously attacked in the media, physically threatened, and attacked financially. We have been called liars, "Trumpanzees," and worse. We have had FBI special agents, and special agents who work for Pennsylvania State Attorney General Josh Shapiro, show up at our doors. We have been sanctioned and sued. The January 6th Committee is rounding up "seditionists" and "terrorists" who are questioning the election; former U.S. Attorney General Bill Barr called one of us a liar in his book; and powerful DNC insiders have donated $2.5 million, and committed $25 million, to the "65 Project" to directly target and attack us, and our attorneys. This is no one's idea of a good position to be in. But we have persisted, and meticulously assembled our cases, with professionalism, and modest warrant.

Our allegations are undeniable, backed by physical evidence, including documents, video, audio, photos, emails, sworn testimony, affidavits, and admissions. We hope you will avail yourself of the video links and websites we include, even if you are reading this on paper.

We do not claim to be special. We are common citizens who value anonymity. But we recognize that for America to be saved, and our constitutional republic restored, requires that enough ordinary people stand up to be counted. For that to happen, the American people need to know what really transpired on November 3, 2020.

Many charges have been made here in Pennsylvania, and in other states, since election day. Simultaneously, a great many people, both Republican and Democrat, have asserted that there was no fraud, or, more carefully, not enough to make a difference.

But eighteen months later conclusions are starting to change in several of the affected swing states as evidence accumulates and finds its way to the public record. As private citizens and intervenors we were required to patiently "exhaust administrative remedies" and proceed on dictated timelines that did not allow publication of this book until now. We submit that authorities who, at the time may have felt that it made sense to accept whatever the results appeared to be, for the sake of political peace, (or because Donald Trump seemed too threatening to continue in office), might be ready to re-evaluate what actually occurred.

We know that decertification of the fraudulent vote here in Pennsylvania and in other States may not occur, and power may not change hands in Harrisburg, PA, or Washington, DC, as a result of accepting what we believe is the truth, as it should. But this is a bigger issue than who governs for a few years. What is at issue is whether, going forward, we will have a Republic, or a totalitarian government, put in place with fake elections, as is common among such regimes. We want the truth to be known to fix our corrupted system.

As we write, it looks like a Republican sweep should be coming in 2022, in response to the fraud, and the across-the-board polarizing far left policies of the Biden Administration. *But* -- what difference will it make who citizens vote for, if elections are decided by fraudulent processes?

And why would people who succeeded in using fraudulent processes to gain and hold power change their behavior if no one believes that they did it the first time?

They won't.

We have done this work, and authored this book, with everything to lose, and nothing to gain -- except the restoration of our Republic.

N.B. For those readers eager to get straight to the evidence, please see the "Election Day," "Parallel Election," first and then "Appendix A"

1

THE "UNIPARTY" AND THE DELAWARE COUNTY "MACHINE"

Delaware County, Pennsylvania sits just south of Philadelphia. It is known by those who live here as "Delco."

There are just over 570,000 people in the county, and the median household income is $74,477. The county is comprised of a pretty ordinary bunch of suburbs, and a few larger townships, like Chester, which have significant minority populations.

Where Delco differs from your average suburban county, is that it has been run by a political machine for going on 150 years. For the first century, that machine was solidly Republican. In the past several decades it has become mixed: GOP and Democrat.

THE UNIPARTY RULES DELAWARE COUNTY

The Uniparty is a central figure in the events of November 3, 2020. <u>It is the villain in the story</u>. To understand how politics work on a normal day in Delco, you need to understand how the Uniparty machine works, because it is responsible for the career trajectories of most politicians who get elected to office. And it is certainly responsible for ensuring that voting occurs on election day – and how that happens, and then it is responsible for counting the vote.

The machine that ran Delaware County for more than a century, starting in the 1870s, was wholly Republican. That may seem odd, since most of us are used to histories of big Democrat political machines, like Tammany Hall, in New York City, or the Prendergast Machine in Kansas City, Missouri. Those were wiped out, partly by the New Deal, which handed out the goods that party bosses had previously provided, and with some deliberate intent by FDR; and partly by the long decades of low immigration, which cut the 'client base' of the ward bosses. The next generation familial patronage houses like the Daley and Kennedy Machines went to ground or dissipated by attrition. But some non-urban machines survived and quietly flourished by flying under the radar, like the Four Families of California, and this peculiarly Republican one in "Delco."

The election fraud of 2020 was national in scope, as it would have had to be to guarantee that the Democrat candidate won. But it is necessary to understand how it works at the local level, where the fraud must take place. Whatever large scale political machinations Democrats were up to nationally, and however much local Democrats may have agreed with the specific goal of getting rid of Donald Trump, still, at the local level the fraud depended on the usual willingness to manipulate the election, as the political machine leaders have been doing for decades. Challenging the fraud requires an understanding of a very tight-knit collaboration between the Uniparty and various business interests that include closely held law firms, family accounting firms, local and county law enforcement departments that might be cooperative, local justice departments, and members of the judiciary. All of whom work together when it suits them, and any other personage with a substantial financial interest in creating an integrated political, law enforcement, and justice environment that will be favorable to them in myriad legal and financial transactions between elections. It is within this corporate fabric that the machinations of election fraud are perpetrated.

DELCO'S 150-YEAR-OLD MACHINE

In Delco, this malignant cooperative is referred to as "The Machine," and it's roots are very well documented in the book *Ruling Suburbia: John J. McClure and the Republican Machine in Delaware County, Pennsylvania,* by John Morrison McLarnon III. The machine was founded in the 1870s, by William "Billy' McClure. He ran it successfully till shortly before his death, in 1907, while also amassing a large fortune by controlling the liquor licenses in the county. At his death leadership passed to his then 21-year-old son, John. Though it took John McClure a few years to learn how to run the operation, he stuck at it until his own death in 1965. He was widely respected by the people and institutions that matter in Delco. In those 90 years of McClure rule, the county was reliably Republican, though heavily minority precincts voted for a couple of Democrats for President: notably FDR and John F. Kennedy.

According to *Ruling Suburbia*, McClure's machine "employed a wide variety of forms of election fraud: chain voting, repeat voting, assisted voting, naturalization mills, phantom polling locations, vote buying, police intimidation, the use of rouge, oil, and mirrors on voting machines, and ringing out opposition candidates. An assiduously applied patronage system, a remarkable ability to co-opt dangerous opponents, and a rigorously enforced policy were also integral to McClure's success."

McClure relied on hand-picked lieutenants across the county, not ward bosses. Some were in private industry, some were elected officials, and others were in patronage jobs.

McClure maintained a carefully crafted, ambiguous status for the machine itself. Known as the "Delaware County Republican Board of Supervisors," it was nicknamed "the War Board." This existed in addition to the official corporate party entity, called the Republican Executive Committee. The War Board ruled the county. They "slated candidates, set policy, dispensed patronage, and settled all important political questions."

As the author notes, John McClure had a remarkable career between 1907 and his death in 1965. "The citizens of Delaware County supported and continue to support the machine because the machine delivered...the things that citizens want most." At the turn of the century, those included "food, work and police protection to Chester's European and Black immigrants." (Black 'immigrants' were migrants from the South). During Prohibition, the machine provided liquor, and in the Depression, patronage jobs. "In the 1950s and 1960s, the machine kept taxes low...and discouraged Black people from settling in historically white communities. The trash was collected, the snow ploughed (sic), the streets repaired." Busses ran, little league was organized, and, in short, the machine provided what voters saw as value. In exchange, the machine controlled the entire political apparatus, and plenty of the judicial and law enforcement infrastructure as well. Over the course of the past 50 years, the county has become more Democratic, and the machine has become a bi-party entity, which we will describe shortly.

The point of this brief history of Delco's firmly ensconced political machine is to ensure that readers understand that the mechanisms for fraud were already in place, have always existed, and have always been used.

Nothing we are going to tell you about how the vote was stolen in 2020 is either new, or inconsistent with past elections, though it may sound fanciful and excessively conspiracist to those who believe that honest elections are the norm. In the old days, however, the Republican machine would not have thrown the vote to a Democratic candidate. In the Trump era, many Republican operatives 'identify' as #neverTrumpers. Which explains their willing collaboration in Delco in 2020.

Decades of political chatter have led some people to believe that a centralized global "cabal" controls the world. We found the opposite. The old Tip O'Neill saying is true: "All politics are local." Look no further than your neighbors in the town and county where you live to understand who holds real power, legitimate or otherwise. Celebrity oligarchs, like Soros, Zuckerberg, Gates, Bezos, the Koch brothers, and the Clintons, can certainly take actions that affect outcomes. Their money often makes a real difference, as was the case in 2020. That is particularly true of Soros backed candidates at the state levels who had been put in place; and with the 400 million dollars donated by the Zuckerberg's to ramp up the voter registration (real, or not), in Democratic areas (both of which we will discuss later on).

And that goes double for the tech lords and the media with their mighty power of censorship when problematic stories about the Bidens arose.

But who knows what all that would add up to, in terms of vote tallies, without the compliance and hard work of local politicians. Elections are stolen by people who sit on your County Councils, or work for the Board of Elections, and the folks who count your votes.

WHO RULES DELCO NOW?

The current Uniparty machine in Delco consists of a small group of individuals, with a pedigree that goes back to the 1950s. Political party bosses have worked cooperatively for decades to install candidates to attend to their needs, and to extract jobs, salaries, contracts, pensions, perks, and other monies from government coffers.

For the record, Delco is not unique. Delco's political microcosm is all but identical to what has evolved in many other counties in the United States: relatively small corporate bodies control large swaths of land, money, votes, and big parts of the lives of hundreds of thousands of people. These are modern day political fiefdoms. It's a wonder that no one thought of marshalling them for a national operation prior to the recent past.

You may be thinking, "it makes no sense for Republicans and Democrats to work together." When most people think of the Republican Party in Delco, an image of 159,000 ideologically conservative Republicans comes to mind. What Republican would work in tandem with Democrats to arrange outcomes that don't necessarily favor Republicans? We can't speak to their thought processes. But we can tell you who these individuals are. During the November 2020 election, the RNC in Delco was represented by the Delaware County Republican Executive Committee," the "**DCREC**" for short. This influential committee was comprised of:

- Tom McGarrigle - Chairman 2019-Present. Delaware County Council, PA State Senator, businessman, and owner of G+M Automotive shop and a towing company.

- Andy Reilly – Chairman, 2009—2019. Attorney at Saxton & Stump, in Philadelphia, he was formerly on the Board of the Delaware River Port Authority (DRPA) and Delaware County Solid Waste Authority. He became Chairman of the five-county Southeast

Caucus for the RNC since the election, after passing the DCREC Chairman position to McGarrigle in what he called in press releases a "unanimous vote" (of one).

- John McBlain – Attorney at Saxton & Stump. Former Delaware County Council Chairman. Jail (GEO) Oversight Board Member. McBlain was both an executive and General Counsel of the DCREC during the November 2020 general election, and represented both of us as Certified Poll Watchers, and Intervenors when he filed our first injunction demanding access to ballot canvassing (handling) areas against the three-member Delaware County Board of Elections (BOE). He (and the DCREC) later refused to respond to any further filings or related litigation after the election, and McBlain was subsequently appointed to the Board of Elections (BOE) sometime in 2021, only months after supposedly opposing them on our behalf.

- Thomas Judge was an executive member of the DCREC, and its chairman for 34 years, from 1975--2009, preceding Reilly. He died at age 91 in April

2020, before the May 2020 primary, and was Carol Miller's uncle (see below). Judge was Chairman of the Delaware County Solid Waste Management Authority, Director of the five-county Southeast Caucus for the GOP (now held by Reilly) and was Chairman of President George H.W. Bush's presidential campaign for Pennsylvania.

- Carol Miller - Executive Director/Vice Chair of the DCREC since 1992, She is the niece of Thomas Judge.

The interchangeability between the phrases "RNC," "GOP," "DCREC," "Republican Party," "Republican Party of Delaware County," "Delaware County GOP," and all of the variants in PR releases, campaign materials, websites, and all public facing branding is quite intentional, and meant to condition the citizenry to believe they are all one, blended, singular brand.

But, make no mistake, the Delaware County Republican Executive Committee, *is* the Republican Party, and more precisely, *McGarrigle, Reilly, McBlain, and Miller **are** the party*. They ultimately – and unilaterally - decide who the "Republican Party" in Delco will promote, fund, accept "donations" from, manipulate, direct, and endorse as candidates, and position for primary elections. Their lieutenants, and direct reports are many of the Township and Borough GOP Chairs, and those angling for positions within the GOP.

The DCREC and its lieutenants work a lot like "The Sopranos," the TV series about an organized crime family in northern New Jersey. In that series, the real "boss" of the family, Tony Soprano, installs his uncle "Junior" Soprano, as the public facing head of the family, to divert attention from himself. Much like the show, the DCREC and GOP "boss," is reportedly <u>Bobby Willert,</u> who is a direct familial descendent of the "Machine" that is the subject of *"Ruling Suburbia."* Willert is to Tony Soprano, as McGarrigle is to "Junior" Soprano, and a key figure in the Delaware County "Machine."

<u>Dave White</u> is Willert's "Number One," who runs the current iteration of the Delco "machine" with Willert, and was a 2022 gubernatorial primary candidate for Pennsylvania. White represents himself as a blue collar "working Joe,' and "HVAC guy" when in fact, he is among the wealthiest multi-millionaires and arguably one of the most influential political operatives and "king makers" in Pennsylvania.

The authors of this book are both registered Republicans, but stand (very) far apart from the GOP and DNC corporate machines and Uniparty that have taken over the electoral processes.

So, while Democratic party operatives were the primary orchestrators and executors of the election fraud during the November 2020 election cycle, they were only able to carry it off with the cooperation and collaboration of the GOP, and specifically, the DCREC.

Without an adversarial relationship between parties, and their DNC and GOP corporate entities, we lose much of the checks and balances that were a primary assumption of the authors of the U.S. Constitution.

The "Uniparty" model of politics, which has devolved from reaching across the aisle to sitting in each other's laps, has turned the US election process from a robust competition into mere political theater in many places. When people ask, "How did that corrupt idiot get elected?" the odds are good that the person was not elected, but rather installed by the Uniparty.

Unfortunately, many State Attorneys General, District Attorneys, judges, and members of law enforcement are beholden to, or in the pocket of, today's Delco machine as well.

Understanding that the Uniparty wages political and legal warfare against anyone who opposes them helps to explain why you hear so little about these matters. Political machines like Delco's, deploy intimidation, propaganda, cognitive warfare, and, especially, controlled opposition, to great advantage, both here on the home front, and across the country.

HOW IT WORKS NOW

The GOP, DCREC, and DNC Uniparty corporate entities leverage their respective minions to select, endorse, and install their people into County Council, the body that administers and directs all monies and contracts in the county. The largest expenditures in Delco's $794 million budget (and most other Pennsylvania counties), are:

- "Social Welfare" (Prisons, Water Authorities, Schools, and Waste Management)

- "Courts" (judges, lawyers, and solicitors)

- "Transportation" (Roads and infrastructure).

In Delco, the prisons were privatized and are operated by "GEO Group, Inc." (formerly Wackenhut), which slurp up tens of millions of dollars annually, from Delco's $100 million social welfare budget. DELCORA, the Delaware County Regional Water Authority, is another prime beneficiary of Uniparty largesse. County controlled boards and especially school systems are also ripe plums for patronage and solicitorships where favored Uniparty lawyers suck up large legal fees. Port Authority and Waste Management services, and a few other big budget entities are on the list as well, but for illustrative purposes we'll focus on the prisons and water authorities, though all of the county services provide patronage financial fuel for the Uniparty.

The Chester Water Authority (CWA), DELCORA (also water), and GEO (prisons), are all willing landing pads for politicians in between positions, and also serve as retirement stops for cash outs for political operatives and politicians.

Tom Killion, PA State Senator for whom I (Gregory) was a poll watcher, withdrew his litigation for November 2020 election violations by the Board of Elections, after he lost his incumbency, when "all his people had found homes," and he had reportedly landed at DELCORA or CWA. Killion had introduced a bill to grant CWA $100 million in CARES Act funding shortly before the 2020 election.

Andy Reilly and John McBlain resigned from the DCREC since we filed our litigation and are reportedly idling one and two counties from Delco at their respective water authorities. McBlain was appointed to serve out Jim Byrne's term as GOP minority member on the Board of Elections (BOE), that he first sued for election violations and fraud on behalf of the DCREC, Leah Hoopes and Gregory Stenstrom, and then inexplicably dropped, declaring "there was no fraud" as he exited, stage left, to take on his new political patronage positions, solicitorships, and prizes.

HOW CORRUPTION OPERATES TODAY: GEO GROUP'S LONG HISTORY OF ABETTING CORRUPTION

(The description below is detailed and complicated. In a nutshell it tracks the way the DCREC gets money allocated to the private prison services company called GEO Group, and then the way that it sends politicians who are retiring, or out of office, off to GEO Group, to fill actual jobs, or serve on the board. This material, with much credit to the investigative prowess of "Nik the Hat" and "Your Content" News, is here to illustrate the actual transactional corruption of

Delco politics, and politics in the state of Penn-
sylvania, on any normal day.)

On November 12, 2009, Pennsylvania GOP State representative, and former House Speaker, John M. Perzel, was charged with 82 counts of theft, conflict of interest, conspiracy, obstruction of justice and hindering apprehension or prosecution. Perzel had been a member of the board of directors of GEO Group, the nation's second-largest private prison firm, for years.

Perzel, his brother-in-law, a nephew, two former chiefs of Perzel's staff and five other people with ties to the Pennsylvania House GOP caucus (including two former district attorneys) were charged with spending approximately $10 million in State funds to develop advanced computer programs that were used by the GOP to commit election fraud to their benefit.

Perzel resigned as a member of GEO Group's board, a position he had held since 2005. Perzel was paid a salary of $20,000 a year as a GEO board member plus board fees and options; those fees and options were worth $147,953 in 2008.

As a separate matter, and fast forwarding from 2008 to the time of authoring this book, federal prosecutors have reportedly convened at-least two grand juries to consider whether criminal charges can be lodged against former Delaware County lawmakers, political party bosses and their consultants.

The statewide sting operation involves a large group of whistleblowers ranging from law enforcement to former court clerks and consultants, one source said, noting she testified before both state and federal grand juries about the evolving situation. The probe involves former and current elected officials spanning across Pennsylvania who partook in 'pay-to-play' style scandals throughout their political careers.

Prosecutors are specifically interested in Delaware County, where the private prison industry was born in the '90s before being replicated throughout the United States. 'Ground Zero' as prosecutors called it, appears to be Upper Darby Township.

George Wackenhut, former FBI agent, and founder of Wackenhut Security, which became one of the largest private security firms in the United States, would later branch out into corrections, and evolve into today's biggest global name in private imprisonment: GEO Group.

"It all comes down to greed." They almost got away with what the prosecutor described as "the greatest and largest conspiracy in modern history."

The ongoing grand jury investigations resembles 2014's Operation Mississippi Hustle, named for then-Mississippi Attorney General Jim Hood, who coordinated the FBI investigation, where conspirators devised pay-to-play private prison schemes that involved a chain of command - a lobbyist, a lawmaker, a commissioner, and a judge. The commissioner works hand-in-glove with local political power players to award private prisons - such as Florida-based GEO Group - lucrative multi-million-dollar contracts. From there, when legislation or an executive action impacts prison capacity at privately-owned facilities, a lawmaker advocates against the regulation - and, if unsuccessful, that's where the judge comes in.

In the 2020 election iteration of the "Mississippi Hustle," elected officials at all levels then intentionally lose reelection, resign, or retire after receiving job offers from private prisons through their cronies who offer lucrative and unusually hefty signing bonuses for turning against President Trump. *Since its beginning - GEO Group has picked up 344 office holders at the end of their tenure.* The GEO Group is apolitical, and funds whichever party has the most turnout or potential in the region.

Similarly, in Maricopa County, Arizona - GEO Group funneled cash to Arizona Gov. Doug Ducey in 2014 - and shortly thereafter, prison executives were awarded a contract worth over $70 million a year.

Several Pennsylvania lawmakers received strings of large donations from individuals with affiliations to GEO Group, in addition to Speaker of the House, and Republican State Rep. John M. Perzel mentioned above.

Pennsylvania US Senator Pat Toomey involved himself in a questionable 'shell donation' scandal involving two other lawmakers and a lobbyist. He received $22,392 from Stewart company employees, who lobby for GEO Group.

At the federal level, campaign finance data tracked by the Center for Responsive Politics show Stewart employee money went not just to Toomey but also to Rep. Scott Perry ($17,000) and former Rep. Todd Platts ($25,000), both PA GOP, since 2006.

GEO was awarded a contract in two of the senator's jurisdictions, and Platts was elected and sworn in afterwards as a York County (PA) Common Pleas Judge, despite having no obvious qualifications for a judgeship, displacing a highly experienced judge.

This is just a small list of ugly transactions which have broken through in the media, or are being investigated by some legal arm of the state.

We could fill another book with cases of private-public corruption and the relationships and finances at county level authorities like the CWA and DELCORA. GEO is just one representative example.

We want you to understand what the game is, and how seriously it is played, in Delco and elsewhere.

2

ELECTION DAY, NOVEMBER 3RD, 2020

GREGORY STENSTROM

On November 3, 2020, I showed up to watch the polls to which I had been assigned. I was assigned as the sole GOP poll watcher for 36 precincts (1-1 through 11-6), located in Chester City, Pennsylvania, of which I was able to inspect and observe 22 precincts.

If this seems like a lot, it was. But I am a professional data and forensic computer scientist, and experienced in security, fraud, and corruption investigations, among other things, so I was comfortable with the assignment. Because I have this specific professional background, I know what I am looking for when I serve as a poll watcher. I strove to be scrupulous in doing my job with both the letter and the spirit of the law in mind.

The Delaware County Board of Elections had provided me with a notarized certificate of appointment as a poll watcher on behalf of PA Senator Tom Killion. I presented it when requested at the polling locations in Chester City on Election Day.

On November 3rd, I observed poll workers in multiple assigned Chester City polling places, which included the 1-3, 1-4, 1-6, 2-1, 2-2, 2-3, 11-2, and several others, providing regular ballots, rather than provisional ballots, to voters who were told they had registered to vote by mail, without making them sign in the registration book. I challenged the practice in those precincts where I observed it, and while I was present, they then stopped the practice and began providing provisional ballots.

People were waiting patiently in lines, excited to vote. Despite Chester City being a historically Democrat stronghold, there appeared to be some voters in the mix who planned to vote Republican based on campaign provided clothing, accessories, and more than a few (surreptitious) thumbs up. I was informed at each polling location by their respective judge of elections that I was the only GOP poll watcher they had seen in this 2020 election, or any other election they could remember.

At about 6:00PM I went to the Delco "Wharf Building" counting center in Chester City located on Seaport Avenue on the Delaware River, with my certificate, to observe, as the sole poll watcher from the Tom Killion Campaign, as authorized and tasked to do so by Killion's campaign manager, Cody Bright. Bright had been informed, and he informed me that throughout the day that there were "a dozen national level GOP poll watchers" at the counting center, observing and monitoring ballot canvassing. This turned out to be untrue.

I checked into the building and took the elevator from the ground floor to the 1st floor counting room, where I was denied entry, to which I objected, and was then surrounded first by four municipal Park Police, and then an additional five joined them. I presented my poll watcher certificate and refused to leave, at which point I was threatened with physical removal and arrest. I calmly stood my ground to the perplexment of the (9) police officers, and firmly stated I was a certified poll watcher, lawfully carrying out my duties, and that it was unlawful on their part to attempt to remove me from a canvassing area. Deputy Sheriff Mike Donohue joined the police officers, taking charge, and instructed me to leave - without explanation - and then further stated that if I did not comply, they would physically remove me, and arrest me. Being surrounded by law enforcement officers, and being threatened with (unlawful) arrest is an occupational hazard when performing physical security assessments and government corruption and fraud investigations, and I took the threat in stride. Police officers are trained professionals, and instinctually respond positively to command authority and quiet professionalism, which I in turn have been trained in.

As a former US naval officer, executive officer and commanding officer of special operations and special warfare units, I am quite experienced in asserting authority, even without a uniform or badge. While I would not recommend a civilian without those skillsets refuse to comply with a police officer, I stated amiably that while I didn't want a physical confrontation, that that would be what it was going to take to make me leave, and that I would try not to injure any of the (9) officers. That de-escalated the situation and got a few chuckles and an easing of body language among the (much younger) officers. I include this detail both because it happened, and to indicate how a civilian can stand his ground successfully. The incident was the primary reason I was uniquely able to move about and gain access that watchers in other voting centers across the country were denied.

With a break in the tension, Sheriff Donohue, who was also chuckling, stated he didn't want to remove or arrest me, and informed me that there was a separate list for "observers," and I had to somehow get on it before they could allow me in.

I asked Mike (we were buds now) if there were any GOP poll watchers in the building at all, and he told me that there were two inside. I asked to speak to them, and one man came out. I asked him how he got on "the list," and he stated he had volunteered via email and been told to go there, with no other explanation as to what he was supposed to do other than "watch," and that he was leaving shortly, and he didn't think any other GOP observers were coming. I asked him if he knew what he was supposed to be "watching." He stated that he had "no idea," and "couldn't see anything from behind the barriers anyways." I thanked him and Mike and went back to the ground floor to call Leah and figure out how to gain access.

Leah connected me with Tom King and Phil Kline, of the 501C3 Project Amistad organization, and after apprising them of the situation, Phil stated that Project Amistad would pay for a lawyer to join us and urged Tom to get one as fast as possible. We agreed that Leah would be the point person.

While on the ground floor waiting for an attorney, or for Leah to figure out another way to get me and several other observers waiting with me, including Mike Majewski and Joe Masalta, on the access list. I saw workers carting in boxes of ballots via the main elevators, the separate garage loading dock elevators, and some to and from the back doors closest to the Delaware River, without any supervision or chain of custody.

Figure 1 - Inner Entrance to Delco Vote Counting Center - Note Delco County employee John Barton approaching to stop photo

There was no apparent process integrity, or obvious way for anyone to determine the origin of any of the rolling racks

with USPS boxes filled with mail-in ballots, or their ingestion into, or egress out of the system. They weren't escorted,
and many wore semi-official paper "Voter Protection" badges
around their necks that had been issued to hundreds of Democrat operatives on election day, many of whom I had been
informed, had been bussed into the county from unknown
whereabouts.

Several workers, also with "Voter Protection" badges,
casually sat at cafeteria tables with USPS boxes of mail-in
ballots spread over the table while they looked at the front
part of the envelope. We later found out that they had been
tasked with checking to see if there was a signature – any
signature – on the envelope. That should have already been
accomplished, or otherwise assigned to a Bureau of Elections
employee tasked with manually entering the information at
a terminal connected to the Pennsylvania SURE system to
verify its receipt, and that it was valid. They should have
been updating the database before it could be allowed to be
counted. There was absolutely no reason for Democrat "Voter
Protection" volunteers to be handling mail-in ballots – unobserved and unsupervised – in the ground floor cafeteria to
ostensibly "check for signatures."

Figure 2 - "Voter Protection" Badge

As will be described in a further chapter, I suspected the only plausible reason for this process might be a "Kansas City Shuffle" - a possible switch of racks and ballots or shuffling fake ballots into the mix. This could easily be accomplished by bringing in racks of ballots from other floors, from any one of three different unobserved elevator banks in different parts of the building. There was absolutely no repeatable process, or chain of custody, or even reasonable diligence in keeping track of the racks, the USPS boxes filled with mail-in ballots, who was moving them, where they were coming from, or where they were going.

I later found out that the Board and Bureau of Elections did not even have a complete list of the hundreds of "Voter Protection" volunteers that worked and strolled about the counting center without a second look by election officials, nor had they asked for any identification or credentials. While I was required to have a certified poll watcher certificate that the Board of Elections had verified for my name and address after being vetted by Senator Killion and the GOP, before notarizing it a week before the election, unvetted Democrat "Voter Protection" volunteers were given free and unlimited access to roam about as they pleased.

I witnessed organized chaos with rolling racks of mail-in ballots going in different directions with some going to the cafeteria, and some going to and from the boxes of mail-in ballots, while yet others collected and pushed the rolling racks around.

Joe Masalta, one of the other observers who had accompanied me, and who is a US Navy SEAL, took videos and photos of this operation, which received millions of views on Facebook and YouTube, and completed an affidavit. It is included among our litigation exhibits. At 10PM, a balding, middle-aged man in a disheveled suit approached us. Leah had pressured King and Kline to attend to us. So, this was our attorney. He identified himself as John McBlain, and confidently promised to straighten things out. I accompanied him back up to the first floor counting room. He did not disclose that he was an executive board member and general counsel for the DCREC, and I had no idea he was the former Delaware County Solicitor, and the former County Council Chairman.

Figure 3 - Racks of Mail-In ballots in boxes of 500 rolled throughout the Wharf building counting center on election day without supervision, or rational reason or documented process.

Figure 4 - John McBlain, DCREC General Counsel

We were met by Delaware County Solicitor William Martin and Sheriff Donohue. Martin ignored me, and with great hostility attacked McBlain, loudly stating that no one who was not on "the list" was permitted inside the counting center. What happened next was dumbfounding to me – McBlain, who had been a fountain of confidence on the way up the elevator went to water. His knees started shaking, and he broke out into a sweat, and would not hazard a word aside from unintelligible mumbling in response to Martin's verbal assault – which Martin was visibly enjoying. I physically took his arm, moved him aside and confronted Martin, which enraged him to the point where spittle was coming out of his mouth, and he screamed and demanded we leave, while McBlain trembled next to me. Mike Donohue seemed concerned that the confrontation might get physical with Martin. We were face to face with him yelling and not moving. Donohue intervened and asked, "how do they get on the list to come in?" to which Martin responded by stalking off to the back room. It was a surreal exchange, and one that would repeat multiple times over the coming weeks with Martin, who speaks with loud exasperation as a matter of course. McBlain took Martin's departure as his cue to leave and was headed back to the elevator leaving Mike and I looking at each other with astounded "WTH?!" expressions, and there was little else to do but follow McBlain to the elevator.

We rode down and walked to the waiting area where the other observers who had accompanied me were assembled. McBlain finally said he had to make some calls to find out how to get on the list.

When McBlain returned he informed me that the gate-keeper for the entry list was DCREC Executive Chair Carol Miller, who we would later learn was McBlain's peer on the DCREC, and she had called in my name and the other four observers with me to County IT network administrator John Barton, who was responsible for checking us into the first floor counting center.

We were finally allowed in at approximately 11PM, five hours after our 6PM arrival, and were deflated to learn that the five-hour wait, and the "entry pass," only got us 20 feet further into the room, where we were restricted to an "observers' pen." At that point, with what I had thought was only an hour or two before the election results would be called, the better part of valor was observing and learning as much as we could.

We were the only GOP observers in the room, which was otherwise packed with Democrat employees, volunteers, and DNC "Voter Protection" poll watchers standing in the small, square "observers' pen."

Trays of ballots were still coming in through the three doors that appeared to lead from a back office, and a second back-office supply room; there were also doors leading from an outside hallway, with separate elevator access from the public elevators and the garage loading dock elevators.

Figure 5 - The BlueCrest Sorting Machine Loading Tray section

I had no meaningful opportunity to observe any part of the count: the sorting appeared to have been done elsewhere, and the machines were too far away from the observation position to see the mail-in envelopes or ballots. I observed opened ballots going out the second back office closest to the windows in red boxes after handling and sorting by volunteers, some being placed in green boxes, and ballots from the green boxes being placed in scanners like the scanner I had used to vote. But it was too far away (30 feet) to be sure. I asked Deputy Sheriff Mike where the ballots came from, and where the ones that were leaving the room went, and he said he did not know.

I asked Laureen Hagan, the elections official in charge of operations, where the ballots were coming from and how they were being processed. She responded that I was only there to observe, and that I had no right to ask any questions. I said that I wanted to observe the activity in the seques-

Figure 6 - Laureen Hagan, Director Bureau of Elections

tered back room where I could glimpse activity when the door opened, but she denied my request, stating that the law prohibited access to that room by poll observers, and we were restricted to the observers' pen. I responded that there was no law denying access to observers from canvassing areas, where ballots were being handled and processed, and she then said that it was "a COVID thing." I pointed out that I had a mask on, and so did the people visible through the door when it opened. She then informed me that she wanted to prevent us from "interfering." I responded that I was only there to observe and not to interfere, and to make a statement if I observed something wrong. Hagan said, "I assure you that everything's fine. There's no fraud going on," and left to go to the back room.

Shortly after this exchange with Hagan, "Voter Protection" volunteers, accompanied by deputy sheriffs, started bringing in semi-opaque bins with blue folding tops that contained transparent plastic bags, approximately 10" square, with each bag containing what appeared to be some sort of cartridge, a USB vDrive, and a paper tape from the voting machines. They were brought to the computer tables which contained four computer workstation towers on tables connected to four wall mounted monitors, with one workstation tower on the floor under the tables that was not connected to a monitor.

A flurry of workers started disassembling the bags and separating out the USB sticks, cartridges, and paper tapes from the plastic bags, and dropping them in open carboard boxes, with two workers sticking the USB drives into the computers to start the election day counts. I immediately objected, and directed McBlain to challenge the process, and he again retrieved. Hagan to hear my objections. I asked why the returned items had not come with the sealed bags from the judges of elections, and she explained that they had been taken out of the bags at the three county election processing centers by the sheriffs, who were collecting them "for ease of transport." I stated that that was a break in the chain of custody, to which she shrugged her shoulders. I then asked her why they were separating out the USB drives from the cartridges and paper tapes, which was destroying any forensic auditability and further corrupting the chain of custody, and she said, "that's how we have always done it." I knew that was a misrepresentation because it was the first time the counting center had been used, and reconciliation and tabulation had previously been performed at the precinct level where everything had been put in canvas bags, sealed with a plastic zip lock, and brought to the garage at the Media, PA Government Center by judges of elections. I told that to Hagan.

She again stated I had no right to interfere, and was only permitted to observe, turned, and walked away. I pleaded with

McBlain to intervene and at least demand that the USB drives remain with the cartridges and tapes in the plastic bags so we would not have to reassemble and compare them during the official tabulation scheduled for that Friday. He did nothing except look at the floor and sweat.

It is noteworthy that dozens of Democrat "volunteer" workers constantly streamed through the counting area un-accosted, with no check of either ID's or names, still wearing their "Voter Integrity" lanyards and badges, while the certified poll watchers were restricted to the pen. They walked about unrestricted, with no scrutiny, many handling ballots and carrying boxes of unopened mail-in ballots back and forth. This turned out to be the arrangement that Democrats set up at the new counting centers in many swing state cities and pivot counties across the country.

Despite multiple exchanges, elections officials continued to refuse access to the back rooms or a line of sight to any-thing meaningful, and we were stuck "observing" in the pen where we could essentially see nothing. I again conveyed to McBlain that I wanted to pursue immediate legal recourse to gain meaningful access, and he left the roped off area to seek Board of Elections Solicitor Manly Parks. Somehow, Dela-ware County Solicitor Martin had deemed it a good idea to name Parks the Board of Elections Solicitor, even though Parks was also the Solicitor of the Delaware County PA Democrat Party.

At approximately 2:30am Mc-Blain returned and said he had had a conversation with Parks and the President of the Board of Elections, Gerald Lawrence, and

Figure 7 Manly Parks, Board of Elections Solicitor

they had agreed to allow us access to the "back office" and "locked "ballot room" at 9:30 AM the following morning. By that time and given that any other legal recourse would have taken as long, or longer, and there was nothing meaningful to observe, I reluctantly agreed to the 9:30AM meeting. We were then informed that they were closing down for the night and that everyone had to leave.

I was incredulous, and refused to leave, and called a senior executive in President Trump's campaign, who immediately answered. I told him that if we couldn't get lawyers and federal law enforcement involved to stop them from locking us out, they could steal the election. I was informed that other counting centers had already shut down for the night, and they were stopping the count nationwide. Frankly, I could think of no logical reason for shutting down and stopping the count – aside from an intent to cheat.

I will never forget that conversation. They were already celebrating what looked like an overwhelming victory based on the election day voting, and he was ebullient and a little slurred, and I could hear loud, excited celebratory chatter in the background.

> *"Greg, Trump is 657,000 votes ahead, and there is no way they can win."*

To which I replied:

> *You know me, and I'm telling you, President Trump may be winning by 657,000 votes right now, but if we don't stop them from shutting down the voting centers, he'll be losing by 100,000 votes by tomorrow, or whenever they stop counting."*

> *"Greg, please, relax, don't get yourself arrested, and go home, everything will be fine."*

We lingered as long as we could to see if election employees and volunteers were leaving, and when we saw the counting center empty out, we left.

WEDNESDAY, NOVEMBER 4TH, 2020

As agreed only seven hours prior with the Chairman of the Board of Elections Lawrence, and Solicitor Manly, I returned at 9:30AM with Leah, who we had also added to the entry list as an official poll watcher for Craig Williams. McBlain wouldn't show up until 11:00AM.

Counting appeared to have continued through the night, or some additional votes were otherwise entered in the tabulation servers, because the count on the tally screen had increased to approximately 140,000 for Biden, and 85,000 for President Trump, but with all Republican candidates of all other "undercard" races still leading their opponents.

I approached Deputy Sheriff Donohue with Leah and informed him that we were there to go to the sequestered backroom offices, as agreed the previous evening with the BOE Chairman. Mike was expecting us and told us he had been instructed to keep us in the observer's pen. I asked him to retrieve Manly Parks or Chairman Lawrence, who had agreed to let us in, as McBlain was late, and he posted several Park Police to keep an eye on us and went to the back room. The elections officials ignored us for two hours. Donohue did not return, and not a single official stuck their head out of the closed door to the back room. During this time, as I continued to press for access to sequestered canvassing areas and con-

tinued to question the pedigree and chain of custody for boxes of ballots coming into and leaving the room from various vectors, I drew the ire of Delaware County Solicitor Martin. Martin was appointed County Solicitor April 1st, 2020, by motion of Council made by Vice Chair Kevin Mad-

Figure 8 - William Martin

den. Like most professional bureaucrats, Martin is not used to being challenged, and is incredibly thin-skinned. He was growing frustrated with my repeated requests to know why Voter Integrity volunteers were moving about the large room with boxes of ballots, both unopened and opened, with no defined process.

Boxes of ballots were being fed into voting machines that lined the wall, without any means to explain how they got

there, where they came from, and how they were being reconciled. It was a free-for-all. To his credit, Mike Donohue would
dutifully bring my concerns to the back room, and usually
return with a shoulder shrug and no answer. But on one oc-
casion, Martin came storming out and started screaming that
I was "interfering" with the election, that quicky escalated to
"Arrest this man! Arrest this man!" to which both Park Police
and deputy sheriffs responded, and I found myself surrounded (again). I yelled back in deep voice "you are a Democrat
Solicitor and have no more authority to order my arrest than
I do to order your arrest, you toddler. Why don't you let the
grownups talk!" and I turned away from him dismissively,
then looked back to see him shaking he was so mad. I turned
towards Mike, away from Martin. This drew a carefully concealed, but obvious grin from Mike, and the other officers
who were now snickering at Martin, who was furious, but
emasculated, and he stormed off to the back room. I relate this
short story not as some petty bravado, but to illustrate that the
easiest way to defang an imperious bureaucrat is to refuse to
comply and refuse to be drawn into a (losing) fight. Just say
"no." An effective tactic in dealing with toadies – especially
when police might be hovering and deciding how to respond
– is to treat them like the petulant children that they are, frame

the absurdity of it, and then ignore them and press forward. Of course, this is only a smart tactic if the child in question can't serve up a healthy dose of pay back in the future, but in this case it was appropriate.

McBlain finally arrived, and we apprised him of the situation. He exited the pen, and went into the back room, where apparently, the election officials were waiting us out. At 11:30 AM, Ms. Hagan emerged from the room, and informed us that she would give a tour of the Chester City counting center to Leah and me and a few Democrat poll watchers who had joined us in the pen. I stated that I did not want a tour of the facility, and that I only wanted them to honor their agreement to allow direct access to the sequestered counting room. She ignored us. Hagan, along with Ms. Maryann Jackson, another elections official, did not allow us to enter the sequestered counting room. Instead, they walked us in an approximate 20-foot circle directly in front of the roped off pen we had been restricted to, discussing the basics of election balloting but provided no insight into the purpose of the sequestered counting room.

One comment made by Hagan led me to think that "pre"-pre-canvasing happened in the back room. The comment indicated that all ballots had been checked before going downstairs to the ground floor cafeteria for pre-canvasing, before being brought back to the 1st floor counting area, and entering the main counting room, for accuracy/sufficiency of signature, date, and barcode label, and entry in the Commonwealth SURE system. This made no sense and was redundant of the Bureau of Elections data entry employees who could just as easily have checked the envelopes as they entered their receipt into the SURE system. It was also an obvious break in chain of custody and a vector for fraud.

I specifically asked Hagan whether the names and signature were matched, and whether the dates and barcode label were also checked. She replied in the affirmative. I then asked whether the names were checked against the voter registration rolls, and she again answered in the affirmative, indicating that people in the back room did the checking and data entry.

From my vantage point I observed approximately ten people in the back room through the door when it was opened. Hagan confirmed that no ballots went through the BlueCrest sorter without first being checked for name, date, signature, and barcode.

I could see 4000-5000 ballots in bins on the racks next to the BlueCrest Sorter, and I asked both Hagan and Jackson in front of the group:

"If all of the mail-in ballot envelopes are checked for completion, as you stated, then why are there multiple large bins of ballots on the racks next to us between the BlueCrest sorter and ballot extractors labeled "No Name," "No date," and "No signature," on the bins?"

The election officials, red faced, declined to answer. The bins mentioned above were removed shortly thereafter. Several Democrat observers who had joined us on the "tour," including Richard Schiffer, who were intently listening to the exchange, spoke with Leah and me, stating that they were also now not comfortable with the ballot ingestion process, or the fact that the back room had been sequestered from all certified poll watchers sight. They demanded to see the back room with us.

With this new development, Hagan and Maryann Jackson abruptly ended the "tour" to "take a conference call" upon the direction of Solicitor Manley Parks who had been hovering within earshot. I asked Solicitor Parks when that "phone call" would be done so that we could see the back rooms as promised, and he said he did not know. I asked him if he intended to grant us access as promised, and he simply turned around, and walked into the back room without further comment. Hagan, Jackson, and Solicitor Parks never returned, and we left after two hours, having been denied access to the back room.

I insisted that McBlain, our attorney, secure an immediate court order providing access to the room, and he finally agreed to do so. He texted me that the court order had been signed by Common Pleas Judge Capuzzi at 9:30 PM, and the court order required that observers receive only a five-minute observation period in the sequestered room once every two hours. I told McBlain that Leah and I would return to the counting center at 8:30AM when they opened.

We would later learn that there had been a hearing that afternoon that included McBlain, Manly Parks, and William Martin with Judge Capuzzi, after an inadvertent admission by Martin during a later BOE meeting. We had been required to request a transcript of any formal hearing for our later appeal before the Commonwealth Court of Pennsylvania and were informed there was no official record, and that a hearing had not been held. We had assumed McBlain had independently secured Judge Capuzzi's order.

THURSDAY, NOVEMBER 5TH, 2020

I returned the following morning at 8:30 AM with Leah, with a copy of the court order in hand, and McBlain was, again, nowhere to be found. Sheriff Mike was waiting for us, again, and told us he had been instructed to bar entry despite the court order, and we started arguing when I demanded he comply with the Judge's order. Solicitor William Martin emerged from the back room, red faced, and rapidly approached and screamed that we would not be allowed in the back room under any circumstances, and with Park Police and Sheriffs edging toward us from every direction, I decided it would be best to get ahold of McBlain or Judge Capuzzi. McBlain did not respond.

I then contacted Judge Capuzzi's chambers directly and explained to his secretary that the elections officials were not complying with his order. She suggested that I consult with my attorney (McBlain) and said she could not discuss the matter further with me.

When I returned upstairs to the pen, some new areas had been cordoned off, and John McBlain unexpectedly came out from the back room and stated he had conferred with Solicitor Manley Parks, and they had agreed to bring all ballots in from the sequestered room to the main room so that we didn't have to go into the back room. I was stunned at his duplicity in not joining us in our demand to enforce Capuzzi's order, as well as the fact that he had ignored our calls for almost two hours.

McBlain informed us that the elections officials were going to bring 4500 of the 6000 total ballots in the back room out to the main room and leave 1500 remaining spoiled ballots in the "spoilage room" with no explanation of what or where that might be. I made McBlain confirm that the "universe" of remaining ballots in the back room that remained to be processed was, in fact 6,000, and further made him affirm that he had personally seen those ballots -- *and no others* -- in the back rooms and storage rooms. He re-affirmed this multiple times to me in front of multiple witnesses.

McBlain further explained that "their new plan" was to re-tabulate the 4500 ballots by re-filling them out with a pen so that they could be read by voting machines, so we could "see everything." I followed him out of the counting room, to the sidewalk outside of the building lobby, and continued to press him if it was, in fact, legal to cure ballots. I was unconvinced that this was the case, and asked him to challenge it, but he assured me it was "normal" procedure and then abruptly walked towards the parking lot without another word.

Meanwhile, Leah, who had remained behind in the counting room observed Jim Savage, the Delaware County Voting Machine Warehouse Supervisor, walk in with about a dozen USB drives in a clear unsealed bag. She called me to immediately come back up to the counting room. I ran up the stairs, and she showed me photos she had been able to surreptitiously take (no photos or camera use was permitted anywhere in the counting rooms despite live streaming cameras throughout the room, and the fact that it was a (very) public ballot canvassing area, which the law explicitly permits).

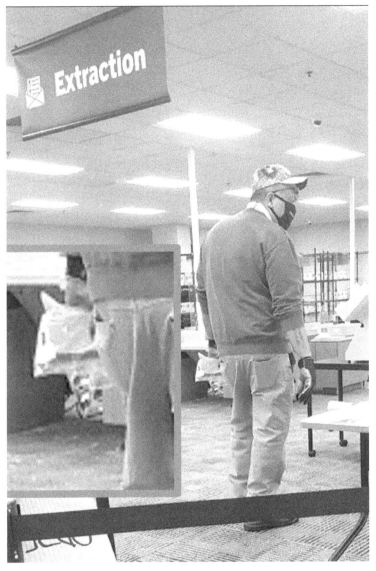

Figure 9 - Delco Voting Machine Warehouse Manager Jim Savage
holding bag of USB drives Thursday morning

Savage was the former President of the United Steelwork-
ers (USW) 10-1 in Philadelphia, and as a leading member of
the USW National Oil Bargaining Committee had led the first

national strike in 35 years against the Philadelphia oil refinery industry in 2015. An elected delegate for Bernie Sanders, he

was an outspoken socialist. He was arrested in the 2011 Occupy Philadelphia movement, and in 2012 worked with the Obama administration to induce the Carlyle Group private equity firm to take over the refinery from Sunoco in Philadelphia. He had taken over as Delco Voting Machine Ware-

Figure 10 - Jim Savage

house Supervisor in April 2020 – a job well beneath his experience and skill sets. I knew the above background on Savage, and also knew he loathed President Trump, from Leah and the Delco Watchdog group.

As further context to the events that follow, shortly after the 2021 primary, and his participation in the destruction of November 2020 election fraud evidence, Savage was again given a high compensation job as a lobbyist in Washington D.C. for the USW in June 2021, punctuating an assignment of a little over a year as the Voting Machine Warehouse Supervisor during which time he had complete control over the physical results of elections. Savage was captured on video admitting to his role in the election fraud, plotting the destruction of evidence with the Supervisor of Elections (Jim Allen, an import from Chicago), and at one point boasting that "we" blew up the Philadelphia oil refinery. Savage was assigned as the Safety Supervisor of the Philadelphia oil refinery, and was at ground zero of the explosion that caused over $1 Billion in damage and shut the plant down.

As such, Leah and I had locked on Savage when he came into the Wharf building, and closely observed his actions. He had ducked into the back storage room area out of Leah's sight, and was circling the counting room, before making a dash for the tabulation servers, with USB vDrives in hand when we next spotted him.

I ran back outside to retrieve McBlain, who was gone, and then ran back up to the counting room at which point I observed Mr. Savage plugging USB vDrives into the vote tallying servers. The clear baggie containing those drives was not sealed or secured.

I immediately objected and challenged the uploading of votes from the unsecured drives, and retrieved Deputy Sheriff Mike Donohue with my objection, and he went to the back room to retrieve Ms. Hagan. Hagan again informed me that I could only observe the process but could not make any comments or ask any questions while Mr. Savage was directly in front of us loading USB vDrive Cast Vote Records (CVR's), each containing hundreds to thousands of ballots.

I responded to Hagan in front of Donohue that we were, in fact, observing Savage plug USB vDrives into a tabulation server without any apparent chain of custody and without any oversight from any election officials. It was inexplicable why the Voting Machine Warehouse Supervisor would take it upon himself to load VDrives, with tens of thousands of voting results, independently and unilaterally into the tabulation server. No one stopped the upload, and Savage was permitted to continue this process over two dozen times, and he was then allowed to walk out without any interference by anyone.

As stunning as the number of election law violations over the previous two days had been, this event was beyond the pale.

I called and texted McBlain throughout the day without success to get him back to the counting center to address the USB issue, as well as what was now being reported to me by other GOP observers: that there appeared to be more additional paper ballots in excess of the 6000 that McBlain had assured me were the entirety coming into the office administration area. I wanted him to represent us and get us into the back office and storage room as ordered by the judge. He would not return until approximately 5:30pm.

An hour after Savage had departed, with vigorous demands to see what the result of Savage's uploads were, the monitors displayed an update on the vote. The numbers moved dramatically: from approximately 140,000 Biden and 85,000 Trump in the morning; to now approximately 180,000 Biden and 105,000 Trump after the update.

During that same update, *all* Republican candidates who had previous leads were reversed and flipped.

Having seen the USB vDrive updates, and now seeing paper ballots in the back office, and other observers reporting that they had seen more ballots as well, I went outside and again called Judge Capuzzi's office. Again, I spoke with his secretary and explained the situation, and that McBlain

Figure 11 - Judge Capuzzi

had departed and was nonresponsive to calls or texts, and she asked me what I wanted the judge to do. I stated that I wanted him to demand his order be enforced, and that I would gladly bring my phone back up and hand it to the Sheriff and

Solicitor. She stated she could not provide any legal advice, suggested I seek counsel, and hung up. She did not realize she had not actually terminated the call, and I heard loud laughter from her and a deeper toned laugh from a male before the line went dead and I returned to the counting floor. I would later learn through Judge Capuzzi's own response to our appeal of his later ruling, that he had, in fact, been listening to my call, and was apparently responsible for the laughter.

I went back upstairs and confronted Deputy Sheriff Donohue, and stated that I had just spoken with Judge Capuzzi (admittedly without telling him the result), and said that I was going to inspect the back room in accordance with his order, and that they would have to physically restrain me, with the live stream cameras videoing the confrontation with the court order in my hand, and that he could later explain the potential altercation in court, and he rushed to the back room.

At 1:30 PM, he reemerged with Delaware County Solicitor Martin, and they informed me I would now be allowed to inspect the locked ballot room.

I was joined by Democrat Observer Dr. Jonathan Brisken. On my way to the locked storage room, while passing through what was now referred to as the "back office," I counted 21 white USPS open letter boxes on two racks, on my immediate right after entering the room, labeled "500 ballots" per box. In addition, the approximately 16 cubicles for workers in the same room each contained boxes also labeled "500 ballots," for a total of 31 boxes of 500 in that sequestered room. This is the same room that McBlain had stated had 4,500 ballots in it earlier, most of which had been presumably moved to the front of the counting room for curation. It was supposed to be relatively empty, except for the 1500 ballots McBlain had said were in a "spoliation room." This was a difference of approximately 16,500 ballots in just the first of the "back office" rooms.

Just after the two racks with the 21 boxes of 500 unopened ballots each, I observed an open door to a 20'x30' storage room with dozens of semi opaque storage bins with blue folding tops that appeared to have envelopes in them. I could see through that room to another door that led back into the back corner of main counting room which was the same door I had seen workers bring in red bins full of "spoiled" ballots the previous night.

I also saw one small office shelf just to the left of the locked and secured "ballot room" with four sealed boxes. I lifted one of those boxes before Solicitor Martin objected that I could not touch anything, and it was heavy-- approximately 30-40 pounds. They appeared to match the description of the boxes described to me earlier by poll watcher Joe Driscoll and another observer that they thought might be boxes of ballots. If those boxes did contain ballots, I estimate that if full, could have contained an additional 2,500 ballots per box for a total of 10,000.

Figure 12 - Table with 4,500 opened ballots that would reportedly not scan being sorted and cured. Note approximate 10-foot distance from "observer" barrier

Ms. Hagan unlocked and opened the "ballot room" and Solicitor Martin entered first and started the timer for 5 minutes. Then Briskin and I entered, with Sheriff Donohue following us and closing the door. There were multiple racks filled with thousands of unopened mail-in ballots. We were not allowed to take any photos, so I immediately started counting. Labels on some boxes were visible, mostly with names of districts known to trend Republican, including Bethel and Brandywine. I took the following notes:

- 5 boxes of 500 labeled 10-12

- 5 boxes of 500 labeled 18-20

- 1 box of 500 each, labeled 26-28, 50-52, and 58-60.

- The remaining boxes did not have markings visible, and we were not allowed to touch them to determine their origin.

- Democratic poll watcher Dr. Jonathan Briskin also observed these boxes and confirmed the numbers of ballots, and that the total number of ballots was vastly greater than we had been led to believe earlier in the day.

- I later observed Dr. Briskin working with a female poll watcher drawing a diagram and detailing what he had seen after we were returned to the roped off area in the counting room, and noted it was quite detailed and corroborated what I had observed.

In addition to the boxes of unopened mail-in ballots, I observed another shelf that was packed with open and ripped transparent plastic bags with cartridges, green security ties, and a 16"x16"x28" carboard box labeled "CHAIN OF CUS-TODY RECEIPTS." In total, I estimated approximately 18,500 unopened mail-in ballots, with which Dr. Briskin uncomfortably concurred.

So, after being told the "universe" of total remaining paper ballots to be counted was 6,000 by McBlain, during this first 1:30pm tour, on Thursday, two days after election, and 38 hours after being denied access, having to obtain a court order, and fighting to enforce that order, I saw a total of:

- 16,500 unopened mail-in ballots in the "back office"

- 18,500 unopened mail-in ballots in the locked "ballot room"

- Potentially 10,000 ballots in the sealed 30-40-pound boxes outside of the locked ballot room

- 4,500 ballots being "cured" in the counting room

- ***For a grand total of 49,500 unopened or uncurated ballots***

To my knowledge, and according to the tally monitor, and as reported on the web, 113,000 mail-in ballots had been requested, and 120,000 mail-in ballots had already been counted, with an approximate outcome of 18,000 for President Trump and 102,000 for Biden already recorded.

At that time, I assumed that the approximately 49,500 unopened ballots would also be processed in the pending running of the sorter, envelope-ballot extractors, and scanners, adding those ballots to the overall total.

At 3:30 PM, I again was allowed to re-enter the back rooms, now accompanied by another woman who I later learned was Board of Elections member Ashley Lunkenheimer (and not a Democrat poll watcher). In addition to the boxes I previously observed, which remained undisturbed, I saw an additional two racks had been moved into the

Figure 13 - Ashley Lunkenheimer, BOE Member

room, with another 16 additional, new boxes of 500 unopened mail-in ballots with approximately 8000 more unopened mail-in ballots labeled 5-2, 6-1, 6-2, and 7-2, with some labels not visible from my position. There were three red "spoiled" ballot boxes with several shed ballots visible in one, and the others appeared to be empty, but I could not verify as I was not allowed to touch anything or take any photos. The 21 boxes in the "back office" were still in place, so this brought the suspected unopened mail-in ballot total to **57,500**.

Figure 14 - Val Biancanielllo

I asked Sheriff Donohue when the next machine run that would process the unopened ballots was scheduled and was informed that election officials planned on a 4:00PM start. I could see workers coming in and preparing. I went outside to call GOP officials to see if we could potentially either delay the run or be permitted to get close enough to the machines to see something but was unsuccessful.

When I returned at 5:30 PM for the next 5-minute tour, I was informed that a Delco GOP representative, Val Biancaniello, had been given my place by Solicitor Martin, and upon her return I asked her why she would do that, and what she had observed. She stated she had "not seen any fraud" and I again asked her specifically if she had seen boxes of unopened mail-in ballots, and she said "oh, yes, lots of them," but she could not recall any further details. When I pressed her for more details, she became truly angry, and told me I needed to "relax," and that she had "straightened everything out," and gotten more observers to watch over the re-filling out of the 4,500 ballots that could not be scanned. I asked her if she had taken any notes and she showed me some incoherent scribbles.

As best as I could make out, they said, "Mail In Ballots Dead People;" "Sorted Newtown 30," "Marple in room to be processed stacks of 25," and "They check was 4 precinct 'ready to be scanned'." She would not explain these nonsensical notes and demanded to know who I was and who I was working for, to which I responded I was a certified poll watcher authorized to perform duties thereof, and I ended the confrontation. I retreated, and she continued to vent to John McBlain, who had finally returned, apparently to manage me.

It is noteworthy that at that time I was able to see the table of 4500 ballots being curated and re-filled out, and those I was able to see were all for Biden. Joe Driscoll said he had seen 15 for Biden and 1 for President Trump, before election officials repositioned the barrier and moved us back.

For the next scheduled 7:30PM 5-minute inspection, Val loudly objected to me going back into the room, and demanded to send Attorney Britain Henry instead, who Leah had convinced to come to the center from Bucks County, and who I had been speaking with for the previous hour. Val stated she had "got him down there," which was confusing, but I agreed it would be a good idea for an attorney to corroborate my observations, and briefed him on the layout, my previous observations, and what to look for over Val's increasing objections to my presence.

Attorney Henry returned from the tour and corroborated my observations of tens of thousands of unopened mail-in ballots, and he stated he would prepare a statement of what he observed. I did not understand, and could not reconcile at that time, why the election result counts had remained roughly the same, while the sorters and envelope extraction machines had been running for almost 4 hours, and presum-

Figure 15 - Britain Henry, GOP",
Attorney

ably processing mail-in ballots, and at that time attributed it to the count not being updated on the monitor.

In the presence of Ms. Biancaniello and Attorney Henry, I asked John McBlain to explain how the USB vDrives had made their way to the center carried by Mr. Savage. He informed me that in his experience, some USB vDrives were typically left in voting machines by judges of elections overnight in previous elections, and that Savage had simply found them in the machines that had been returned from polling locations back to the warehouse, including machines that still had all components in them (USB, Cartridge, and Paper Tape) and that the next day he had transported approximately 24+ USB sticks and an assortment of tapes from the voting machines (Proof Sheets) from the warehouse to the counting center.

I pressed him to find out why there had been so many, and why there was no chain of custody, and why Savage would be involved in entering the USB drives into the computers without any other election officials present, particularly Hagan, who had overseen the process previously.

McBlain informed me that he had been told that some judges of elections had left entire scanners – with cartridges, USB vDrives and tapes (Proof Sheets) – and that the moving company had returned them to the warehouse, where Mr. Savage collected everything and put them in transparent plastic baggies, and canvas return bags. This explanation, in part, may have accounted for five (5) large election judge bags that I witnessed being carried in by a Deputy Sheriff that morning. I was able to take photos of him bringing them into the counting center, and another photo that afternoon of five (5) canvas election material bags being removed from the building. It did not explain 24+ USB vDrives.

I informed McBlain in the presence of Biancaniello that I had seen an approximate 50,000-vote flip for Biden after Mr. Savage had plugged in the USB drives earlier, as described above, and asked them both if that was "normal" for previous elections. They did not respond.

Despite my multiple objections to the lack of transparency, and what I perceived to be a significant break down in any chain of custody, I was routinely ignored by election officials, and was met by mostly blank stares and shoulder shrugs by Mr. McBlain.

I could not understand how the mail-in ballot count remained essentially steady at 120,000 when I and multiple others had seen anywhere from approximately 50,000-to-70,000 unopened mail-in ballots AFTER the 120,000 count had already been completed and updated on the http://Delco-PA.Gov/Vote website.

Figure 16 – Presumed USB vDrives, Paper Tape from scanner, sealed with green lock tie, being brought into building on THURSDAY morning, having beenallegedly returned to the warehouse WEDNESDAY morning. Opened without observers in off limits sequestered area

Figure 17 - Five (5) more bags from scanners that had been allegedly "left at polling locations" and brought to counting center THURSDAY afternoon. Sheriff Donohue is on left.

I do not know where the 120,000 envelopes and ballots that had been enclosed in them went from the counting room after being counted, and was ignored by Ms. Hagan when I asked her where they were. I was denied access to see them. At the end of the day on Thursday, after the 7:30PM inspection kerfuffle, I observed the opaque blue lidded plastic boxes I had seen during the 1:30PM inspection in one of the back rooms, all stacked against the wall next to the BlueCrest sorter with what appeared to be mail-in voter envelopes but was not permitted to go near them and find out if they were opened and empty, or still sealed with ballots, or still had ballots in them. They disappeared from the room shortly after I took the photo below.

As a result of the election officials' acts, I was unable to fulfill my responsibilities as an official poll watcher.

I was continuously harassed, threatened, denied access to the room and the ballots, the election officials were openly hostile and refused to answer questions, repeatedly defied a court order to provide access, and obstructed my ability to observe the count in a way that would enable me to identify irregularities, which is the primary purpose of a poll watcher.

3

ELECTION WEEK AFTERMATH: "STAND DOWN!"

On Saturday, November 7th, 2020, I called and texted William McSwain looking for assistance. I was at the Delaware County Government Center observing the challenges and processing of the Provisional ballots, of which there were over 9,000, and that was going poorly.

I conveyed to McSwain that I was certain that approximately 50,000-to-70,000 unopened mail-in ballots were still in the back room of the Wharf building. I was also sure they hadn't had the time to fully fabricate and synchronize the 47+ missing vDrives, for which I had a list by precinct, from what

I believed were used in a fraudulent upload of electronic votes by Jim Savage, the Voting Machine Warehouse Supervisor. I

Figure 18 - William McSwain, Attorney Eastern PA

had only briefly met McSwain at law enforcement friends and family get togethers, but McSwain knew I was credible, and took my allegations seriously.

I provided specific, quantifiable data points, with recommendations that could be executed quickly. I wanted to get forensic images of the vote tabulation machines, among several related devices, and said if I could get authorization from McSwain, I could get an independent team on location to take the forensic evidence (if he couldn't). I was specifically interested in securing the electronic certification records so that they could match up USB vDrives that had been inserted into the tabulation servers with the voting machines the vDrives came from.

McSwain was responsive and supportive, promised to return with an answer as quickly as possible – and was true to his word, despite it not being the outcome I had hoped for.

McSwain was unable to send a team of his own to render the assistance needed or give us approval to move. I suspected that McSwain had likely been ordered to stand down by US Attorney General William Barr, given the media's frenetic insistence that we had just had "the safest and most secure election in history." The assessment turned out to be correct.

McSwain had been instructed to stand down, and to turn over the information to PA Attorney General Josh Shapiro, which we were dumbfounded by, since Shapiro was on the ballot, and a potential beneficiary of the fraud, whether aware of it or not.

Figure 19 US Attorney General Barr "It's all bullshit"

Barr denied he had told McSwain to "stand down," but if that was the case, then the cover your ass" (CYA) memorandum that Barr reportedly sent six days after the election but didn't publish until McSwain's sent a letter of apology to President Trump in June 2021, wasn't very convincing.

The Philadelphia Inquirer and other national press picked up the story, corroborating McSwain's and my version of events. Oddly, Barr included the event in his biography, confirming that McSwain's call to him did, in fact happen, but calling my report of 47+ missing USB vDrives "all bullshit."

At the time of publication of this book, Barr has reportedly reconsidered his initial assessment, and seems to regret not directing a more thorough investigation – or rather, any investigation at all.

Had McSwain, a Marine, stood his ground instead of "following orders from his chain of command," the trajectory of the election might have changed. Because he stood down, he will be forever associated with "The Caine Mutiny" like shame of "old yellow stain," as an epitaph to an otherwise exemplary lifetime of service and accomplishments.

President Donald Trump responded with a strong statement when the revelations of the order to stand down in June 2021 came to light, with the accompanying letter written by McSwain that conveyed that Barr had ordered federal authorities not to aggressively investigate claims of fraud during the election.

"U.S. Attorney from the Eastern District of Pennsylvania was precluded from investigating election fraud allegations. Outrageous!" President Trump said in the statement

"I wanted to be transparent with the public and, of course, investigate fully any allegations. Attorney General Barr, however, instructed me not to make any public statements or put out any press releases regarding possible election irregularities," McSwain wrote.

"I was also given a directive to pass along serious allegations to the State Attorney General for investigation - the same State Attorney General who had already declared that you could not win," the former prosecutor said. "I disagreed with that decision, but those were my orders."

Figure 20 - Josh Shapiro, PA Attorney General

Shapiro predictably denied receiving any reports of credible fraud, from McSwain or anyone else, and had predicted President Trump would lose by 80,000 votes in PA, which was incredibly prescient because that was exactly the outcome.

In addition to the Inquirer, Politico also reported the "mention in McSwain's letter to Trump about being told to "pass along serious allegations" referring to the handling of one complaint, a source told Politico. That allegation involved "Navy veteran Gregory Stenstrom's claim that 47 USB vDrives went missing during the election process in Delaware County, Pennsylvania."

Although I said the USB vDrives could have contained tens of thousands of votes, local officials later falsely insisted that the drives were used for programming voting machines and did not contain votes. Secured, paper confirmations of each vote cast guarded against large-scale fraud, according to the officials. Of course, we now know that was also a lie (by the local officials).

The provisional vote challenges bear mentioning as an epitaph to a bizarre election week. Approximately 4,500 - 5000 voters who had not requested mail-in ballots arrived at polls and were informed they had already voted. Most were furious and demanded to cast a provisional vote. Attorney Goldstein and his partner Britain Henry (who had performed the 7:30PM inspection of the back room at Val Biancaniello's insistence), concluded that there were thousands of discrepancies, inconsistencies between the ballots, reports from citizens, and questions about the SURE system that required a formal challenge and further adjudication in Court, of thousands of provisional ballots.

And then, without explanation, or objection from the DCREC or anyone in the GOP, Goldstein dropped the challenge. The "judicial climate" had changed, due, especially, to the overwhelming media narrative that this had been the 'safest and most secure election in history, which was being

Figure 21 - Jonathon S. Goldstein, GOP Attorney

intoned like a mantra by that time. That seemed to make it a moot point. But it was a tactical legal blunder, bad precedent, and morally bankrupt. Regardless of the expected outcome, a meaningful challenge might have provided important data points to verify that fraud had, indeed, occurred.

When the Moton, Hoopes and Stenstrom litigation and accompanying videos and audios hit the media and Internet in November 2021, it was a gut punch to Delaware County District Attorney Jack Stollsteimer, the Soros $1 million man, who along with PA Attorney General Shapiro, had quashed all investigations.

Figure 22 - Jack Stollsteimer, Delco District Attorney

A little known, and seldom used statute in Pennsylvania law is that DA's and the AG have a fiduciary requirement to investigate election fraud, and that it is itself a crime not to do so. At the time of publication, Stollsteimer, red faced from the public videos and evidence of county officials admitting to election fraud and wantonly destroying evidence, stated it now merited investigation with the caveat and assurance, from Stollsteimer, that he expected not to find anything.

In one of the most blatant attacks by a Delco official on the veracity of our testimony, litigation and evidence, Delco Executive Director Howard Lazarus, another recent pre-election addition to the lineup of County officials eager to deny fraud and "debunk" us, implied that the videos and over 100 exhibits included with the case, were all fabrications themselves and `false.' He stated, "We are confident that in the end

Figure 23 - Howard Lazarus, Executive Director Delco

the allegations will be proven to be fabricated and wholly without merit, and that our systems are worthy of your trust."

On May 18th, 2022, DelCo Solicitor William Martin announced at the Delco Council Meeting that Jack Stollsteimer had completed his investigation on May 5th, 2022, and would bring no criminal charges, and that the evidence presented was all fabricated.

No one from his office ever contacted us.

4

GREGORY STENSTROM – FATHER, SON, AND CITIZEN

I made a choice on November 3rd, 2020, to be drawn into a fight against those who thought they could determine how my family, loved ones, neighbors and country should live, and that we should all comply with their will. You could argue that I made this choice earlier when I agreed to be a poll watcher. Which I did because I knew what the cheating in Philadelphia and Delco looked like in 2016 – robust, but not quite aggressive enough to save Hillary Clinton. I knew that efforts to commit election fraud would be redoubled, refined, and better calculated to win, regardless of what the real vote looked like, in 2020. Because I investigate fraud and secure companies from it professionally, I had been in touch with members of the Trump campaign prior to the election.

My decision to fight after what I witnessed on November 3, changed the trajectory of my life forever. It resulted in great pain, and cost my family dearly, but it also kept me in the fight. I will leave the details for another time because they are too personal to add to the already tragic story of how America lost the ability to elect leaders with honest voting. Suffice it to say that one casualty of my crusade was the loss of a family business in which I was working with my adult sons, Patrick, and Brian. My family's life was further shattered when Brian took his life on February 6th, 2021. This loss of a healthy, beloved son only makes me hate the fraud more. It used to be a family joke that I am "that space between a rock and a hard place." Implacable. Immovable. Unshakeable. A statue wrapped in rhinoceros hide when it came to holding true to my core values. What I was left with was pain, silence, and a laser focus on resolving the issues we fought over. There will be a reckoning. There will be punishment. There will be justice.

After our first case that we filed in December 2020 was summarily dismissed without an evidentiary hearing and we were sanctioned for $50,000, and despite what we had witnessed, and the outcome it contributed to, we were ready to give up. Leah and I couldn't find a lawyer who would take the case, and we were alone. But something in me would not walk away. Four days after my son took his life, I called Leah and told her we were going to file our first Appeal, *Pro Se*, "on our own behalf."

So, we got back into the fight.

I've been in a lot of different fights. It's what I'm trained for, as an Annapolis graduate, former Naval officer, and veteran of foreign wars. More specifically, at this stage of my life I am an experienced professional in security, forensics, and fraud. And I'm good at it.

One formative back story, which provides a sample of my experience dates from January 2010.

Then Philadelphia City Controller Alan Butkovitz was frustrated with his unproductive audit of the Philadelphia Sheriff's Row Office, just as his predecessors, Controllers Jonathon Seidel and Joe Vignola had been during the previous 20 years that Sheriff John D. Green, James Davis of Reach Communications, and a cast of politicians and power brokers, ransacked the City of Philadelphia. I was referred to Alan, and he asked me to take a look. The details of that investigation could fill another book, but the outcome was that in a short time I personally found that Sheriff Green and Mr. Davis, et al, had stolen $220 million during the previous 20 years, and I recovered $53 million of that sum, returning it to the city coffers. The Sheriff and James Davis eventually entered guilty pleas and still have several years left in prison to read this book.

With that success, for a time I became an object of curiosity, a pointed knife of the power elite, and "the man in black" in the City of Philadelphia. I was contracted by other leaders in the Commonwealth of Pennsylvania to conduct similar investigations, the next largest of which saved $63 million in taxpayer money for another state agency.

During that time, I was surrounded by armed officers with drawn weapons and threatened with arrest several times, threatened with financial ruin, followed by men intent on doing me violence, and regularly ridiculed. I rebuffed bribery attempts, was called a "liar" by powerful men and women before their inevitable comeuppances and floated through it all unscathed.

RIGHTEOUS JUSTICE

I gained a grim taste for it, like any other professional who is skilled at his craft. The biggest lesson I learned from that time was that when it comes to getting in this type of fight, with high-level, high-powered corruption, it is a solitary endeavor, without accolades or recognition. It is often painful, and friends are few.

When you fight grand corruption, you fight alone, and there is no meaningful financial gain that comes from it. Just satisfaction for a job well done.

The only ones who benefit are opposing politicians, the uninvolved who always swoop in to take unearned credit, and the inevitable new batch of corrupt officials that move into any vacuum and recommence stealing until they, too, are eventually caught. This is a continuing cycle that dates back to the first time a government had tax dollars to control.

Maintaining cynicism and skepticism, while assuming everyone is lying, is the most productive way to enter any such investigation. You learn that wherever there is "public trust" with money or power involved, there is always corruption.

One moment that would resonate with me for many years, took place in private, behind closed doors, after the Philadelphia Sheriff resigned.

I was alone with Alan Butkovitz, the City Controller whom I had come to like and admire, and whom I had learned was a devout Jew, when he asked me in a hushed voice,

"Who sent you? Where did you come from?"

In this situation, some might recite their resume, but I answered,

"For 20 years, the Sheriff and his cronies stole from those who could not defend themselves; the poor, widows, orphans, and people down on their luck, and they prayed to God for help and justice. I guess he sent me."

Somehow, I knew that Alan would be satisfied with that answer, and he was, and simply responded *"I guess he did,"* and that concluded the conversation.

It was a good couple of years for cleaning out corruption in Philadelphia, and Pennsylvania, and I worked on multiple investigations, some of which made headlines as I quietly turned my work and forensic evidence over to various city and law enforcement agencies to be taken to their conclusions.

When my close friends asked me why I didn't mind others often taking credit for my work, I would reply "I like being the 'Jerry McGuire' of security work, and don't mind being the elbow or foot in the headline photo."

The best security experts and investigators know that their stock in trade, and the most valuable aspect of their work is utter and complete privacy. When you are tasked with sorting out dirty laundry, it is counterproductive to break the bond of secrecy and air it in public. Rule number one is don't embarrass the client who is paying you to help them.

One thing I learned was that the rich, powerful, and "untouchable" elite all have the same arrogance, look, and patterns of behavior when they first learn they are in trouble. All initially called me a "liar." All puff up, posture, and threaten, and a few follow through with their threats.

In the end, all of them cry.

That is admittedly the most satisfying part. There are people who deserve the schadenfreude they provoke. I've seen the crocodile tears flow, as they all suddenly find the Lord -- only after being caught. It is for others to sort through the consequences of their crimes and corruption. That's when the justice that I am compelled to seek happens.

I had conducted "white hat" hacks, security assessments, and fraud investigations, for the preceding decade at many of the largest financial institutions in the U.S., and several foreign countries. Over the decades leading up to the November 2020 general election, I audited global corporations, regional transportation authorities, national SCADA infrastructure, pipelines, electric and communications grids, and government agencies. Those jobs were satisfying, profitable, and my clients were usually grateful. But that work was not as satisfying as exposing the corrupt.

PHILADELPHIA CHEATING

Another investigation, after the Sheriff kerfuffle, took me to Philadelphia City Hall in the summer of 2011, and a nondescript, unlabeled computer server encased in glass with a locked door inside the data center. I had a court order allowing me to take forensic images of computer systems and monitor network traffic flows. After the usual puffing of chests and posturing of worried officials with something to hide, and perplexed uniformed officers they had called to stop me, I cracked open the case and the computer and took forensic images of a dusty hard drive – one drive that would remain untouched for legal evidence, and one "working" drive for forensic examination.

When I spun up the forensic working drive image, I learned that it was the City of Philadelphia Voting Tabulation Server, where all votes for the city were supposed to be aggregated, collated, and counted.

It had not been turned on in a decade.

Draw your own conclusions, but little surprises me anymore.

I know I mentioned above that secrecy and confidentiality are the entire point of my business, but this specific data point was instrumental in bringing me to where we are today, and without it, my subsequent motives and actions over the past year and a half would be unclear.

I had recently watched then fringe presidential candidate Donald Trump at the 2011 White House Correspondence Dinner and noted the look in his eyes and the set of his jaw as he absorbed Seth Meyers and President Obama's non-stop ridicule, barbs, and laughter at him. I have seen the look Donald Trump responded with in two types of situations, one being when a man is set on killing someone, the other being when a man will pay any cost in accomplishing a seemingly impossible goal. I know that look and stored that data point away to draw on later.

In June of 2015, I posted on Facebook "Donald Trump is going to win the presidency in 2016" about the same time as Ann Coulter's recognized his breakout qualities and made her famous proclamation on Bill Maher's show.

THE 2016 ELECTION IN PHILADELPHIA

I contacted a close friend who must remain unnamed, who was a point man for then candidate Trump, and told him I would like to help. I shared my view that, unless Philadelphia had found some way of counting votes through the ether, and based on Obama's 2008 performance there, it was unlikely that the votes were even counted at all in Philadelphia, and it was a waste of time, money, or resources on what was a lost cause. I predicted that Hillary Clinton, the presumed Democrat candidate for 2016 would enjoy an early call of approximately 600,000+ votes for her, to ~100,000 votes for whomever might be the ultimate Republican candidate on the eve of the election.

I met with several campaign executives and strategists working for the GOP and President Trump, during the campaign. I volunteered to make calls in Delaware County, PA, on President Trump's behalf at the local GOP headquarters in Springfield, PA, and trained and prepared to be a poll watcher.

We believed that it was the people who would count the votes that would determine the outcome, and Delaware County ramped up from less than 100 GOP poll watchers in the 2012 Obama-v-Romney race to almost 1,000 GOP poll watchers for a county of 428 precincts.

I spent the entirety of November 8th, 2016, in a Democrat controlled poll in Delaware County, as a poll watcher, where I repeatedly turned away fraudulent voters, and at one point had the Judge of Elections (JOE) eject one Democrat operative who had no credentials, name tag, and whom they refused to identify, who repeatedly entered voting booths and cast votes when we weren't close enough to tackle her, and only after I told the JOE I would have the operative arrested – and her for allowing it - was she escorted out for good.

After the poll closed at 8pm, it took us until 11:30PM for the poll watchers and election workers to count the absentee ballots, go through the machine tapes and tally write-in ballots, and sort through everything, and reconcile the vote, to arrive at a slim lead for Hillary Clinton over President Trump at a poll that had been expected to be overwhelmingly in her favor. It took 3 ½ hours to reconcile a little under 800 votes.

At about 1:00AM on election night I received a call from my unnamed friend, who was presumably with President Trump, and he asked me "can Hillary take Pennsylvania away?" to which I responded,

"No, I don't think so. There are no more votes for her to steal in Philadelphia, Trump has it by at least 40,000 votes statewide, but they will NOT make the same mistake in the next election."

For the next four years, I would repeatedly explain to my friend and several other GOP state and national campaign level personnel to expect that whatever President Trump's lead might be at the beginning of the night, unless they took pre-emptive action, he would likely be losing by the next morning.

No one listened.

Fast forward to May of 2020, and a phone call from Mrs. Leah Hoopes. Leah was a Delaware County, Bethel Township Committeewoman, frustrated with the election law violations she had recently witnessed in the May 2020 primary election, and she had been given my name by a mutual friend, code-name "Dmitri," who we both knew from the Union League of Philadelphia, which had been the hub of my personal and professional life from 2004 through 2011. The motto of the

Union League of Philadelphia is "Love of country leads," and I loved the people there.

Leah had asked "Dmitri" if he knew anyone who could help her sort through the myriad of problems, data, and elements of fraud that might have occurred, and he pointed her in my direction.

I was intrigued, but politely declined.

There should be a photo of Leah under the dictionary word "persistence."

She stayed in touch and called to ask me to come to a demonstration at the Media Court House and Government Center to protest the continued business shutdowns mandated by PA Governor Wolf and acquiesced to by the GOP majority legislature for Covid. I told her, *"I don't do demonstrations, carry signs, or bark at the moon. There are more effective means of demonstrating than walking around in circles and yelling into reporters' microphones and cameras."*

Leah didn't get angry, and she pressed on like the consummate special operator and advocate she was becoming, and threw back *"what would you do?"*

"Well, if you're asking, I would set up a small table, PA speaker system, play patriotic music, do the Pledge of Allegiance, schedule business owners to give speeches, print up

programs, and give the news media as many photo and video opportunities as possible."

"OK, if I do all that, will you help," she asked.

"That was smooth," I said.

How could I say no?

That event went well, and I was impressed with Leah's passion, integrity, organizational skills, and natural leadership abilities. What struck me most was there was nothing demure or artificial in Leah. The facades that most people wear in public were not there. She was 100% authentic and direct. Her eyes bored a hole in your head when she spoke, and if it didn't look like you were paying attention, she would take hold of your arm until you did. She operated at a high frequency and energy level, like me, and I was drawn to her.

She asked me several more times after the protest to get involved in election integrity efforts, and to possibly train people, and I repeatedly said "No."

Leah doesn't easily take a "no" when she wants a "yes" and pressed me for a reason why I would not engage.

I told her that I had been in the same types of fights that I saw coming, already knew what the outcome was going to be, and that my business was going well, two of my sons were working with me, and it wasn't worth the fight. I told her the evidence was walking all around us with people wearing face masks that couldn't block a virus.

"People aren't worth it. I know from experience, that whatever happens, you and I will be ridiculed, called liars, threatened, sued, financially attacked, and at the end of the day, none of the idiots walking around with maxi pads on their faces will lift a finger, and in the end, we'll be alone, broke, and beat to hell."

Leah protested that she believed people were inherently good and asked about the hundreds of thousands of people at President Trump's MAGA rallies, and didn't believe that we could possibly end up alone in any forthcoming fight.

"It doesn't cost anyone anything personally to show up at a rally. It makes them feel good. When it comes to putting their asses on the line, and their money where their mouth is, most people won't do it because it makes them feel bad. Most run. They are happy with their "Matrix" blue pill and will not risk their necks to help us save ours when the shit hits the fan."

In September of 2020, I met privately with a senior member of President Trump's campaign staff, and he said, *"We have information that there is massive DNC mail-in ballot fraud in the works. Is there anything we can do about it here in Pennsylvania?"*

I responded with my standard line for these situations, which was, *"I'm too pretty for jail, and the only effective countermeasures available at this point would be equally illegal. The only thing President Trump can do is win by such a huge margin, that it might neutralize the cheating."*

I was miserable, and sick about it, but thought I was past my "Dudley Do Right" stage. I was working on a large contract after a crushing "covid" year, and just wanted to get fresh revenue flowing into our business and be successful for my family. My sons had both left other opportunities to make a go of working together as a family, and Lilliana, my fiancée, and my soon to be stepchildren, were all counting on me as well.

Leah called again in mid-October, and told me she had been working with the Delaware County Watchdog group she had organized, and gave me a raft of new information they had developed, and relayed that the Board of Elections was intent on doing everything possible to stack the deck for Biden, and asked to meet. Fresh after meeting with my unnamed friend regarding his fears, I agreed to meet Leah.

We met at La Porta, a restaurant on Middletown Road a short drive from my home, and Leah was a fountain of information. There were hardly any GOP poll watchers this go round; the procedures for handling and counting ballots still hadn't been finished with the election only a couple of weeks away; they had learned that the CTCL ("Zuckerberg money") had dumped $2 million in Delaware County, and another $10 million in Philadelphia; and it was looking very grim. She asked that I just help on election day to watch for potential fraud and help them identify it.

I looked her straight in the eye's and told her *"You are asking me to get into a fight, and I'm telling you - again - that it is probably going to be the most painful experience of your life. You will lose friendships, family relationships, and they are going to come after us with hatchets if, God forbid, we actually do see anything. And, in the end, we will be alone – more importantly, I will be alone if you bale out – and it's going to cost a lot personally."*

She nodded gravely, truly mulling what I had said over in her head, and said, *"I'm in."*

Leah had no idea what she was really in for. She is 5'3" on her toes, and a woman in a predominantly man's game, but my gut told me, *"She will stand and fight."*

How could I say no? How bad could it be?

5

LEAH HOOPES – MOTHER, WIFE, AND CITIZEN

I am a natural born networker. I meet people and auto-matically figure out who goes where, and who can do what job. Who will do whatever needs to be done. I'm social, intuitive, and driven. In March of 2020, I was a 39-year-old wife and mother of a then 14-year-old son. I see myself as a momma bear, ready to do whatever is needed to ensure that justice prevails, because I'm not going to leave my son a cor-rupted, unfree world.

I was teaching Krav Maga - Israeli self-defense techniques - at a local gym at the time. But mostly I was working actively for the Republican party, working specifically to elect Donald

Trump in the upcoming election. Starting in 2019 I served as the Republican Committeewoman for Bethel Township.

I'm a lifelong resident of Delaware County, where I was born and raised in a blue-collar family headed by two patriotic, conservative parents. My father was the kind of man who would not tolerate any disrespect for the flag. We all believed in the American Dream, and in fundamental American goodness - which we saw in our daily lives. My mother, a God-fearing woman, taught me how to have empathy, and that when you stand up for your convictions you may stand alone.

I graduated from Delaware County Community College with a Criminal Justice degree and was headed to the Pennsylvania State Police Academy. That was not to happen - God had other plans for me. But I had spent several years working with my uncle - a former state police commissioner - and aunt at the detective agency they ran. Though things took a different turn, that training formed my underlying approach to the world: Check the details. Do the research. See what doesn't line up. Make the charges stick. Get justice. Most of all I was taught to value integrity, tenacity, and the having the sense to follow your gut.

These days my husband and I own a property management business. And, of course, I've spent a lot of time during the past 18 months, working to demonstrate that the 2020 presidential election in Delaware County was a sham.

One reason I found Trump so compelling as a leader, is that I grew up around a lot of the social pathology he discussed and worked to turn around. I spent my early youth watching as friends and neighbors were lost to drugs and alcohol, opioids, and other drugs of despair. I believe that drug abuse is usually a result of mental health issues --- and the mental health issues came from living in a culture in which the life roles for solid working-class citizens were being wiped out. The future was increasingly hazy. Good people we knew could not cope with a world in which their jobs, their places in society, the meanings that defined their lives, were evaporating before their eyes, because politicians on both sides of the aisle thought that exporting jobs to China and elsewhere was smart policy. Throw in the undermining of the nuclear family. Heroin, fentanyl, oxycodone, even Percocet, were substitutes for clear roles, real opportunities, and traditional coping skills. So, when I heard Trump promise to bring back factories, to create real economic growth across the economy, I was sold.

Furthermore, I thought he did a great job in his first term. So, I was eager to see more in a second term. Which is why I could laugh, later, after the election, when one rather crude writer called me - and Greg - 'jilted Trumpanzees.' In the left-wing press, which is a wing of the political establishment, I was dismissed as a nobody, and a mere 'door knocker.' But I saw myself as a watchdog. A patriot. Someone who cares about her country. That is where I was coming from.

DELCO WATCHDOGS

Starting in March of 2020 I began connecting with several grassroots organizations around Pennsylvania. With the pandemic closing in, and rules and procedures beginning to change, I sensed that President Trump's declared enemies were up to no good in this election year. I brought several people together to create the Delco Watchdogs, because it was clear that we were going to have to keep a close eye on Democrats to make sure they didn't steal this election. When a mutual friend told me about Greg's background as a security expert, I knew I needed to have him work with us. So, I reached out. He said "no." I did not take 'no' for an answer.

Our first event together occurred on May 21, 2020. It was a rally in Media, Pa., with citizens and business owners for "getting back to work and worship." We knew they were manipulating us with all the Covid rules. We brought in great speakers, like PA State Assemblyman and Navy vet, Steve Barrar. Of course, nothing changed. But we made our point.

One thing I have learned along the way: there are many people we've met who are just like Greg and me. People who are passionate patriots; they have a strong relationship with God, and therefore with truth, and who had strong gut instincts about what was happening. To these people I want to say, trust your instincts. We're on the right side of history.

I formed the PA WATCHDOGS and approached blue collar average citizens who wanted to get involved, were tired of the good old boys club, and also were angry that our County was turned over to the left wing, by who we would learn was the GOP and DNC "Uniparty." Our members were:

- Karen Elliot, a new committee woman in ASTON GOP

- Wendy Willauer, a geriatric nurse who was deeply affected by Governor Wolf's nursing home orders that resulted in thousands of deaths

- <u>Richard Gibney</u> an EMT with a history of effective activism and calling out government officials in Delaware County

- <u>Jodi Diamond</u>, a single mother of two, she designs tombstones, and is an investigator who assembled data on Jim Savage, CTCL and the Counting Center

- <u>Matt Dadich</u>, a father of four, and committeeman for Lower Chichester GOP

- <u>Stephanie Leone</u>, a concerned mother, and our social media maven

- <u>Gloria Brazell</u>, retired from Scott Paper, board member of the local library, and ex-Committeewoman for years,

- <u>Mark Carroll</u>, a family man, small business owner, and volunteer for then House Rep candidate Ralph Shicatano

CV-2020-006883 CARROLL ET AL (DELCO WATCHDOGS) V. DELAWARE COUNTY BOARD OF ELECTIONS

I was approached by Tom Killion's campaign to investigate and prepare a lawsuit, if necessary, to address pop up voter sites (paid for by CTCL money). We filed lawsuit CV-2020-006883 on 10/14/2020; Carroll et al v. Delaware County Board of Elections and Its Administrative Arm Delaware County Bureau of Elections. The case was dismissed, but we were later vindicated with the Commonwealth Court's decision that the election reforms of 2019-2020 that became Act 77 (and included provisions for pop up voter sites), were unconstitutional, in Doug McLinko, et al. v. Commonwealth of Pennsylvania, et al.

ELECTION DAY AND AFTER

Back to Wednesday, November 4th. Greg and I were fighting the good fight inside the counting center. We got there, and Greg walked right up to Deputy Sheriff Mike Donohue and said, "We are here to go to the back room." Mike said "no," and went to the back room alone to fetch his bosses. They made us wait what felt like forever. Election Clerk Laureen Hagan and interim election director Marianne Jackson came to the front room. Laureen summoned some attitude and told us that we were not going into the back room. John McBlain arrived late, as if it was no big deal that election laws were being violated.

Laureen was adamant that she had no idea about any conversation with Gerald Lawrence, but the compromise was to give us a closer tour of the "Kabuki theater" going on in the front room. It was a complete distraction, and a violation of the Pennsylvania election code. We were impatient with McBlain because these people were blatantly lying and blocking us from going into a back room where a huge number of suspect unopened ballots were stored.

Why wasn't McBlain, who represented the Delaware County Republican Executive Committee, fighting for the two Republican certified poll watchers, and me - a committee woman? McBlain couldn't argue his way out of a parking ticket. He gave us more of an argument than he did to the people breaking the law. It was a disgrace.

There was a clear attempt to manage us. That was the same treatment I have received from Valerie Biancianello, Tom McGarrigle, Dave White, people in my own committee, and others in the DELCO GOP. They pat you on your head, tell you to "knock on doors," be quiet, and "stay in your lane," while they completely pursue their own self-interest.

From the week of the election, to filing our first lawsuit in December 2020, throughout the appeal process, and up until now, time has flown by in a blur. The more we spoke out and stayed ahead of the propaganda and false narratives, the more allies we found. Courage spread like wildfire.

I was still thinking – hoping - we would have a Hollywood-like moment, in which we were heard in court, and appropriate action would follow. Our evidence was clear as day and we were ready to get on that witness stand to present it to a jury. Eighteen months later, we're still fighting to be heard.

To say that I was angry about the way things went is an understatement. I was beyond angry: devastated, frustrated, and horrified at what was going on right here in my home county, which is not some unrelatable, distant corrupt city. And, at times it showed.

If I had a dime for every time some well-meaning person told me that I would be more effective if I "sounded nicer," and that I "could catch more flies with sugar than vinegar," I'd be rich. I'm not defending this, but I'm not apologizing for it either: I was watching evil doers betray freedom and election integrity in my country. I was angry.

And I was a bit scared. Scared for my son, and his generation, who could grow up without the freedoms we were born into. Scared for myself and my husband, considering some of the consequences of my political actions. My persistence in holding people accountable for cheating, led to instances of the FBI and PA Attorney General Josh Shapiro using forceful intimidation tactics at the front door of my house.

After Greg and I investigated, assembled our evidence, and Attorney Deborah Silver filed our first lawsuit in December 2020, I was devastated to watch Republican Judge Capuzzi not allow an evidentiary hearing, or discovery, but add insult to injury, opening the flood gates for sanctions against us.

He used scorching language in his opinion, saying that our actions were 'contemptible,' we had 'unclean hands,' and that 'we didn't have a scintilla of evidence.' But he wouldn't look at the evidence.

This surely undermined our confidence in the independence, integrity, and impartiality of the judiciary. The week following his opinion, the local lefty paper, The Delco Times, put out an article attacking us. Nor did they ask us for our responses. Not a surprise, of course, when a left-wing paper applauds an unfavorable ruling against two Republican poll watchers. We should have expected public humiliation, scrutiny, and ridicule from every progressive in Pennsylvania.

The Republican Party left us high and dry. After the Gettysburg hearings, some of the people from inside the grassroots efforts began turning away from us. We lost valuable time with our friends and families. And of course, our efforts created financial strains for us.

Plus, I didn't like being called a liar and a fraud from both sides of the aisle. I will never apologize for telling the truth.

I have worried about whether my husband will be made to pay for my choices. And I know how much he has worried about me. This fight has been worth the effort. But it's important to understand just how much effort that has been.

I don't really understand what people thought I would gain from this if I were lying. What would that get me? If you are an honest person who has lived a normal life, it is harsh to be accused of making things up for some (invisible) personal gain.

For eight straight months I spent my days and nights talking to thousands of people. Literally - twenty thousand people. I was the central hub, the connector. Interviewing people, being interviewed, my phone was busy for 12 hours a day. Now things are quieter. But I am not giving up on working for the truth to come out.

What do I get? If nothing else, my son will look to his mother and say she never stopped fighting. He will know common people don't need lots of money or power to make a difference. My son will know that when I leave this earth that nobody could stifle my voice; that he is capable of being a critical thinker; that he should continue to fight for his country. I answer to God and to my son.

The truth, my dear son, always matters.

This book may never sell. It may sit on the shelves. without hitting any best seller list. But the truth is written, and it will be a part of history. It will speak to those who have been in our position; those who keep quiet for fear of retribution; those who know that something is not right; those who want to know what really happened in 2020, and how it was accomplished.

Figure 24 - Steve Barrar, Gregory Stenstrom, and Leah Hoopes

6

THE SETUP

"I consider it completely unimportant who in the party will vote, or how; but what is extraordinarily important is this—who will count the votes, and how."

Joseph Stalin, Soviet dictator, said in 1923 (Boris Bazhanov, *The Memoirs of Stalin's Former Secretary* (1992)

The humiliating loss of Hillary Clinton and debacle of the November 2016 election of Donald Trump would never be allowed to happen again, and the GOP and DNC corporate Uniparty set to work immediately afterwards to permanently correct the situation.

Never again, would elections be left to the citizenry to decide.

The Uniparty "ruling class" would henceforth install illegitimate government officials. Ballots would be centrally "collected" and "counted" under the control of partisan DNC and GOP bureaucrats and their solicitors and lawyers. Small, decentralized precincts and wards, which had been the backbone of preventing election fraud for over two centuries, would be eliminated, and vast sums of private partisan monies would be used to extract the public citizenry from the ballot creation and counting process.

TARGETING SWING STATES AND PIVOT COUNTIES

The United States includes 3,006 counties; 14 boroughs and 11 census areas in Alaska; the District of Columbia; 64 parishes in Louisiana; Baltimore city, Maryland; St. Louis city, Missouri; that part of Yellowstone National Park in Montana; Carson City, Nevada; and 41 independent cities in Virginia – for a grand total of 3,139 voting districts (which we will refer to collectively as "counties" for consistency's sake hereafter).

Among the reasons much of the US citizenry was initially uncertain of the extent of the November 2020 election fraud was that only a small number of "swing" states needed to be targeted to change the outcome of a national election, and these "swing" states could be broken down even further into only a few dozen, primarily metropolitan, "pivot" counties to control the outcome for all 3,139 Counties and 50 States in the US.

This is why the bulk of all campaign monies and advertising - over 90% - is poured into these specific "swing" states, "pivot" counties, and metropolitan areas, and why the DNC has historically only needed to "win" a small percentage of the total counties in the US, to win an election. Examples of recent elections for Obama (18%), Hillary (15%) and Biden (13%) percentages for wins in the schema of total number of national counties barely registered, in election cycle after election cycle, for approximately 2600 out of the 3,139 Counties.

Delaware County has been a "pivot" county, and an oversized influence in Pennsylvania and national politics since the 1870's as discussed earlier, and the electorate has been reliably delivered to the ruling class. It was a matter of convergent destiny - and perhaps "bad luck" (for them) - that Leah and I would become witnesses to the fraud that the DNC and GOP Uniparty "ruling class" would execute in November 2020 to ensure their full control over the nation.

The "swing" states for 2020 included Pennsylvania, Georgia, Arizona, Michigan, Wisconsin, Ohio, Florida, and North Carolina.

"Swing" states can vary from presidential election to presidential election voting cycles, and we can forewarn based on our findings for 2020, that in 2024, Ohio, North Carolina, and Florida will be highly contested, and were major beneficiaries of the 2020 private Zuckerberg CTCL financial largesse.

The pivot counties targeted for fraud in 2020 to "swing" the results of the national election, and their coincident metropolitan areas, and counties, by State were:

- Pennsylvania - Philadelphia, Chester, Delaware, Allegheny, Montgomery

- Georgia - Clayton, DeKalb, Douglas, Fulton, Cobb, Gwinnett

- Arizona - Maricopa, Pima

- Michigan - Wayne (Detroit), Ingham, Oakland, Muskegon, Washtenaw

- Wisconsin - Milwaukee, Dane (Madison)

- Ohio - Franklin

- Florida - Miami-Dade, Leon, Broward

- North Carolina - Durham, Orange, Buncombe

This list of eight (8) "swing" States and these twenty-seven (27) pivot counties are interesting, and important to consider with regard to the case made herein for massive election fraud, for multiple reasons:

- The list of counties for each state above is in exact order by the size of private grants from the Center for Tech and Civic Life (The "CTCL" PAC financed by Mark Zuckerberg).

- The top counties in each state all implemented centralized Counting Centers, virtually identical in make up to the Delaware County, PA, Wharf Counting Center, and with the exception of only a couple, most pivot counties had centralized counting centers.

- ALL swing states legislatively implemented "no excuse" absentee ballots during the period between 2016 and 2020.

- ALL swing states legislatively implemented almost identical, major election reforms, to expand absentee ballots, drop boxes, "pop up" voting, "curbside" voting, centralized counting centers, takeover of election official duties by partisan bureaucrats, and centralization of previously decentralized precinct voting operations.

- ALL swing states, and most of the respective pivot Counties, were the subject of allegations of massive election fraud, which were disregarded in the "safest and most secure election in history."

- The swing" states and pivot counties in Pennsylvania, Georgia, Arizona, Michigan, and Wisconsin that went to Biden and the DNC undercard (most notably the Congress) ALL denied Poll Watchers access to canvassing areas.

- **Every single one of these pivot counties, targeted by the DNC and GOP Uniparty, and the CTCL, ALL went to Biden in 2020, and the DNC congruently dominated in "undercard" races.**

THE WHITEBOARD

In the government, as in corporate America, most strategic and tactical plans start out with a problem at the upper left of a whiteboard, with the desired outcome on the bottom right, and a linear Gantt flow chart that gets fleshed out in between.

It's both a strength and a weakness of government, defense and US intelligence agencies, the strength being that there is a plan to begin with (which is more often NOT the case), and the weakness being that for those that have seen enough of them, they become easily recognizable - and predictable.

Pick any failed plan implemented by the "ruling class" over the past few decades, and overlay them into a linear flow chart, and they ALL fail and get derailed when they hit an unexpected obstacle – which most often comes down to a person, or persons, which stop the plan, and cannot be threatened or otherwise made to change their minds.

One example of this would be former President Clinton being spotted on the airport tarmac with then US Attorney General Loretta Lynch.

Another would be the recent Durham report that exposed and revealed the corruption and criminality of Hillary Clinton, and the weaponization of intelligence agencies by Obama.

The "Fast and Furious" operation executed by Obama and then US Attorney General Holder to implement gun control in the US by sprinkling automatic machine guns like fairy dust on Mexican drug cartels, hit the end of the workflow when an investigation into the murder of a US Border Control Agent blew apart their planned narrative.

The easiest way to spot the next, or latest guffaw or disastrous kerfuffle of the "ruling class" is to simply read the front pages of the "news," watch our propagandist "mainstream media," and look for the key phrases of *"conspiracy theory,"* or *"debunked,"* or any *"fact checking"* performed by propagandists like Snopes, PolitiFact or Factcheck.org. Just take the opposite tack for any narrative that includes those phrases or those actors and assume the worst.

If those narratives fail to move the needle, there is high likelihood that those trying to reveal truths potentially damaging to the ruling class will be smeared, arrested on any number of fabricated charges, impeached where possible, sued, sanctioned, and if all that fails, will commit suicide with two shots to the back of the head, or hang themselves under guard with any surveillance cameras disabled. But that is the subject of multiple other books, and only included here for illustrative reasons.

It is because of the regular failure of centralized whiteboard-based Gantt linear workflows, and now laughable - almost pathetic - attempts by the "mainstream media" to quash anything that makes the "ruling class" appear to be the boobs and buffoons they are at their core, that the US military and intelligence agencies have gravitated towards nonlinear, "asymmetric" warfare and operations.

When properly executed, nonlinear, asymmetric, multi-layered plans, that rely on a decentralized, flat organization of highly trained people are virtually unstoppable.

However, we're dealing with a highly centralized DNC and GOP Uniparty "ruling class" that is chock full of narcissists, miscreants, and criminals of every sort. So even when they attempt to implement a nonlinear, asymmetric plan, what they end up with is a bunch of cobbled together linear Gannt chart plans doomed to failure as a collective in any dynamic environment.

We do not make these denigrating observations out of schadenfreude, or to dismay the naysayers that might have made it this far into this book from reading on. Rather, we have outlined how readily transparent the plans of the Uniparty "ruling class" and their willing sycophants in the media (both far left and far right) are, as part of the overall blueprint for both the massive election fraud that is the subject of this book, and almost every "Keystone Kops" ruse they inflict on the citizenry.

Imagine a whiteboard with a problem at the top of the board that lists the problem as simply "**Trump**," and end result on the bottom right that says, "**Remove him from office in 2020.**"

If you're going for the sure thing, you can't rely on the old fashioned, tried, and true means of voting fraud that didn't work in 2016, because the charismatic Trump blew all the norms, percentages, and curves, with 80+ million Twitter followers.

BY THE NUMBERS

In 2016, President Trump won 2,652 of 3,139 counties in the US, leaving Hillary with 487 counties. He didn't just win the majority in those counties, but took them by margins of 68% to 96%, in a total blow out.

Figure 25 - President Trump MAGA Rally

Hillary was one of the most universally unlikeable candidates put forward by either the DNC and the GOP since George McGovern (1972) and William Taft (1912) respectively. And yet, Hillary still somehow "won" the popular vote with 65,844,610 votes to Trump's 62,979,636, with a difference of 2,864,974 votes in only 15% of 3,139 counties.

The total number of votes for other candidates was 7,804,213, for a grand total of 136,628,459 votes for all presidential candidates. Clinton captured almost as many votes as Barack Obama did to win in 2012 (65,915,795), but she lost the electoral college by a wide margin, with only 227 electoral votes compared to Trump's 304.

I remember Hillary and Bill the evening of the election, dressed in the purple of royalty, purple dress, purple suit, purple tie, and perfect lighting for "ruling class" royalty. Their expectations of a win were dashed, and Hillary was stomping around like Rumpelstiltskin, furious that she had lost an election that had been a "sure thing," if not bought and paid for outright.

Comparing 2016 to 2020, and voting totals of 81,282,916 from 520 Counties for Biden, 74,223,369 from 2,564 Counties for President Trump, and 2,891,441 for other candidates, and a grand total of 158,397,726 votes – an astounding 21,769,267 more votes cast that in 2016 – was statistically outside of all norms and broke all curves for credibility.

Let's round those numbers up for ease of reference, and we have 65 million Clinton, to 63 million Trump, and 137 million total votes in 2016, compared to 81 million Biden, to 74 million Trump and 158 million total votes in 2020.

As incredible and manufactured as those numbers appear at an instinctual gut level, the problem when using statistically anomalous numbers in litigation is the adage that: *"Statistics don't lie, statisticians do."*

Cue the mainstream media and their immediate assertions of anything running contrary to the election of their anointed ones, and the phrase "conspiracy theorists," and "debunking," and graphic after graphic from their statisticians contradicting other statisticians – and it all amounts to unintelligible gibberish and a headache for the citizenry, the majority of which have been conditioned to move on. And they do.

One of the tenets of election law and civil law concerning elections, and a litigative hurdle that all election fraud cases must overcome in both the lower courts, and especially the Supreme Court of the United States (SCOTUS) is that election fraud must be proven to have quantitatively changed the outcome of an election.

CRITERIA FOR A "SURE THING"

Going back to our figurative whiteboard, we can add multiple parameters that must be considered to survive litigation, make a fraudulent election "stick," get through the certification process, and install the illegitimate "winners."

Criminals are clever, but not especially smart - and our "ruling class" is full of them. If they were smart, they wouldn't have to needlessly risk their liberty or necks to achieve financial objectives. There are exceptions, of course, but criminals, and corrupt politicians, in general, are not especially imaginative, and think linearly, when they think at all.

If only they could find a way to overcome the US Constitution and allow millions of "no excuse" mail-in ballots, and take full control over all the counting, and electronic tabulation of votes, it would make things much easier logistically, and reduce the number of trigger men and bag men required. The downfall of every otherwise great plan is that while it might be designed by smart people, it is most often executed by idiots.

So, what would you need to put on a whiteboard to be able to execute on the objectives above and control all ballots?

Well, first, you would not only need no excuse absentee ballots, but there would also need to be a situation where most people would have an incentive to vote by mail. We can only walk through one conspiracy theory at a time, but it is a factual statement that Covid-19 and the lockdowns of 2020 assured a substantial percentage of the ballots would be mail-ins.

Then you would need to control who would process and count the ballots and remove the citizenry from being able to observe the ballots and election.

You would need a simple means of applying formulas and statistical ratios to ensure everything matches up to previous elections (regardless of whether they were also fraudulent), so consolidation of ballots into a single "up ballot" and "down ballot" to be able to add and modify ballots as necessary to ensure that reconciliation of ballots would make sense statistically, would be critical.

Most importantly, you would have to centralize everything into voting centers, and consolidate voting districts and centralize them to ensure data smoothing and ratio formulas could be maintained.

Lastly, the number of ballots printed would have to be almost doubled - or at least allowed to be printed ad hoc on demand - to ensure that the entire election could be fabricated if necessary.

LEGISLATING "TRANSFORMATIVE" ELECTION REFORMS

The holy grail of such a whiteboard plan would be to create a completely closed system where electronic counting machines and tabulation machines all automagically synchronize and ultimately reconcile with state voter rolls in a push-or-pull exchange, as required, to completely mask any fraud, and thwart any semblance of a forensic audit.

With all of this in mind, the "ruling class" Uniparty would need to introduce corresponding legislation into the swing states between 2016 and 2020.

Leah and I would learn that Act 77 was not "hijacked by the Democrats," as alleged by the GOP and most notably, gubernatorial candidate Doug Mastriano. That was an outright lie. It was the #NeverTrumpers, RINOs (Republicans In Name Only), and the merely ordinarily corrupt who traded their country for a few pieces of silver, patronage, and political favor. They were the ones who would give Democrat Pennsylvania Governor Wolf an easy layup.

Enter key members of the Pennsylvania State Senate, with their 2016 and 2017 Election Reform recommendations to the committee that set up election reform bills for the 2019 - 2020 Regular Session of the Senate on January 29, 2019.

Thirty-one (31) Senate Bills that subverted the law were introduced to the GOP majority PA Senate for "election reforms" between 2019 and 2020.

Less than six months after President Trump took office on January 20th, 2016, the Pennsylvania GOP led Senate put forward Senate Resolution No. 394 of 2016 directed Joint State Government Commission (JSGC) to study the issue of voting system technology.

Specifically, the resolution directed that the study should include "information gathered from other states regarding the administration of elections and technology, a survey of counties in the Commonwealth regarding the administration of elections, and information regarding the cost to administer elections and to improve, upgrade, modernize or replace election system technology."

Which, we have learned is "politicianese." When translated for civilians, it means "partisan lobbyists will provide the language for election reform, for which we will haggle and negotiate concessions to forward our careers and add to our personal wealth, and betray the citizens and constituents we represent."

Leah and I can state that condemnation of the PA Senate legislators listed herein without fear of being sued for slander or libel because their prospective betrayal was included in their "transformative reforms" in the very body of their lobbyist crafted recommendations and reports, to wit:

The Advisory Committee recommended – in 2016 – "that the act of June 3, 1937 (P.L.1333, No.320), known as the Pennsylvania Election Code, be amended:

- to provide a greater incentive to poll workers to attend training

- to allow counties to conduct elections more efficiently by taking into account actual voter participation levels when determining how many ballots to print

- to improve election security and integrity.

- to provide funding to assist counties in the purchase or lease of new equipment.

- to create a commission to advise the General Assembly regarding proposed amendments to the Pennsylvania Election Code as well as other election- related matters.

- to change Article 5 of The Constitution of the Commonwealth of Pennsylvania to prevent ambiguity and inefficiency regarding the way justices, judges, and justices of the peace are listed on ballots for purposes of retention elections (adding the judges to the partisan ballot).

The full report, which would not be released until October 2019, directly referenced materials produced by the George Soros funded "Democracy PAC," a super PAC to support and/or oppose conservative federal candidates in the 2020 elections. Soros contributed $5.1 million to the group through June 7, 2019.

Previous to that effort, Soros was the principal financier for Delaware County, PA District Attorney Jack Stollsteimer, giving him $1,000,000 to unseat incumbent Katayoun M. Copeland. Soros further gave Philadelphia attorney and notorious leftist Larry Krasner $1.7 million for the same November 2019 election. These Soros funded District Attorneys would be responsible for investigating (or not investigating), and prosecuting (or not prosecuting) any election fraud that might occur in Philadelphia and Delaware Counties, PA in November 2020 during the Presidential election.

A summary of the "election reforms" the Joint State Government Committee recommended were:

- Early Voting

- Voter Centers

- No Excuse Absentee ballots

- All mail voting

- Automatic Voting Centers

- Same Day Registration

- Online Registrations

- Electronic Voted Ballots

- Voting machine examinations and replacement

PA SENATE ELECTION REFORM BILLS

The key members of the recommendation committee were Senator Mike Folmer, Sen. Judith L. Schwank, Sen. Thomas H. Killion, and Sen. Patrick J. Stefano. They crafted the following election reform recommendations, which were curiously identical to election reform recommendations presented to legislatures throughout the country, most likely because they were created by the same lobbyists. Compare and contrast the recommended Senate Bills (**SB's**) with the previous "perfect" linear plan for executing massive election fraud in the 2020 election:

- **SB411** Change State Constitution to allow "no excuse" Absentee Ballots (Folmer/Schwank)

- **SB412** "Given the challenges elections officials have in finding poll worker volunteers, this provision is an additional – and unnecessary – headache," that should be repealed from the State Constitution, so they can be replaced by paid (partisan) bureaucrats currently excluded from being poll workers (federal, state, county, and municipal employees serving as poll workers). (Stefano/Folmer)

- **SB413** Repeal separate ballots for justice, judges, and justices of the peace, and make them part of the partisan, endorsed political party, "down vote" – making a single ballot for all races (Martin/Folmer)

- **SB414** In addition to "no excuse" mail-in ballots, reduce the requirements when applying for absentee ballots; mail absentee ballots earlier; give voters more time to return absentee ballots (past election day); eliminate the public posting of absentee voters, and remove other restrictions. (Schwank/Folmer):

- **SB415** Permanent Early Voting List. Once a voter opts in, he or she automatically receives an absentee ballot for all future elections. (Folmer)

- **SB416** Vote Centers/Curbside Voting - voters can cast their ballots at any Vote Center in the county, including temporary "curbside" centers for disabled voters that cannot physically enter a polling location, and "pop up" centers – regardless of their home address (Killion/Folmer)

- **SB417** Number of Votes to Qualify as a Write-In Winner would require successful write-in candidates receive the same number of write-in votes as would be required if they had filed signed nomination petitions (Martin/Folmer):

- **SB418** Number of Ballots to Be Printed - give counties the discretion to print 10% more than the highest number of ballots cast in the previous three Primaries or General Elections in an election district (Stefano/Martin):

- **SB419** Consolidation of Smaller Precincts - give counties the option of either mailing ballots to voters in precincts with fewer than 250 registered voters or allowing counties to consolidate election districts under 250 registered voters. In other words, in person voting would be replaced by mail-in ballots. (Folmer).

THE LEGISLATORS

Let's review the folks who crafted the above Senate Bills that would ultimately become ACT 77 in Pennsylvania:

Michael Folmer (born January 2, 1956) is a convicted sex offender. He represented the 48th district in the Pennsylvania State Senate, which includes all of Lebanon County and portions of Dauphin and York Counties, from 2007 to 2019. He was a member of the Republican Party. In September 2019 he was arrested on child pornography charges and resigned his State Senate seat.

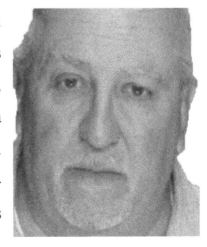

Figure 26 - PA Senator Michael Folmer

In July 2020, Folmer was sentenced to one to two years in county prison.

Thomas H. Killion (born 1957), a Republican, was a member of the Pennsylvania State Senate for the 9th Senatorial District from 2016 until 2020. He previously served as a

member of the Pennsylvania House of Representatives for the 168th district from 2003 to 2016. I (Greg Stenstrom) was a certified poll watcher for Tom Killion. Given the election fraud reported to Killion and Cody Bright (Killion's campaign man-

Figure 27 - PA Senator Tom Killion ager) by Stenstrom, Killion drafted a complaint to challenge the vote, but inexplicably withdrew it, never talking with me directly, and explaining via Cody Bright that "all of his people have been taken care of and found homes, including Killion."

Killion, who introduced PA Senate Bill 1234 in August 2020 to provide $100 million to the Chester Water Authority (CWA), reportedly went to work for the Authority, after the election. Dave White (2020 candidate for PA Governor) was reportedly overheard that he stands to profit $54 million if the

Chester Water Authority Trust is sold to Aqua America. Bright subsequently was elected and installed as an East Goshen Supervisor, and graduated to a senior advisory role and State Director for the Mehmet Oz for US Senate campaign.

Republican Scott Martin, a member of the PA State Senate for the 13th district since 2016, previously served as Lancaster County Commissioner and chairman of the PA Republican County Commissioners Caucus. On December 11, 2021, Martin announced his intention to seek the office of

Figure 28 - PA Senator Scott Martin

Governor, and then withdrew from the primary in February 2022.

Patrick J. Stefano (born 1965/66) a Republican, is currently a Pennsylvania State Senator for the 32nd district. Prior to being elected to the State Senate in the 2014 election, Stefano served as vice president of the Fayette County Chamber of Commerce.

Figure 29 - PA Senator Patrick J. Stefano

Figure 30 - PA Senator Judith Schwank

Judith Schwank (born 1951), a Democrat, was elected to the Pennsylvania Senate from the 11th district in a special election on March 15, 2011 to succeed the late Michael O'Pake. The district includes the city of Reading and most of eastern Berks County.

With most of the heavy lifting, and lobbyist work completed in the working Senate sub-Committee, we can now move forward to the full Senate State Government Committee for 2019-2020 that would introduce the bundled-up Senate Bills described above and further tuned as described below, into Act 77 when signed (in record time) by Pennsylvania Governor Wolf.

THE PA SENATE STATE GOVERNMENT COMMITTEE

The PA State Government Committee is a standing committee of the Pennsylvania State Senate. Standing committees are more important than others in terms of the impact and leverage of the bills that they consider. The central focus of both the PA House and Senate State Government Committees for 2019-2020 were election reforms.

The 2019-2020 Senate State Government Committee was GOP majority controlled and comprised of:

- Mike Folmer Chair - R

- Kristin Phillips-Hill Vice Chair - R

- John Gordner - R

- Doug Mastriano – R (2022 Gubernatorial Candidate)

- Patrick Stefano - R

- Judith Ward – R

- Anthony Williams Minority Chair - D

- Maria Collett - D

- Katie Muth - D

- Lindsey Williams – D

Figure 31 - PA Senate State Government Committee

Senate State Government Committee

Tuesday, June 18, 2019, 12:00 noon

East Wing, Hearing Room 8E-B

A summary of the Meeting Minutes tells the rest of the story and the coup de grace to honest elections in Pennsylvania: To consider Senate Bills

No. **300**, **411**, **414**, **418**, **421**, **422** and **693**; and House Bills No. **448** and **1461**.

- **Senate Bill 300 (Scarnati)**: Amends the Election Code to permit open primaries.

- **Amendment #A02032**: Clarifies both the definition of "unenrolled elector" and also the procedure for unenrolled electors to cast primary ballots.

- **Senate Bill 411 (Folmer)**: Amends the Pennsylvania Constitution to reform the provisions relating to absentee ballots.

- **Amendment #A01729:** Makes clear voters wishing to vote by absentee ballot need not be outside their municipality in order to qualify for an absentee ballot by making a technical change and by adding: "a law under this subsection may not require a qualified elector to physically appear at a designated polling place on the date of the election."

- **Senate Bill 414 (Schwank/Folmer)**: Amends the Pennsylvania Election Code to make statutory changes to process for unexcused absentee ballots.

- **Amendment #A02142:** clarifies an absentee ballot must be mailed no later than the Friday before the election so that absentee ballots will be counted with other ballots on Election Night; makes a technical amendment to clarify a certain citation.

- **Senate Bill 418 (Stefano)**: Amends the Election Code to change the number of ballots to be printed for an election.

- **Amendment #A01540:** Amends the bill to clarify the calculation for the number of ballots to be printed based upon gubernatorial, Presidential, and municipal Election years.

- **Senate Bill 421 (Boscola)**: Amends the Election Code to eliminate straight-ticket/party voting in Pennsylvania.

- **Amendment# A01865**: Changes the applicability section to state that the Act shall apply to elections commencing on or after January 1, 2020.

- **Senate Bill 422 (Vogel)**: Establishes the Pennsylvania Election Law Advisory Board.

- **Senate Bill 693 (A. Williams)**: Amends the Election Code to allow for shifting judicial ballots in Philadelphia.

- **House Bill 448 (Kaufer)**: Adds the Director of the PA Emergency Management Agency and the Commissioner of the PA State Police to the PA Commission for the U.S. Semiquincentennial and extends a report deadline.

- **Amendment #A02135**: Clarifies that the Commission is commonly known as "America250PA" and extends the report deadline to three years instead of two.

- **House Bill 1461 (Fee)**: Amends the Administrative Code of 1929 to allow the Office of Inspector General to investigate and combat all avenues of public benefits fraud.

AN UNCONSTITUTIONAL AMENDMENT

The problem with the process was that any amendment to the PA Constitution – and especially regarding election law - must be put onto the ballot as a referendum for the citizens to vote. For this reason and others, the Commonwealth Court of Pennsylvania would later rule in McLinko v Commonwealth of Pennsylvania (Bonner v. Commonwealth) that "Act 77,"', and in its entirety, was unconstitutional, and that specifically, the GOP and GOP majority PA Senate bypassed the PA Constitution and denied and infringed on the rights of the citizenry.

ACT 77

In review, the PA GOP introduced this to the Senate via Senator Folmer (R) with his memo for SB 419 as the collective of election reforms; and the PA GOP then sent it through both chambers (PA House and Senate) and to the floor as SB 421, which was passed nearly unanimously, and it then went to Wolf's desk to become ACT 77 in October 2019.

Only two brave PA GOP Representatives (House) would refuse to sign SB 421 election reform bill, House Rep Dave Zimmerman (99th Legislative District , Lancaster) and House Rep Steven Mentzer (97th Legislative District) - despite the entire PA Senate and House having been briefed and advised that it was unconstitutional – and that elections would essentially be turned over and be highly vulnerable to fraud with the implementation of "no-excuse" mail-in ballots, with the 2020 Primary elections only months away, and the General election only one year away.

It would be these same GOP PA Senators that ALL signed Act 77, led by Senator Doug Mastriano – who was in the Committee responsible for crafting Act 77 – that would assemble in Gettysburg after the election in November 2020, and hear what they had wrought – and then do absolutely nothing to remedy until long after the election.

Mastriano would amazingly state during his gubernatorial campaign that he had been "forced" to sign Act 77 "by the powers that be" and that it did, in fact, result in a grossly fraudulent election, and further stated that he was "fighting" to remedy it. He ultimately did little but talk and send a letter requesting an audit of election results, until pressed to repeal it stating it had been "hijacked." True, or not, the House and Senate members who passed Act 77 had a "duty to know," and act decisively to correct it.

SUMMARY AND KEY COMPONENTS OF THE LEGISLATIVE SETUP:

- No Excuse Mail-In Ballots

- Drop Boxes and "Pop Up" and "Curbside" voting

- Election Officials can be unelected partisan bureaucrats or unsworn partisan "volunteers"

- Eliminate straight party **voting** option when voting electronically

- Add judiciary elections to the same partisan election ballot for all (no longer separated) – Judges are now party members included in the party ticket.

- Increase the number of ballots allowed to be printed and allow for ad hoc, unlimited printing as necessary

- Ballots may be processed AFTER election day with no definitive "end" to election period

- Consolidate and centralize precincts

- Allow centralized "Counting Centers"

- Online and Same Day Registration

- Early Voting

All of these "transformative" election reforms were necessary to take elections away from the citizenry, and permit partisan bureaucrats to print any number of ballots or create any number of electronic ballots they deemed necessary, and unilaterally count them, without oversight and meaningful observance by poll watchers. The removal of virtually all checks and balances that might involve the citizenry and public scrutiny were all just Gantt chart lines from a figurative whiteboard crafted by those intent on destroying our Republic and doing away with our Constitution.

Why should it be any surprise that this legislative takeover of elections in the US would yield any other reactions or result from the Courts and Judges - now beholden to partisan politics and Uniparty ruling class approval and endorsements - would refuse to hear a single filed election fraud lawsuit, and deny any evidence to be submitted, or allow discovery in any of the "Swing" States and "Pivot" Counties that passed these election "reforms?"

How could it be a surprise that not only Common Pleas Judge Capuzzi in Delaware County, PA, would issue an inexplicable order that there wasn't a "scintilla of evidence" of election fraud without even allowing for a hearing, but every single partisan Judge, reliant on the endorsement and largess of the Uniparty "ruling class" would rule identically along partisan lines, across the country.

NO REAL ELECTION

The only possible answer is that there was no election in November 2020. It was a coup d'état, which resulted in the installation of an illegitimate government, secured by a judiciary and justice system beholden to the culprits that executed the coup, and State legislatures and Congress that allowed it.

This chapter has focused on the mechanics and legislative tasking, and groundwork required to execute the fraud, which by its nature requires a qualitative and subjective approach. In the next, and in subsequent chapters of this book, we will provide the quantitative proof and evidence of massive election fraud in Delaware County, PA, from which others may extrapolate to the other swing states and pivot counties.

We leave you with the summary results of the Presidential election of November 2020 in the Pivot Counties for the reader to review and digest.

All following tables were built using election tallies and data from CNN, and align directly with CTCL grants and donations described earlier in this chapter:

CTCL AND SOROS TARGETED SWING STATE PIVOT COUNTY RESULTS

Sorted in order by donation and amounts. The private grants and donations of the CTCL that went primarily to development of counting centers ("Big Stores") and counting machines (BlueCrest sorters) directly correlated to flipping swing states, and were also directly correlated to levels of reports of fraud. Soros funded and installed District Attorneys ensured no meaningful investigations would occur. Not a single county favored by the CTCL, and Soros resulted in a Republican win.

Pennsylvania	Biden	Trump	Difference
Philadelphia	603,790	118,532	485,258
Chester	182,372	128,565	53,807
Delaware	206,423	118,532	87,891
Allegheny	430,759	282,913	147,846
Montgomery	319,511	185,460	134,051
Pivot Total	1,742,855	834,002	908,853
State Total	3,459,823	3,378,253	81,670

Figure 32 - Pennsylvania Pivot County Results for November 2020

Georgia	Biden	Trump	Difference
Clayton	95,466	15,811	79,655
DeKalb	308,162	58,377	249,785
Douglas	42,814	25,454	17,360
Fulton	380,212	137,247	242,965
Cobb	221,847	165,436	56,411
Gwinnett	241,994	166,400	75,594
Pivot Total	1,290,495	568,725	721,770
State Total	2,473,633	2,461,854	11,779

Figure 33 - Georgia Pivot County Results for November 2020

Arizona	Biden	Trump	Difference
Maricopa	1,040,774	995,665	45,109
Pima	304,981	207,758	97,223
Pivot Total	1,345,755	1,203,423	142,332
State Total	1,672,143	1,661,686	10,457

Figure 34 - Arizona Pivot County Results for November 2020

Michigan	Biden	Trump	Difference
Wayne(Detroit)	597,170	264,553	332,617
Ingham	94,212	47,639	46,573
Oakland	434,148	325,971	108,177
Muskegon	45,643	45,133	510
Washtenaw	157,136	56,241	100,895
Pivot Total	1,328,309	739,537	588,772
State Total	2,804,040	2,649,852	154,188

Figure 35 - Michigan Pivot County Results for November 2020

Wisconsin	Biden	Trump	Difference
Milwaukee	317,527	134,482	183,045
Dane	260,121	78,794	181,327
Pivot Total	577,648	213,276	364,372
State Total	1,630,866	1,610,184	20,682

Figure 36 - Wisconsin Pivot County Results for November 2020

The 2022 and 2024 elections in Republican States of North Carolina, Florida, and Ohio, have all been positioned to flip.

Ohio	Biden	Trump	Difference
Franklin	409,144	211,237	197,907
Pivot Total	**409,144**	**211,237**	**197,907**
State Total	**2,679,165**	**3,154,834**	**(475,669)**

Figure 37 - Ohio Pivot County Results for November 2020

Florida	Biden	Trump	Difference
Miami-Dade	617,864	532,833	85,031
Leon	103,517	57,453	46,064
Broward	618,752	333,409	285,343
Pivot Total	**1,340,133**	**923,695**	**416,438**
State Total	**5,297,045**	**5,688,731**	**(391,686)**

Figure 38 - Florida Pivot County Results for November 2020

North Carolina	Biden	Trump	Difference
Durham	144,688	32,459	112,229
Orange	63,594	20,176	43,418
Buncombe	96,515	62,412	34,103
Pivot Total	**304,797**	**115,047**	**189,750**
State Total	**2,684,292**	**2,758,775**	**(74,483)**

Figure 39 - N. Carolina Pivot County Results for November 2020

7

THE PARALLEL ELECTION

Wan man ȝevit þe a pig, opin þe powch (When a man gives thee a pig, open the pouch)."

- "The Proverbs of Hendyng" 1275 AD

Con artists and criminals are clever but not especially imaginative, and once you learn basic cons and fraud strategy and tactics, they become easy to spot with experience.

If we were using the election fraud we observed in Delaware County, PA in November 2020, as a basis for a new *"Ocean's 14"* movie and whipping up some snappy dialog between Danny Ocean (George Clooney) and Rusty Ryan (Brad Pitt), then they would call this grift "A Big Store Pig in a Poke, with a Pidgeon Drop, and a Kansas City Shuffle."

We've simplified this to a "Parallel Election."

A "pig in a poke" is a thing that is bought without first being inspected, and thus of unknown authenticity or quality. A "poke" was a term for bag in the High Middle Ages, this idiom was explained as a confidence trick where a farmer would substitute a cat for a suckling pig when bringing it to market, so the image of a "pig in a poke" is of a concealed item being sold.

When the buyer discovered the deception, it was described as "letting the cat out of the bag." That is what Leah and I have done.

"The Big Store" is not so much specific to a particular con, but rather the scope of the con. The Big Store is a technique for selling the legitimacy of a scam and typically involves a large team of con artists and elaborate sets. Often a building is rented and furnished as a legitimate and substantial front for a business. That would be the remote "Wharf Building" on the Delaware River in this case. The "betting parlor" setup in the Paul Newman and Robert Redford movie "The Sting" is an example of a "Big Store" con.

A "Pidgeon Drop" in most basic terms is substituting one item, or container, for another item, or container. In our case, which would be the Tupperware tub full of vDrive USB drives of unknown pedigree, and forged return sheets and machine tapes (proof sheets). The real ones were replaced with fake ones.

In a "Kansas City Shuffle", the mark must be aware of, or at least suspect that he is involved in a con, but also be wrong about how the con artist is planning to deceive him. When the boxes of 500 mail-in ballots were brought up and down three different elevators on multiple racks on election eve at the Wharf Counting Center in Delaware County, without any chain of custody, or honest explanation for what the "volunteer" election workers were handling, or why, or what they were looking for, there was a "Kansas City Shuffle" in play. As demonstrated in video exhibits of volunteer election "helpers" in our lawsuits, they sheepishly state they are examining signature blocks to determine if they are "real" and "valid" without any logical or reasonable explanation of how they are supposed to accomplish that task without the ability to compare signatures or match them to voter rolls. It was a Monty Pythonesque task that made no sense to anyone, given that every mail-in ballot was already supposed to have been verified and entered in the PA SURE system and the BlueCrest sorter evaluated signature blocks. Only a functional idiot would assert that they were doing anything meaningful.

In fact, what was happening, was that the unobserved "pre-canvassing" ballot signature "inspection" process on the ground floor cafeteria of the Wharf Building allowed rolling racks of ballots to be "shuffled" from elevator to elevator, and floor to floor, to ultimately get them to the first floor BlueCrest sorter ballot ingestion intake despite the fact that they were from sources unknown.

The telltale of the "Kansas City Shuffle" in Delaware County, PA, and Philadelphia, PA, and GA, MI, WI, AZ, OH, FL, and NC, was that no poll watchers or certified "intervenors" were allowed anywhere near the ballot ingestion area.

Let's assume, for argument's sake, that the "ruling class" could not entertain the possibility of allowing the citizenry to cast votes, perhaps because old-fashioned means of cheating -- like ballot box stuffing -- would not be enough to secure the desired election result in key counties. The White Board would require a "SURE THING." What is more of a "sure thing" than pre-filling out 120,000 mail-in ballots and storing them in the Wharf Building counting center before the election?

In 2016, the "ruling class" could not deliver a fraudulent election to Hillary using the precedential fraud ratios of a 6-10% election swing against President Trump, who was winning at 300-1000% margins. Gone were the days of a roughly equivalent division between Democrats and Republicans, and roughly 50-50 voting that could be manipulated and changed by small, incremental fraud like stuffing a ballot box, or having 2 or 3 fraudulent voters per voting machine, for 1,000 machines across 428 precincts in Delaware County, PA. President Trump pummeled Hillary and completely destroyed Biden in "real," election day voting.

Shuffle multiple racks of 120,000 fake ballots in from somewhere in the Wharf Building counting center to the ingestion area of a BlueCrest sorter, with a confederate loader, or even someone too indifferent or callous to glance at the signatures on the envelopes, and it only took a few hours to have 102,000 votes cast for Biden and 18,000 ballots cast for President Trump. It wouldn't matter if the signature block had Mickey Mouse or Donald Duck, penned in. Once the ballot inside the envelope was injected into the tabulation process, it was a mindless, fired bullet, without conscious or pedigree.

Immediately destroy and dispose of the 120,000 outer envelopes with the barcodes, signatures, and forensic pedigree of where the ballots came from, and you have a perfect "Kansas City Shuffle." And you have a 5-to-1 fraudulent margin of swing to mitigate the actual, 5-to-1 election day pummeling that Trump voters had inflicted on the agenda of the ruling class.

The roughly ~70,000 "real" mail-in ballot envelopes, observed in the back rooms, remained available for an audits where they might have to produce a subset of "real envelopes, but could not suffice to explain where all ~120,000 envelopes that were counted went, and a resulting approximate ~50,000 envelope deficit in a full count, as requested in our litigation hold.

We've covered "The Big Store," the "Pig in a Poke," and the "Kansas City Shuffle" aspects of the con, and we only have the "Pidgeon Drop" left to explain.

The grifters – and specifically Jim Savage - withheld 47+ vDrive USB cards that comprised 50,000-to-100,000 electronic votes they would need, depending on what voting tabulation results they determined they should program them with. So, they waited.

Despite massive fraud that gave Biden an unimaginable 81,000,000 votes, he was still behind in PA, WI, MI, AZ, and GA, and way behind President Trump in electoral college votes, on election night.

Biden needed a minimum of 40,000 votes to "win" in Pennsylvania, and 80,000 votes to bring the tally high enough to negate the "normal," mundane election fraud that could result in successful challenge by President Trump. Remember that election fraud that does not exceed the threshold that would change the outcome of an election is essentially just noise.

Now comes the "Pidgeon Drop," and Voting Machine Warehouse Supervisor Jim Savage strolling into the Wharf Building counting center two days after the election with a transparent plastic baggie full of vDrive USB Cast Vote Record (CVR) sticks.

Had the vDrive USB cards come in sealed precinct ballot bags with custody sheets and a pedigree and proof or origin, with an explanation that 47+ vDrives had not been turned in, then this might look quite different. But instead, as with all "Pidgeon Drops," 47+ fraudulent vDrives that were wholly fabricated electronically to infuse and flip the vote by 50,000 votes from President Trump to Biden, were swapped in for the real vDrives.

As an expert in fraud, and a student of con artists and swindles, I immediately recognized the drop for what it was, and we challenged Savage, and notified the Deputy Sheriff (Donohue) and Clerk of Elections (Laureen Hagan) to try and stop the upload of the fraudulent votes. For that we were rebuffed and physically restrained.

Photographs were "banned" by Delaware County Solicitor William Martin. That order was rigorously enforced by the Sheriffs, who immediately surrounded anyone that attempted to take pictures of what was most certainly a public area, where government officials and election workers had no right or expectation of privacy, and it was unlawful of Martin to "forbid" photographs. But from a practical perspective, Sheriffs would have physically and forcibly ejected poll watchers that took photos.

Leah and I took photos anyway – which was a lawful exercise of our rights and our duties. Martin did not want any evidence of Savage uploading the vDrives, and I was swarmed and blocked by officers who tried to block my view of Savage.

Once Savage started uploading vDrives, I emphatically pressed election officials – and specifically Delaware County Solicitor Martin and Clerk Laureen Hagan – to update the count so we could see the impact of Savage's fraudulent Pidgeon Drop. I again threatened to get an emergency injunction, and the culprits finally relented, and the 50,000-vote flip for Biden was put up on the board.

In summary, we have the following con elements:

- **"The Big Store"** – The Wharf Building Counting Center

- **"The Pig in a Poke"** – 120,000+ fake ballots in boxes on racks in the Wharf Counting Center pre-stationed and ready to be swapped in for real ballots (see Project Amistad "Jesse the Truck Driver" testimony).

- **"The Kansas City Shuffle"** - Inexplicably bring dozens of racks of ballots up and down three elevators to introduce the 120,000+ fake ballots into the system, and move the 70,000 real ballots into the locked back room

- **"The Pidgeon Drop"** – After bringing in Tupperware tubs of loose USB vDrives and uploading a large quantity of electronic ballots on election evening, Savage strolls into the counting center two days later, and substitutes fake, fabricated USB vDrives, with tens of thousands of votes, for real ones, infusing them into the system to further flip the vote another 50,000 ballots to steal PA from President Trump, and give it to Biden.

Let's simplify even further. While all the shenanigans and fraud of previous elections went on as a diversion, the

REAL fraud was as simple as injecting 120,000+ fake mail-in ballots and 50,000 fabricated electronic votes into the counting process.

This only required external confederates to set things up by legislating centralized counting centers, and no excuse mail-in ballots, which was accomplished with a handful of lobbyists and bags full of cash. Then, only a couple of bagmen (the BlueCrest sorting machine loader, and Voting Machine Warehouse Supervisor, cum former Union President, Communist, and Trump hater Savage), to insert the USB vDrives and destroy the Mail-in ballot outer envelopes.

Mission accomplished, assuming no one challenged them.

Enter Stenstrom, Hoopes, and the whistle blower, and our challenge.

Now – the culprits need to make the results they fabricated out of thin air match election day voting documents and materials, which was predictably an impossible task. But, that part of the story doesn't come until later, and we need to review from the beginning within the context of describing the con:

PUTTING THE PLAN ON A WHITE BOARD

The 2016 Trump versus Hillary election showed the ruling class that they could not afford to leave the election in the hands of the citizenry to elect their own representatives to govern them.

The "old school" small cons of ballot box stuffing, raising the dead to vote, and using off the street hacks to impersonate voters, could not be relied upon. Even if we assume that some subset of voting machines were logged into remotely, via the illegal modems and internet network connection hardware that were included in voting machines and voting machine tabulators, it was not enough to deliver the election to Hillary in 2016.

It's relatively easy – child's play – to swing an election by single digit margins of 4-to-8 percent. In a county the size of Delaware County, PA, where primaries and undercard elections are won by only hundreds or even a few thousand votes, with 428 precincts, it only takes a few wayward votes per precinct and basic multiplication of flipping a few votes per precinct to make up thousands of votes.

But what happened in 2016 is that Hillary energized a disenfranchised movement of "deplorables" that Trump readily harnessed and energized, to completely blow the margins from single digits to proportions that could not be overcome with overwhelming election returns of upwards of 96% of some precincts voting for him. Hillary was so repugnant a candidate, that voters –Democrat, Republican or Independent – came out in droves for Trump. Precincts that historically were roughly divided 50-50, plus or minus 10% or even 20% became overwhelmingly impossible to mitigate using the old cons.

A significant problem for the white-boarders and their linear Gannt charts was that old cons that had taken decades to perfect and implement could not be stopped, and were still necessary in most locales. Old dogs cannot learn new tricks, and disrupting those cons would have been more perilous than leaving them alone.

So, they let them all go forward on the same old trajectories. They complemented the new Big Store con because they would distract and draw fire away from the bolder bigger con.

The "normal" election – Election Number 1 – proceeded forward, with little change to the game plan, with the added benefit of drop boxes and pop-up voting boxes providing visible evidence that thousands of mail-in ballots were being added to the universe of votes as cover for the Big Store con.

Those votes – the old con votes – could not be relied upon to deliver the margins required to ensure the ruling class candidates would prevail, and they could NOT afford to even count them in targeted Pivot counties.

What they needed to do – to ensure winning – was to totally fabricate ALL mail-in ballots and then infuse electronic ballots, as required, in targeted Swing States and Pivot Counties to deliver a "sure thing" and run a Parallel Election Number 2.

This is even easier than it sounds, and would require only a handful of confederates to implement. In Delaware County, PA, they would only need to fabricate 120,000+, or so, fake mail-in ballots, and a few dozen – 45-to-60 – vDrives to deliver the desired "sure thing." Each USB vDrive for each precinct contained hundreds-to-thousands of votes in the Cast Vote Record (CVR). With the consolidation of precincts, it was an easy math problem to determine which vDrives to manufacture and fabricate an outcome, and which ones to hold back for a few days while determining how many votes would need to be electronically programmed to assure victory.

Post-election, the voting machine tapes (proof sheets), vDrives, custody sheets, and return sheets could be manufactured, and/or destroyed, to synchronize with the reported election results in relative leisure.

Past election margins could be maintained, but tens of thousands of votes added, by simply increasing the total number of votes in targeted precincts. For example, a precinct that had 1000 total votes in 2016 with 67% (670 votes) for Hillary, could increase voter turnout by 1000 votes (to 2000 total voted) for a net gain of another 670 votes in 2020 while still maintaining the illusion of keeping a "67% majority" while pumping up the actual numbers of votes required to swing the state. For instance, at a macro level, simply increasing voter turnout totals by 30,000 from 2016 to 2020 in a Pivot County, using the same exact percentages and ratios, could yield an additional 20,000 votes for Biden (67% of 30,000).

Wait a couple of days to determine how many votes Biden would need for a win in PA, and then just add the number of voters using the previous election's percentages and ratios, and "Voila, winner, winner, chicken dinner."

A parallel election of the "old con" and new "Big Store" con had the added benefit of providing dozens of fruitless rabbit holes to occupy investigators and harm their credibility.

We had "krakens," and "router logs," mail-in drop box stuffing, and ballots that hadn't been folded or used different paper and inks, and "risk limited audits" (just recounting ballots that had already been illegitimately injected in the system). What those rabbit holes could not provide were hard numbers to quantify the extent of fraud. Without those quantitative numbers, the thresholds for declaring a fraudulent election could not be legally defined.

At the whiteboard high level, any negative fallout could be mitigated by:

- Destroying evidence

- Dismissing litigation, not permitting any evidence to be submitted

- Delay, Deny, "Debunk," Threaten, Intimidate, Gaslight – employing all the same old tricks until people give up.

These mitigative responses could not be achieved without certainty that law enforcement and justice would not investigate or hear evidence.

THE NATIONAL SETUP

The math of winning an electoral election is easy, and it was then only a matter of targeting swing states and counties to cement control of the 2020 election, and future 2022, and 2024 elections.

Soros' money was poured into these targeted swing states and counties in outlandish quantities, and millions of dollars were expended to secure the District Attorney positions in 2017 in Philadelphia (Larry Krasner), and 2016 in Montgomery County (Kevin R. Steele), and in 2019 in Delaware County (Jack Stollsteimer). Politics and prosecutorial records aside, Soros' funded District Attorneys all had one thing in common.

None conducted meaningful investigations of election fraud, and in fact, allegations of fraud were ridiculed and quashed. Multiple documented reports of election fraud were formally documented and reported to these District Attorneys, and Leah and I went so far as to write a formal letter, delivered by certified mail, and included in our lawsuits that Jack Stollsteimer (District Attorney), Josh Shapiro (Pennsylvania Attorney General-elect), and William McSwain (US Attorney for Eastern Pennsylvania) had been "inexplicably mute" and "perceptibly impotent" in their choices to NOT investigate any reports of election fraud.

Leah and I assisted over a hundred citizens who had witnessed election fraud in filing HAVA (Help America Vote Act) violation reports – which by law, the PA Attorney General must investigate, and has a fiduciary duty to respond to the complainant and report. Shapiro did no such thing, and instead obnoxiously kept repeating that there was "no election fraud."

With the key county-level law enforcement prosecutors and LEO's taken out of the picture for the 2020 general election by the ruling class using Soros' money, the next step in the big con was setting up the "Big Stores."

While the Covid-19 pandemic was an ideal situation for scaring people to stay home and use mail-in ballots, and set up "Big Store" counting centers, it wasn't a requirement, and just made the con easier to pull off. If they never had any intent of counting any of the ballots in parallel election 1, only of using ballots in parallel election 2, then Covid-19 provided good cover with lockdowns, and consolidation of precincts and counting centers, but was not a critical path obstacle in executing parallel election 2.

For the purposes of this book, and to deflect at least one "conspiracy theory" barb we will leave the Covid-19 aspect of the election alone and continue forward discussing the essential elements of the big con.

"THE BIG STORE"

Going back to the whiteboard, they needed big – huge – centralized counting centers with labyrinths of halls and multiple elevators. They also needed voting machine/election warehouses that were off the beaten path.

Let's look at the counting center Wharf Building at 2501 Seaport Drive, Chester, PA, 19013, in Delaware County. It is one of the most isolated areas in Delaware County, with low risk of any pesky cameras from local businesses picking up comings and goings, and no prying eyes for almost a half-mile, or more, in any direction.

DELAWARE COUNTY, PENNSYLVANIA COUNTING CENTER
2501 Seaport Drive, Chester, PA, 19013

Figure 40 - "The Big Store" Wharf Building - Rive

Figure 41 - "The Big Store" Wharf Building – Parking Lot view

The commonalities between Delaware County, Pennsylvania and the targeted "Pivot" counties throughout the country were Counting Centers and Voting Machine Warehouses that strongly favored a low probability that what was happening inside – and outside – could be meaningfully observed. Some might argue that the pool of buildings that would meet the functional requirements to be Counting Centers and Voting Machine Warehouses would result in the buildings being uniform in types of locations. We have included photographs for several building locations in the "Pivot" counties and will leave it to the reader to decide for themselves the similarities, and appropriateness for a "Big Store" con.

DETROIT, MICHIGAN
1 Washington Blvd, Detroit, MI 48226

Figure 42 - Interior of Counting Center Detroit Michigan

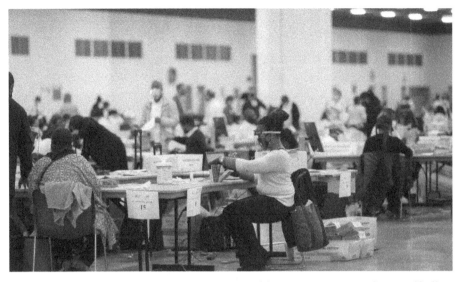

Figure 43 - Counting tables Detroit MI, Note boxes of ballots

MILWAUKEE, WISCONSIN COUNTING CENTER

1901 S. Kinnickinnic Ave, Milwaukee, WI 53204

Absentee vote counting in the city of Milwaukee. Photos by Jeramey Jannene.

Figure 44 - Interior of the Counting Center in Milwaukee, WI

FULTON COUNTY, GEORGIA COUNTING CENTER

736 Cleveland Ave SW, Atlanta, GA 30315

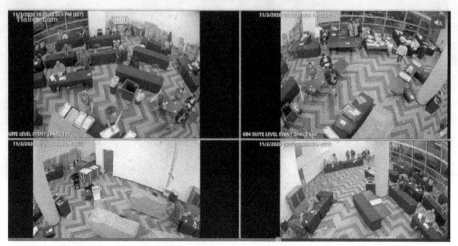

Figure 45 -Fulton County GA State Farm Arena Inside

Figure 46 -Fulton County GA State Farm Arena Street View

MARICOPA COUNTY, ARIZONA BALLOT COUNTING CENTER

510 S. 3rd Ave, Phoenix, AZ 85003

Figure 47 - Maricopa County MCTEC Ballot Counting Center

PHILADELPHIA, PA CONVENTION CENTER

1101 Arch St, Philadelphia, PA 19107

Figure 48 - Philadelphia Convention Center Street View

Figure 49 - Philadelphia Convention Center Inside

From a "Big Store" con perspective, each "Counting Center" uniformly had limited exterior, local cameras that might record the comings and goings of commercial trucks, USPS trucks, with parking lots, covered parking garages, and loading docks, and commercial structures creating a "moat" that isolated the buildings, even in urban areas where traffic was so heavy, it offered security through obscurity.

"THE PIG IN A POKE"

To ensure a predictable outcome in Parallel Election 2, only two primary components of the con needed to be addressed.

The first being that any mail-in ballots that were going to be counted on election day would have to be in the building beforehand so they could be inserted/ingested into the entry point of the counting system.

Using the analogy of the pig in a bag being replaced by a cat that would appear the same to an observer, the counterfeit "fake" ballots (the cat) would only need to be pre-staged and stacked neatly in the Wharf Counting Center, waiting to replace the "real" ballots (the pig).

Multiple reports were made nationwide of independent shops producing filled in fake ballots tens of thousands at a time, and then being shipped via USPS to distribution centers. These stories, like most everything reported in this book as conveniently "debunked" by factcheck.org and PolitiFact used virtually no data points for their "debunking."

Postal subcontractor Jesse Morgan on Oct. 21 moved 144,000-288,000 completed mail-in ballots from Bethpage, New York, to Lancaster, Pennsylvania, where his trailer holding the ballots disappeared, after he had driven it almost daily for 18 months previous.

Postal subcontractor Nathan Pease was told by two separate postal workers on two separate occasions that the USPS in Wisconsin was gathering over 100,000 ballots on the morning of Nov. 4 to backdate the ballots so that the ballots would be counted even if they arrived after the statutory deadline.

Postal workers in Traverse City, Michigan; Coraopolis, Pennsylvania; Erie, Pennsylvania; and Elkins Park, Pennsylvania, indicate widespread malfeasance in the Postal Service including backdating ballots, ordering that Trump mail be interdicted to be placed in the 'Undeliverable Bulk Business Mail' bin, and emphasizing that Biden mail be delivered on time.

It was relatively easy for a media anxious to maintain their narrative of the "safest and most secure election in history" to attack and pillory witnesses.

Jesse Morgan, in particular, was viciously attacked by the media for having a troubled past and for having been a subject of a documentary on the paranormal.

I met both Jesse and Nathan and spent the better part of two days with them. Both were modest, earnest men, who had nothing to gain at all with their claims, and were apolitical, with no allegiance or even strong feelings one way or another towards any party or candidate. In Jesse's case, he worked long, hard hours every day, drove his truck and trailer for the USPS, and lived a quiet life. He knew he was going to be ripped to shreds by the media, and that it would negatively impact his life, potentially impacting custody arrangement of his children, but he came forward anyways, with specific testimony regarding the pallets of ballots he had inspected and carried.

What was shameful about the media's investigation and personal attacks on Jesse, was that they concentrated so heavily on their ridicule and "debunking" of Jesse's personal history, that they never actually attempted to investigate his story.

Regardless of the mechanics of how tens of thousands of fake mail-in ballots may, or may not, have been manufactured and fabricated prior to the election, multiple election day, election week, and post-election data points corroborate and support the allegation of tens of thousands of fake mail-in ballots being injected and introduced in bulk in centralized counting centers.

The BlueCrest sorters are leased equipment that are paid for by County Bureaus and Boards of Elections by the number of mail-in ballots processed.

As described in detail in our litigation, the Delaware County BlueCrest sorter had over 220,000 unique mail-in ballots run through it.

220,000 minus the 120,000+ mail-in ballots reported as received by the Delaware County Board of Elections on Election Day is a difference ("delta") of 100,000 unexplained ballots.

Figure 50 - "There are no fake ballots here..."

The BlueCrest sorter was set only to check that there was a signature on each envelope, whether a fictitious "Donald Duck" or "Mickey Mouse" or a simple scribble, and was configured to inspect whether a signature was present, or not, but was not configured for signature verification with the PA SURE system.

The 120,000+ mail-in ballots that the Delaware County Board of Elections reported having been received by election day were run through the BlueCrest sorter, and afterwards, all 120,000+ exterior envelopes with signatures and barcodes on them "disappeared" and were reported to have been destroyed according to statements by a GOP official and other Bureau of Election personnel.

Further, the photographic images of each enveloped taken and saved on the internal BlueCrest sorter hard drive were ordered to be destroyed and "wiped" by Jim Allen, the Supervisor of Elections shipped in from Chicago after the November 2020 election to "clean up," and carried out reluctantly by County information technology staff.

Figure 51 - Jim Allen, Supervisor of Elections

No poll watchers were allowed anywhere near the feeding tray of the BlueCrest sorter or within sightline of the boxes of mail-in ballots being loaded into it. Instead, Board of Elections and County solicitors and lawyers (Manly Parks and William Martin, respectively) set up an 4' X 4' "pen" and two chairs on the OPPOSITE side of the feeding tray and visible elements of the sorter, and poll watchers could only observe the back of the machine – and see nothing.

The Board of Elections would inexplicably state that the number of mail-in ballots mailed to voters was approximately 136,000-to-150,000 post-election week, when just two weeks previous had reported only a little over 100,000 mail-in ballots had been mailed out.

Curiously, the number of ballots reported mailed out by the Board of Elections (a high of ~150,000), when added to the ~70,000 unopened mail-in ballots sighted by Stenstrom, Hoopes, and multiple other witnesses, including Democratic Poll Watchers, and attorney Britain Henry, is ~220,000 ballots – equal to the number reportedly run through the BlueCrest sorter post-election.

This begs the question of both where did the mail-in ballots come from, and where did they go after the election? The fact that 120,000+ mail-in ballot exterior envelopes were illegally destroyed, and the BlueCrest sorter hard drive image was illegally destroyed, and 70,000 unopened mail-in ballots cannot be accounted for by the Board of Elections, are all corroborative data pointing to the allegations of fake mail-in ballots being manufactured and delivered via truck in pallets – in large bulk – to Lancaster, PA for distribution to Delaware County, Montgomery County, and Philadelphia.

The media and PA AG Shapiro voraciously attacked individual data points, and made personal attacks on the witnesses, poll watchers, truck drivers, USPS workers, and other credible witnesses as "crazed Trumpers" and "conspiracy theorists, and part of a mass conspiracy" being run by President Trump to "steal" the election from Biden.

A more likely scenario – supported by the evidence – is that 120,000+ fake mail-in ballots were staged in the Counting Center by one or two confederates and introduced into the BlueCrest sorter, who then immediately destroyed the fake envelopes after the ballots were extracted from them.

The "mad Trumper conspiracy" would require dozens of coordinated conspirators, whereas the "Pig in a Poke" con would only require one confederate to deliver the fake mail-in ballots in their envelopes, with one or two confederates to physically handle the fake envelopes and introduce them into the ballot canvassing process.

"THE KANSAS CITY SHUFFLE"

Mail-in ballots were loaded into USPS crates and red and green coded trays in lots of 500, and could be loaded in single stacks 16 to a rack, or if double stacked up to 32 boxes of 500 per rack.

The 120,000+ mail-in ballots reported being received by the Delaware County Bureau and Board of Elections, would only require 8 to 16 racks of boxes and ballots.

The Wharf Counting Center Building had three banks of elevators, the bank elevators for the office areas, a bank of elevators for maintenance and delivering packages and furniture, and an elevator for the parking garage – for a total of three elevator banks.

For inexplicable reasons, the Wharf building ground floor cafeteria was set up as a "Pre-Canvassing Area" and rolling racks of boxes of 500 ballots each were brought up and down ALL three elevator banks from the upper floors (the counting machines were located on the first floor) for volunteer election workers to examine each envelope to see if there was a signature in the signature block.

With 120,000+ fake ballots staged in the building and approximately 70,000 real ballots locked in the back storage room – as later admitted by Delaware County attorneys - it would be an elementary task to shuffle racks of trays of real ballots up and down the elevators to the "pre canvas" cafeteria area where volunteers "verified" a signature in the signature block on the envelope, and then have the same racks returned up to the back room on the first floor, and for fake ballots to be rolled in racks into a separate door to the feeding area of the BlueCrest sorter out of the line of site of poll watchers.

Figure 52 - "The Kansas City Shuffle"

The flaw in this structured con is that the multi-million dollar "BlueCrest Sorter" purchased by Delaware County Board of Elections in August of 2020 using Center for Tech and Civic Life (CTCL) "Zuckerberg money" not only checked each envelope for a signature, but also took an image of each envelope, and in future elections will synchronize with state SURE voting registration rolls and dynamically update the associated databases.

Which rack has "real" mail-in ballots,
and which is fake

What practical reason could there be for moving tens of thousands of ballots on dozens of rolling racks going up and down multiple elevator banks to manually inspect the signature blocks of mail-in ballots to ensure there was something scribbled there, when a multimillion-dollar machine was purchased and configured to automagically scan tens of thousands of envelopes per hour and inspect, image, and evaluate all aspects of the exterior envelope?

"THE PIDGEON DROP"

We have addressed the physical mail-in ballots, which using Parallel Election 2 delivered a "sure thing," which in the case of Delaware County were 5-to-1 vote swings (100,000-to-20,000 votes per candidate that benefitted most from the fraud). This provided a solid, core number of votes and an almost unbeatable lead that would have delivered the desired result of the ruling class in any other previous election.

To seal the deal though, they would have to wait until they had a solid count, and knew exactly how many more votes would be required to deliver the election to Biden and the DNC undercard, most importantly in PA, that being PA AG

Josh Shapiro, upon whom it would fall post-election, to investigate any reports of election fraud, from which he himself benefited.

With the Soros funded District Attorneys in place to manage any investigations at the county level, and Shapiro installed at the state level, the inside confederate (Jim Savage in Delaware County), could be brazen in further perverting the election results.

"The Pidgeon Drop" essentially requires a mark to believe something that was "lost" has been "found" and incorrectly believe that the "found" item has a higher or different value or count in this case.

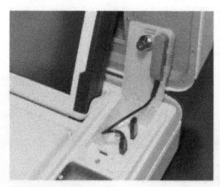 

Verity Scan's vDrive/USB/Modem compartment, open, showing modem with USB connection and vDrive.

Verity Scan's vDrive/USB/Modem compartment, closed and locked.

Figure 53 - vDrive / USB / Modem Compartment and Location in Hart Intercivic Voting Machine

"Find" 47+ USB vDrives two days after the election that had been "lost" and brazenly walk into the Counting Center and upload them into the voting tabulation servers, and it was an easy task to "flip" and adjust the vote to deliver the required number of votes and false victory to Biden, Shapiro, and the rest of the undercard chosen by the ruling class.

Which USB vDrive containing 2,000 votes
is "real." and which is "fake"

Having recognized the elements of the con and the fraud, it was relatively straightforward for us to know exactly where to look in developing proof and collecting hard physical evidence of the fraud.

I (Greg) have a long history of being a professional participant in multiple Internet and computer forensic fraud cases, and other cases where defendants had wantonly destroyed physical and electronic evidence, and had to develop and rely on civil law precedents on spoliation. I not only suspected that officials from the Bureau and Board of Elections, and law enforcement, and elected officials would destroy evidence of election fraud and other felony level crimes – I was counting on it.

I was not disappointed.

It is a much easier case to present, and win, when the defendant in a civil case has wantonly destroyed evidence that would exonerate them. In cases where physical evidence exists, and has not been destroyed, a morally flexible attorney and defendants can create doubt over even the most incriminating piece of evidence and draw jury trials out so long that an exhausted and befuddled jury may not arrive at the verdict that best aligns with the evidence.

In a spoliation case, where evidence that is required to be maintained for 22-months under federal and state law, or for the duration of any active litigation, litigation hold, or court order for preservation – has been purposefully destroyed – the litigant who destroyed the evidence is ruled upon adversely. In other words, if a piece of evidence could potentially exonerate a defendant, but the defendant wantonly destroys it, then the Court must reasonably presume it was incriminating towards the defendant.

If the defendants – in this case the Delaware County Board of Elections, et al, - which fraudulently and illegally certified an election, destroys all evidence that the election was lawful, auditable, and verifiable, the only verdict supported by law and precedence is that they are guilty of the fraud and crimes of which they are accused.

<u>More simply put, the destruction or alteration of evidence, IS evidence</u>.

Delaware County was the last county of 67 counties in PA to report 2020 election results, and before they reported, Biden was still behind President Trump by approximately 8,000 votes, with a similar deficit ratio margin for PA AG candidate Shapiro in his race.

The 207,000 votes for Biden and 118,000 votes for President Trump reported by Delaware County, and that 89,000-vote surplus for Biden, gave Biden his 80,000-vote margin over President Trump, which once certified, illegitimately delivered 20 electoral votes to Biden, and the presidency itself.

It is appropriate that the massive election fraud, and fraudulent certification that enabled the illegitimate installation of Biden, and the Congress, and further cemented Uniparty (primarily DNC) control over Delaware County, PA, if decertified, would almost singularly undo the fraudulent November 2020 election.

SUMMARY OF WHAT WE CAN PROVE:

22. CTCL (Zuckerberg) money that targeted swing states and pivot counties to install centralized Counting Centers and finance BlueCrest Sorters directly provided over $2 million and directly influenced election processes and outcomes in Delaware County, PA.

23. In the years between the 2016 and 2020 election, Soros donations of millions of dollars installed District Attorneys in targeted Swing States and Pivot Counties who would later refuse to investigate reports of November 2020 election fraud.

24. Approximately 70,000 unopened mail-in ballots were stored in a back room at the Wharf Counting Center in Delaware County, PA and those ballots were likely the "real" ballots.

25. 120,000+ "fake" ballots of unknown pedigree and chain of custody were run through the BlueCrest Sorter and Ballot opening machines ("slicers") to separate the outer envelopes from the ballots.

26. 47+ USB vDrives containing "ground truth" Cast Vote Records (CVR's) were, in fact, "missing" on Election Day, Election Week, and Certification dates for both Delco and PA, and were not even recreated until April-May 2021 in response to RTK requests, and in anticipation of upcoming primaries.

27. Jim Savage, Voting Machine Warehouse Supervisor, illegally uploaded 24+ USB vDrive CVR's comprising a net gain of approximately 50,000 votes for Biden on Nov 5th to the Hart Voting Tabulator machines at the Wharf Building Counting Center.

28. ALL voting machines were set to accept ANY ballot from ANY Precinct, making Reconciliation of the vote IMPOSSIBLE.

29. The majority of election materials used to certify the vote do not match. The return sheets, proof sheets (paper tapes), and official results – which should match exactly – are grossly different.

30. Delaware County Board of Elections attorney and other operatives in their employ admitted on video and audio that they fabricated the election.

31. There was NO Chain of Custody – at all.

32. Delaware County Bureau of Election officials wantonly fabricated November 2020 election results both electronically and with mail-in ballots and went to extraordinary lengths to destroy as much evidence as possible.

33. The Board of Elections Chairman (Lawrence), a Biden Elector, knowingly made multiple false statements and unlawfully certified the November 2020 election.

34. District Attorney Stollsteimer refused to investigate until allegations were made public in November 2021, and subsequently concluded his "investigation" without contacting Stenstrom, Hoopes, their Attorneys, or examining any of the Exhibits or evidence, simply stating everything was fabricated. He also refused to release any elements of the closed investigation in response to Right To Know (RTK) applications, citing he had performed an "internal investigation."

35. PA Attorney General Shapiro publicly denied that US Attorney McSwain had turned the report of allegations over to his office, or that he had conducted any investigation at all in Pennsylvania, calling all allegations of fraud a "Big Lie."

SUMMARY OF METHODS FOR EXECUTING A PARALLEL ELECTION:

1. Remove threat of investigation or prosecution by subverting the election of District Attorneys and law enforcement officials in targeted counties.

2. Enact "election reforms" to consolidate "counting centers" and centralize smaller precincts into larger ones.

3. Parallel Election 1: Run all the old scams and cheat "the old-fashioned way" in ALL States and Counties.

4. Parallel Election 2: Fabricate the entire election in targeted Swing States and Pivot Counties, which comprise less than 2% of all Counties in the US, and few as 31 Counties (1%) out of 3,139. Introduce pre-

staged fake mail-in ballots. Infuse fake vDrive Cast Vote Records (CVR's) as required.

5. Destroy ALL evidence required by federal and state law, and litigation hold, to be retained (spoliation).

6. Falsely state that all evidence of election fraud is false and has been "debunked," viciously attack any citizens who exercise their duties and rights to investigate, refuse to hear any court cases or perform any investigation by law enforcement agencies, and disbar any attorneys with temerity to represent such cases.

7. Repeat for all elections going forward.

8

HOISTED WITH THEIR OWN PETARD

There's letters sealed; and my two schoolfellows,

Whom I will trust as I will adders fanged,

They bear the mandate; they must sweep my way

And marshal me to knavery. Let it work,

For 'tis the sport to have the engineer

Hoist with his own petard; and 't shall go hard

But I will delve one yard below their mines

And blow them at the moon. O, 'tis most sweet

When in one line two crafts directly meet.

—Hamlet, Shakespeare

Shakespeare's turn of the phrase "hoisted with his own petard," means that it is good to see schemers and villains defeated by their own schemes.

Justice delayed is justice denied. After over a year and a half, our litigation and evidence have not been allowed to be heard. Leah and I have been relentlessly pilloried and defamed as private citizens by public officials and the media with impunity, with no interest on their part in sorting out the truth. This book, and particularly this chapter, is decidedly one sided, and our version of events, and not by our choice. We want nothing more, and look forward to, both sides being presented before a trier of fact.

William Martin, the Delaware County Solicitor, admitted in a January 2022 public hearing that he met with the Common Pleas Court with Manly Parks, the Board of Elections Solicitor that Martin appointed to that position, and John McBlain, who was ostensibly there representing Leah and me as poll watchers and intervenors, to "amicably" decide how to handle our demand for a court order to lawfully enforce our rights to observe all ballot canvassing areas, and further implied in other public statements that they had again addressed our case (sans the actual plaintiffs) amongst themselves, and we had been "thrown out" of court. He publicly repeated multiple times that we had been "thrown out," "debunked" and were simply harassing County and BOE officials and employees with baseless, "specious" allegations.

As it would turn out, McBlain would be appointed to the Delaware County Board of Elections only months after the November 2020 election and was unresponsive to any queries on the litigation regarding election fraud from our lawyers Bruce Castor and Deborah Silver, Leah and me, and from the Commonwealth Court of Pennsylvania, which subsequently ordered that McBlain and the Delaware County Republican Executive Committee be removed in their entirety from the appeal due to their refusal to respond.

So, in essence, Delaware County and the Delaware County Board of Elections unilaterally presented their one-sided collective case to the Delaware County Court of Common Pleas, leaving Stenstrom and Hoopes, the plaintiffs and intervenors totally out of the equation in what can only be perceived as either a violation of our rights, or they all missed the same day of law school that litigation is an adversarial plaintiff vs defendant arrangement, and not solely decided by the defendants attorneys and would-be-attorney. This left the draconian Uniparty unchallenged, to cement a manufactured election without evidentiary hearing, discovery, investigation, jury, or transparency.

At the Court of Common Pleas, Judge Capuzzi emerged from the meeting with the County and Board of Elections legal counsel after considering our lawsuit and allegations of election violations and fraud, without any input from the intervenor plaintiffs, or evidentiary hearing. The assertions by Capuzzi relied solely on the (false) assurances of Martin, Parks, McBlain and participants in the election fraud, and resulting fraudulent certification.

Leah and I were accused of "unclean hands," "vexation," frivolity, and not having a "scintilla of evidence," despite never having been permitted to testify or present evidence. We were also sanctioned for $50,000, and disbarment procedures were initiated against our attorney Deborah Silver, by Martin. This gave leave to many media outlets to claim that we had been "debunked," as was reported by FactCheck, Snopes, Politi-Fact, CNN, Rolling Stone, the Philadelphia Inquirer, New York Times, Washington Post, and others, based on blanket, unsupported assertions by Delaware County "spokesmen" that there was "no election fraud" and it had been "the safest and most secure election in history."

Not a single media outlet ever mentioned, or apparently read, the litigative responses and admissions of election law violations and fraud, or contacted us or our attorneys, or investigated further than regurgitating the statements from the architects, enablers, and co-conspirators who committed the massive election fraud.

What changed over time, in the face of testimony, and early disclosures of physical evidence of election fraud in social media, and conservative mainstream media, was that Delaware County and the Delaware County Board of Elections initial position of "no fraud" gradually morphed into admissions and rationalizations of the violations and fraud within the body of their litigative responses to us.

Manly Parks, the Board of Elections Solicitor, in a sworn affidavit as a witness included as an Exhibit (B) in defendant BOE's initial response, misrepresented "compliance" with Judge Capuzzi's order, by composing multiple pages of how they set up additional pens ("observer areas"), with the most egregious claim being that they set up an observer area "6 feet from the sorting machine" (BlueCrest Sorter), omitting the fact that the 4'x4' pen was situated at the back of the machine completely blocking any view of the ingestion area which was on the opposite side of the sorter from the main observer pen.

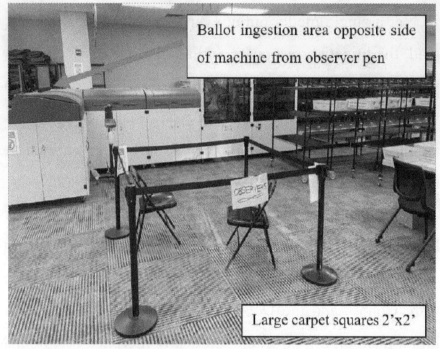

Ballot ingestion area opposite side of machine from observer pen

OBSERVERS

Large carpet squares 2'x2'

Figure 54 - BlueCrest Sorter "Observer Pen" on opposite side of ballot ingestion / loading

Park's other characterizations included multiple other mis-representations of "compliance" of observer areas in the back room (two chairs that observers could not leave once seated), omitting the fact that they had refused entry into the locked storage room until 1:30pm (for 5 minutes) sixteen and a half hours after the judge issued the order, and five hours after being presented with the order (at 8:30am) by Leah and myself; and that Bureau of Elections workspace cubes completely blocked observation of canvassing.

Figure 55 - Back Room Canvassing Area "Observer Chairs"

The Board of Elections attorneys initial filings also depicted photographs within the body of their responses of poll watcher observation areas, categorically denying all allegations and asserting we were lying that there were a large number of unopened mail-in ballots in the back rooms after the election counting was reportedly over, and that there was no requirement for a chain of custody, and implying that we were lying about there being any missing vDrives with official Cast Vote Records (CVR's) on them. Rather, Parks completely ignores and misrepresents our allegations that multiple (24+) USB vDrives of unknown pedigree were inserted into the tabulation server by Savage, stating that we thought he was inserting a single USB vDrive with mail-in ballot tabulations versus election day results (2 days previous), a (mis)fact not in evidence, completely ignoring all factual statements we alleged.

The problem with their assertions was that there were plainly thousands of unopened mail-in ballots in boxes of 500 in photographs in the BOE respondents own legal responses.

In their rush to "debunk" us, and point out that the BOE had "complied" with Judge Capuzzi's order to allow poll watchers access for 5-minutes every 2-hours, and set up chairs and small pens for observers, they inadvertently missed the boxes of unopened mail-in ballots in their own photographs, and contradicted themselves in the body of their own defense regarding the missing vDrives.

The County solicitor (Martin) and Board of Elections solicitor (Parks) in subsequent filings later took the opportunity to remedy those misrepresentations and belatedly acknowledge the unopened mail-in ballots.

It was the Delaware County Board of Elections (BOE), Board Chairman Lawrence's testimony and Board Solicitor, Manly Parks supporting litigative response, that there were NO missing USB vDrives, and that all electronic vote uploads were completed in accordance with law, when they certified the vote, in response to our highly publicized testimony at Gettysburg, yet in Manly Parks response for the Delaware County BOE, a month and a half after certification, Parks states:

> *"Petitioners make several allegations concerning an (sic) USB drive that they alleged was used "without any apparent chain of custody and without any oversight," despite the fact that neither the Order nor the election code require the Board to present chain of custody evidence to party observers and the fact that the USB drive in question allegedly contained Election Day votes from polling places,"*

Which is it? Were electronic votes from missing USB vDrives uploaded two days after the election on Thursday morning and dozens of others unaccounted for? Or were the original assertions by Parks and the BOE that there were no missing vDrives during the certification hearing? It is difficult to discern the incongruencies in Parks' representations from paragraph to paragraph, and document to document. In all previous litigation filings, public statements, and statements by Board of Election members, Bureau of Elections, attorneys, and "spokesmen" regarding certification, they plainly stated vDrives we're either not missing, or "no longer missing."

The public statement by the BOE to news media in response to my allegations of 47+ missing vDrives plainly stated that was false, and subsequently all leftist media, "FactCheck.org," and PolitiFact gleefully stated that we had been "debunked" despite not a single phone call or any attempt to verify the facts. The most obvious question any responsible journalist or "fact checker" might ask is why I would make such an outrageous allegation with such specificity (47+ vDrives missing and 24+ surreptitiously uploaded), for which we had a BOE memorandum listing the missing drives by precinct number in hand? Any responsible journalist or law enforcement investigator merely had to ask for the list and then ask the BOE to produce the vDrives in question for inspection. More curious and outrageous is that Judge Capuzzi accepted the BOE's Bart Simpson "I didn't do it" defense, and unsupported "liar, liar, pants on fire" responses without permitting an evidentiary hearing, and jury trial we requested.

"No longer" implies that the vDrives were either found, recreated, or forged. Video and audio exhibits subsequently included in the Common Pleas docket with our separate January 2022 complaint showed election officials conspiring to create different versions of November 2020 records and re-creations and fabrications of Return Sheets, Proof Sheets (tapes) and vDrives, contrary to their public statements, and contradictory statements related to certification of the vote and election. It was a blatant misrepresentation of election code to state that poll watchers could not question or challenge chain of custody, and lawfully intervene to question election violations and fraud. Again, Parks intentionally convolutes "interfere" with "intervene," the former being forbidden by law, and the latter being the purpose of poll watchers to begin with.

Parks falsely and coyly refers to the vDrives in the singular in his written response, demonstrating his intent to minimize the number of vDrives that were uploaded to tabulation servers after the election. But he is contradicted by multiple sworn statements that dozens of vDrives were missing – and are still missing. Their lies and perjurious testimony are further exposed by the photograph of Jim Savage holding the plastic bag of USB vDrives that plainly shows a plurality, not a singularity (why would he need a bag at all for a "single" USB vDrive stick?). Video, testimony, and documentary evidence has been entered into the Court docket that irrefutably proved they hadn't even bothered to replace or recreate the still missing vDrives from the November 2020 general election for the May 2021 primary.

Parks further falsely states that the law does not require a chain of custody. The law requires that voting machines and voting machine procedures be certified. The Pennsylvania Secretary of State must approve the voting machines and certifications under force of law, and did so in the May 7, 2019, Commonwealth of Pennsylvania Department of State report.

COMMONWEALTH OF PENNSYLVANIA
DEPARTMENT OF STATE

REPORT CONCERNING THE EXAMINATION RESULTS OF HART VERITY VOTING 2.3.3 WITH VERITY SCAN PRECINCT SCANNER, VERITY COUNT TABULATING AND REPORTING SOLUTION, VERITY CENTRAL - CENTRAL SCANNING SOLUTION, VERITY TOUCH WRITER DUO BALLOT MARKING DEVICE, AND VERITY DATA ELECTION DATA ENTRY SOFTWARE AND VERITY BUILD ELECTION DEFNITION SOFTWARE

Issued By:

Kathy Boockvar
Kathy Boockvar
Acting Secretary of the Commonwealth
May 7, 2019

The certification – with force of law – states in section X, Y, and Z that:

*"X, Jurisdictions implementing Verity Voting 2.3.3 must ensure that the USB devices and any other removable media used for election activities are maintained with a **<u>strict chain of custody</u>**. There must be a process to manage the removable media inventory to avoid misplaced and lost media."*

*"Y. Jurisdictions implementing Verity Voting 2.3.3 must ensure that poll worker training emphasizes the need for maintaining the **<u>strict chain of custody</u>** on USB devices (verity keys and vDrives) used at the polling place. County election officials must include processes to ensure that all supplied media is returned at the end of the election day."*

"Z. Jurisdictions implementing Verity Voting 2.3.3 must work with Hart to ensure appropriate levels of training for election officials are planned on implementation. Counties must en-

> *sure that the trainings adhere to the "Minimum Training Requirements" specified in Attachment D of this document."*

As the BOE Solicitor, Parks had a **duty to know** the law, and lawful procedures for elections, and is further required to comply with Pennsylvania law Title 204, Chapter 81, 204 Pa. Code Rule 4.1. Truthfulness in Statements to Others. Which states:

> *In the course of representing a client a lawyer shall not knowingly:*
>
> *(a) make a false statement of material fact or law to a third person; or*
>
> *(b) fail to disclose a material fact to a third person when disclosure is necessary to avoid aiding and abetting a criminal or fraudulent act by a client unless disclosure is prohibited by Rule 1.6.*

At this point in our book, and chapter, we leave it to the reader, and legal professionals, to review the legal filings and public statements of Delaware County Solicitor Martin, BOE Solicitor Parks, District Attorney Stollsteimer, and Pennsylvania Attorney General Shapiro, to consider their compliance with Pennsylvania law and Rules of Professional Conduct. Specifically, while all clients of lawyers, whether plaintiff or defendant are entitled to vigorous advocation and defense respectively, there is a definitive line between representation and participation that has been blurred or crossed regarding the November 2020 general election, and subsequent elections.

In the most recent May 2022 primary election, the loading of USB vDrive Cast Vote Records in Delaware County was conducted completely outside of any observance by poll watchers, candidates and other potential intervenors in a back room. We, again, leave it to the reader and legal professionals to determine whether this blatant violation of election law, and Pennsylvania Secretary of State voting machine certification procedures requiring "strict chain of custody" was a result of Leah and my allegations and litigation. If not, what other plausible explanation might their be?

Returning to BOE Solicitor Parks representations in his litigative response, he offers no explanation for why Jim Savage, who was not a sworn election official, uploaded dozens of official vDrive Cast Vote Records with tens of thousands of votes without pedigree, and knowingly, falsely states as a fact not in evidence that Savage loaded a <u>singular</u> USB vDrive, completely ignoring our allegations that Savage loaded <u>multiple</u> USB vDrives.

Attorney Parks continues, by falsely representing to the Court that we were afforded meaningful representation and were active participants in the decisions of the Court. Parks then makes multiple false statements in an attempt to paint us as omitting facts not in evidence.

> *Petitioners present non-contextual facts and use innuendo to attempt to create the appearance of impropriety. See, e.g., id at ¶ 32 ("There were plenty of questionable things witnessed by the poll watchers...") For example, Petitioners allege that Petitioner Stenstrom "returned at 8:30 a.m. on November 5, 2020" and was denied access, without stating whether the canvassing process had even started. Some of Petitioners' allegations explicitly occurred before the Order was entered, a fact Petitioners omit in order to*

> *create the appearance of impropriety. See, e.g.,*
> *id. at ¶ 25 (containing allegations regarding*
> *ballot counting on November 3).*

The order, was in fact, entered at 9:30pm the evening of November 4th (which comes before the 5th), and dated as such. Parks intentionally conflates that I claimed I was denied access to the counting center when it was quite clear the subject of interest in the order was the sequestered back rooms and ALL canvassing areas. The Wharf building and counting center were already abuzz with workers and canvassing, and was indeed open for business at 8:30AM. It is another blatant, outright misrepresentation of the facts by Parks that in the absence of a hearing, served its purpose of deceiving the Court(s) and achieve a smear of Stenstrom and Hoopes.

Parks goes on to admit that Jim Savage was uploading vDrives – a fact that has been vehemently denied publicly by the Board of Elections, Bureau of Elections, and media. He not only admits that missing vDrives and ballots (plural) were unlawfully uploaded by Savage, but falsely accuses me of breaking the law for "interfering" (misstating the word "intervene" that was in the body of our complaint) and requesting that he be stopped by the Clerk of Elections, Solicitors, and Sheriff, to explain the pedigree, chain of custody, and origin of the USB vDrives, and how dozens ended up in Savage's hands in the election Counting Center, and for which they had no explanation. Parks conveniently omits that Leah and I were certified poll "watchers" and not "observers" within the context of his responses. Parks finished off with a flourish, conflating election code specifying poll watchers could not object to a "single ballot," with a vDrive containing tens of thousands of ballots, and revealing his false representation of a "single vDrive."

Petitioners make several allegations concerning an (sic) USB drive that they alleged was used "without any apparent chain of custody and without any oversight," despite the fact that neither the Order nor the election code require the Board to present chain of custody evidence to party observers and the fact that the USB drive in question allegedly contained Election Day votes from polling places. This demonstrates that the Petitioners are seeking not to enforce this Court's Order, but to challenge it and re-litigate the issues addressed at the hearing on November 4.

In fact, it was Petitioners - not the Board - who violated the Order, as they admit in paragraph 35 of the Petition where they acknowledge that Petitioner Stenstrom objected to and attempted to interfere with the process of <u>ballots</u> being uploaded. *See id. at ¶ 35; see also Ex. A at ¶ 4 ("Any observer may not interfere[ ] with the process, nor may any observer object to individual ballots.").*

Figure 56 - Jim Savage with bag of USB vDrives Thursday morning

Manly Parks is apparently oblivious, or comfortable with his incongruent misrepresentations between paragraphs and documents in which he first personally cites his affidavit and standing as solicitor that they complied with Judge Capuzzi's order, and in the body of his response that there were no unopened mail-in ballots or missing vDrives; and that there was no missing chain of custody and then just as quickly admits that there were unopened mail-in ballots, and missing vDrives, and they were not required to provide a chain of custody. He meticulously uses vDrive in the singular, and cites election code about a "single ballot" and then either sloppily or intentionally refers to ballots in the plural.

More incredible – in the same document – he claims the fact that we saw thousands of unopened mail in ballots is inadmissible and should not be considered by the Court, because Judge Capuzzi erred in his order allowing us and other poll watchers access for 5 minutes every two hours, because it was not a canvassing area (another gross misrepresentation). He further falsely claims the counting center is not technically a "polling location" after the day of the election, again intentionally conflating and convoluting the law and premise that polling locations were previously open for only one day (until 8PM) and that counting occurred the same evening by the judge of elections and poll watchers, with the brand-new iteration of a never before used centralized counting center canvassing (processing) ballots for days after the election.

Applying Parks' logic, why bother to canvass and process votes on election day at all, as long as they were going to steal the election? They may as well have waited until the following day, locked the doors to everyone, and had an "*Animal House*" double secret probation count.

Parks admits in the paragraph below from his response that McBlain directly represented Stenstrom's and Hoopes' interests, and was their counsel, which is confusing because both Parks and McBlain waffle between alternately acknowledging and then denying our standing, observations, and testimony.

> *Petitioners' proposed intervention is nothing more than an attempt to re-litigate the Order. The Petitioners now seek to independently re-litigate the issue through the guise of an intervention, despite the fact that the Delaware County Republican Executive Committee directly represented their interests. It is merely because that relief did not go far enough for the Petitioners*

liking and because they want to use this Court and this proceeding as a vehicle to attempt to cast doubt upon the election results that they now seek to intervene.

In the very next paragraph, Parks states the DCREC, the GOP corporate body in which McBlain is an officer, while supposedly representing us as intervenors, is a separate entity from "Stenstrom and Hoopes.

Tellingly, the Delaware County Republican Executive Committee has not made any allegation that the Board of Elections failed to abide by the Order. The Delaware County Republican Executive Committee, representing the same Republican Party to which Petitioners belong, negotiated for and worked with the Board to implement the Order. It negotiated with the Board to secure additional accommodations for its observers during the ballot canvassing process, above and beyond those set forth in the Order.

Under these circumstances, intervention would only frustrate the purpose of the original Order and the interests of the actual Plaintiff in this case.

Again – which is it? Are "all parties" only Manly Parks, John McBlain, and William Martin and solely the "Esquires" that need to be satisfied with the outcome and have a pow-wow amongst themselves, which was essentially the BOE adjudicating and self-curing the BOE violations? Or do they even include the DCREC, Stenstrom, Hoopes and the candidates?

Parks varies from paragraph to paragraph depending on what tale needs to be woven. When he says, "all parties agreed," he means solely McBlain (who would shortly join the BOE) and Parks and Martin (who represented the BOE). When he is admonishing the Plaintiffs (Stenstrom and Hoopes), we are separate from the DCREC.

UNOPENED MAIL IN BALLOTS

It was both the BOE (Manly Parks) and DCREC's (John McBlain) contention during the election, and again during certification, and again in December 2020 in response to media reports, that there were no unopened mail-in ballots in the back room after processing and counting the ultimately final recorded number of 129,210 mail-in ballots, and that ALL mail-in and drop box ballots were moved to the main front room with observers, and that there were no unopened mail in ballots in the sequestered back rooms.

To further clarify, they (Parks and McBlain) admitted during the election week, that there were approximately 120,000 ballots already counted by Thursday midday, and approximately 3,000-6,000 unopened mail-in ballots and sliced ballots that needed remediation that had been moved from the back room to the front room, as discussed in previous chapters, for a total "universe" of about 126,000 mail-in ballots.

Again, in later reviewing their filings, the Delaware County Solicitor (William Martin), and BOE Solicitor (Manly Parks) must have noted that they had inadvertently included boxes with THOUSANDS of unopened mail-in ballots in their own photographs of the back room and attempted to fix this in the body of their appeal with a set of paragraphs and mental gymnastics that defy logic.

In essence, they argue that the Wharf building, was not, in fact a polling location, and after Election Day, they were not required to provide ANY access to observers (despite shutting the vote down on Election evening), and that the fact that there were inexplicably thousands of unopened mail-in ballots (in multiple boxes of ~500 ballots each) in the back room was not admissible or of consequence – because (despite Judge Capuzzi's order) – no Poll Watchers, observers, or intervenors were allowed in the back room, since they were not "technically" canvassing, and it was after election day.

Despite vigorous denials by the BOE Chairman (Gerald Lawrence, a Biden Elector), and Delaware County Solicitor (William Martin), and Delaware County Board of Elections Solicitor (Manly Parks), and other elected officials (Perrone) that there were no missing vDrives, and that there were no uncounted mail-in ballots in the back rooms, as witnessed by us and multiple other witnesses that filed sworn affidavits – the BOE and Park's own legal filings and responses include both photographic and written evidence of these ballots.

In fact – just as we alleged, there were dozens of missing vDrives containing CVR (Cast Vote Records) comprising tens of thousands of ballots, and tens of thousands more of unopened mail-in ballots, totaling approximately 100,000-to-120,000 unaccounted for ballots.

The video, audio and photographic evidence collected by the whistleblower is not the only evidence that corroborates the Board of Elections elected officials and counsel's OWN admissions, with another of the most obvious below:

> *Petitioner (sic) Confuse Their Private Right of Access With the Access Afforded By the Order and Pennsylvania Law.*
>
> *To the extent Petitioners base their request for intervention and relief on Petitioner Stenstrom's alleged lack of access to the "back room" **where uncounted <u>ballots</u> were stored** see e.g., Petition a ¶ 41, this claim fails.*

Parks again admits - in his own filing - that there were uncounted ballots stored in the back room, AFTER all mail-in ballots were counted, despite initially vehemently denying my (Stenstrom's) allegations that there were tens of thousands of unopened (uncounted) ballots in the back rooms at 1:30pm,

3:30pm, 5:30pm, and 7:30pm on the Thursday afternoon two days after the election - within the same document.

Referring to the Pennsylvania laws regarding Rules of Professional Conduct, it is incomprehensible how any reasonable or logical layperson or lawyer could reconcile the misrepresentations and statements, or not at least suspect Parks crosses the line from representation to collusion and participation in Delco BOE violations and fraud. It certainly doesn't help their case that the BOE Chairman of the Board is a DNC Biden Elector, and that Delco Solicitor Martin appointed Parks as the BOE Solicitor despite Parks simultaneously being the Solicitor of the Delaware County PA Democrat Party. In that light, the statements that "there was no fraud" and it was "the safest and most secure election in history" ring hollow.

Manly Parks and William Martin assert in their responses to Stenstrom and Hoopes complaint that:

"THE BUREAU OF ELECTIONS OF-FICE IS NOT A POLLING PLACE"

Finally, Petitioners lack standing because the Bureau of Elections office where the ballot can-

vassing occurred, and which is the subject of the Petition, is not a polling place under Pennsylvania law, and any alleged rights Petitioners claim were violated do not attach in such an environment. See In re Canvassing Operation, 241 A.3d at 347 (explaining amendments to Election Code that permitted <u>observers</u> to remain in the room at a polling place while ballots were canvassed). Under prior iterations of the code, observers could view ballots during canvassing at polling places; these provisions no longer apply. See id. at 349 (acknowledging that Section 3146.8(g) (1.1) and (2) apply to the ability of watchers to observe ballot canvassing activities).

Because the Bureau office is not a polling place as a matter of law, Petitioners had no rights of access to it based on being approved poll watchers. None of the rules regarding the 10 (sic – incomplete) The Board respectfully requests that this Court take judicial notice of this fact, which is maintained in a public record (a list of polling locations) located on the Del-

aware County Board of Elections website. See
Voter Resources, DelcoPa.gov (accessed Janu-
ary 5, 2021)

Apparently, Parks either intentionally makes false statements, or intentional misrepresentations, or did not actually
read his own citations. He cites as a matter of fact and law,
paragraphs 347, 348 and 349 of *In Re: Canvasing Obser-*
vation, which is merely a reiteration of the argument of the
Defendant Philadelphia Board of Elections in that case, and
NOT the actual findings, opinion and order of the Court.

By NOT citing the analysis or finding of the Court, but
rather repeated the argument of the Board of Elections in Philadelphia, Parks makes it appear that Stenstrom and Hoopes
were in the same conflated class of "observers" as plaintiff
Attorney Jeremy Mercer in *In Re: Canvassing Observation*
despite the Court's actual opinion that the rights and responsibilities of certified poll "watchers" were NOT a matter before
the bar in that case. This intentional conflation is regrettably
not limited to Delaware County's Martin and Parks, and is
a regular citation by other Board of Elections officials and
attorneys intent on blocking certified poll "watchers," falsely lumping them in the same class as public "observers" and

campaign attorneys. In short, *In Re: Canvassing Observation* does not apply to certified poll watchers like Leah and me, and we were, in fact, permitted by law to observe individual ballots and examine signatures and mail-in ballots. To wit, the Court finding and opinion *In Re: Canvassing Observation* specifically states:

> *As a threshold matter, given the specific issue in this case — the degree of access required by the Election Code for an "authorized representative" of a candidate to the precanvassing and canvassing proceedings of an election board — we regard Sections 3146.8(g)(1.1) and (2) of the Code to be the governing statutory provisions, as they directly set forth the rights of such individuals. Section 2650, offered by the Campaign, by its plain terms is inapplicable, as we are addressing the right of access of a campaign's representative to canvassing proceedings, not a candidate or his "attorney in fact". Section 3146.8(b) is likewise not controlling, given that it applies only to the right of "watchers" to be*

*present while ballots are canvassed. **The Election Code contains specific certification requirements for an individual to be appointed as a "watcher," see 25 P.S. § 2687 ("Appointment of watchers"), and there is no evidence of record establishing that Attorney Mercer met these requirements**, and, critically, he did not identify himself as a watcher, but rather as "one of the representatives designated by the Trump campaign... to observe the pre-canvass." N.T. Hearing, 11/3/20, at 20-21A*

SUMMARY OF "HOISTED WITH THEIR OWN PETARD":

The arguments made by Delaware County Board of Elections defendant attorneys are packed with misrepresentations, perhaps the most brazen being that Hoopes, Stenstrom and all poll watchers and candidates should not have been allowed in the Wharf counting center at all, because it was not a polling location. They then circularly admit that the Wharf Center was, in fact, a polling place, but that polling places can only exist on Election Day and once poll watchers were ejected from the counting center on the night of the election, they should not have been allowed to continue their duties as poll watchers and intervenors no matter how long it took them to count the votes.

Most outrageous, is that the Board of Election attorneys mistakenly included incriminating photographs that included boxes of thousands of unopened mail-in ballots taken well after the election was over, and all mail-in ballots were supposedly accounted for, and counted, Upon apparently realizing their error, they attempted to cure this by stating Leah and I should not have been permitted to see them, as if they did not exist, contradicting their earlier filings and assertions that they had complied with Judge Capuzzi's order. Even in light of the minimal transparency granted by Judge Capuzzi permitting 5 minutes of observation every two hours, they state he had "erred" in his order falsely stating it wasn't a polling location at all, and that they were not required to allow any access after election day to observe canvassing.

Despite multiple public statements and sworn statements that there were no missing USB vDrives containing tens of thousands of electronic ballots, and that Leah and I were "debunked" in our testimony that they were infused into the official tabulation days after the election, Delaware County Board of Elections attorneys admit in their own filings that our allegations were, in fact, true.

The Board of Elections and other defendants of both the initial December 2020 and separate January 2022 complaints admit in their own documents and filings that they violated election law and substantiate and corroborate our allegations that there were tens of thousands of unaccounted for mail-in ballots and electronic USB vDrives. Yet the BOE, attorneys, District Attorney, PA Attorney General, US Attorney General, the courts, and the media continue to assert that there isn't a "scintilla of evidence," and that our lawsuits were "frivolous," "vexatious," and "moot" when it comes to any expectation that there is any remedy to the fraudulent election.

The County and Board of Elections paraphrased arguments have gone from "Stenstrom and Hoopes are liars" to "well, we lied about everything, and we fabricated the entire election, and destroyed as much evidence as possible, but trust us, there was no fraud."

We close this chapter with annotated photographs that the Board of Elections lawyers submitted in their own filings to corroborate the statements within this chapter.

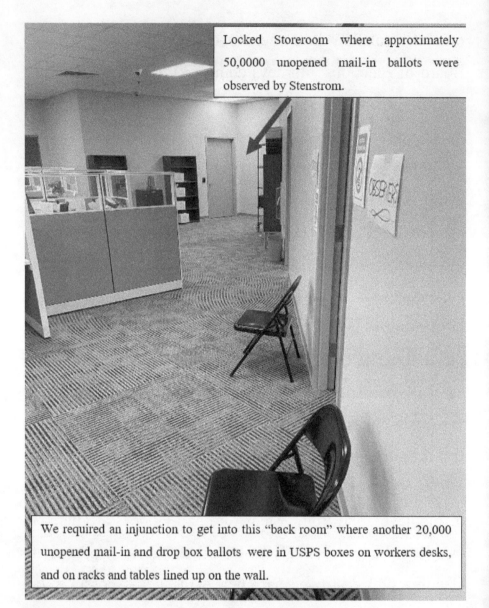

Locked Storeroom where approximately 50,0000 unopened mail-in ballots were observed by Stenstrom.

We required an injunction to get into this "back room" where another 20,000 unopened mail-in and drop box ballots were in USPS boxes on workers desks, and on racks and tables lined up on the wall.

Figure 57 - Back Room SURE Canvassing Area (Off Limits)

These photos were taken AFTER all mail-in and drop box ballots had been counted. Note that there are UNOPENED mail-in ballots in USPS boxes of 500 on wall and red "remediation" boxes on SURE entry worker desk.

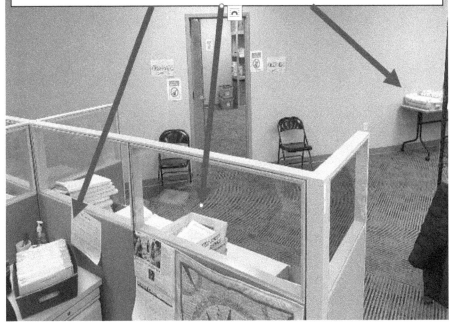

Figure 58 - Back Room SURE Canvassing Area (Off Limits)

The BOE Solicitor (and also Pennsylvania State Democratic Party Solicitor) Manly Parks, included photographs of thousands of mail in ballots (where there should have been none, zero (0), in their rush to show that observer stations (chairs) were set up to "comply" with the Judge's order to allow 5 minutes observation every 2 hours.

These photos were taken AFTER all mail-in and drop box ballots had been counted. Note that there are UNOPENED mail-in ballots in USPS boxes of 500 on wall and in red, yellow, and green "remediation" boxes.

Figure 59 - Back Room SURE Canvassing Area (Off Limits)

Multiple boxes of 500 unopened mail-in ballots are in multiple places in the sequestered back room as evidenced by Defendants OWN photographs AFTER all unopened mail-in ballots were recorded as counted, or being "curated" in the front room.

9

KABUKI THEATER IN GETTYSBURG; LEAH HOOPES

The pivotal post-election moment for us was our testimony at the election fraud hearings at Gettysburg, Pennsylvania, on November 25th, 2020. The unexpected testimony of first-hand experience of fraud that Greg and I delivered, in reasoned tones with evidence, electrified people who were suspicious of the election results. That was the public's first look at real, hard physical evidence and testimony, which confirmed the suspicions of many citizens, who did not believe that Joe Biden got 81 million real votes.

I was invited to the Gettysburg hearings by then PA State Senator Doug Mastriano, (R-Franklin). I had spent a few months getting to know him and working with him on the election. We met in April 2020, at the Re-Open PA rally in Harrisburg, and texted and chatted back and forth at length, starting in September 2020.

Doug Mastriano is a retired army colonel who was a personal protege of former PA GOP Chairman, Val DiGiorgio. DiGiorgio had been the former Chairman of the Chester County GOP, and a partner in the Philadelphia law firm Stradley, Ronon, at which PA Attorney General and gubernatorial candidate Josh Shapiro was also a partner. Shapiro was the Montgomery County Democrat Commissioner at that time, as well. Both Chester and Montgomery Counties are part of the Philadelphia metropolitan area. They border Delaware County, and combined, the three counties represent a larger voting base than Philadelphia by 120%.

Mastriano, with DiGiorgio's tutelage, first ran for the PA House unsuccessfully in the 13th district, placing fourth, and then with DiGiorgio's nod he won a special election for the PA Senate. Mastriano won the GOP nomination May 21st, 2019. Val DiGiorgio stepped down June 25th, 2019, after accusations of sexually explicit texts.

When I met Doug, at the Re-Open PA rally, I was deeply impressed by his presence, the way he spoke about God, and his willingness to fight for the people against the awful policies of Governor Wolf. He wore a big hat, and had his wife, Rebbie, pray over every rally. Later I saw that it was just schtick, and he repeated the exact same thing for a full year.

But in November we were still working together. Mastriano had invited me, and I had told him that Greg needed to be on the list too. So, there we both were, at the first big hearing after the election.

SETTING UP

Upon arriving at the Eisenhower Hotel and Conference Center, we were directed to a large conference room. We saw that the room was packed with media, which we'd been told would not be the case. The makeup of the brightly lit room was primarily liberal establishment media (CNN, MSNBC, ABC, NBC, CBS) with an underrepresentation of conservative media (Fox, Newsmax, OAN, NTD, Epoch Times). We met with Jim Fitzpatrick, and Greg stated:

"This is NOT what we were informed was going to happen, and this is not a hearing. It's a public execution, and I will not take part in it."

Fitzpatrick retrieved retired Colonel Phil Waldron, and Greg continued: "Every Senator sitting up on the dais at the front of the room voted for Act 77 (the Covid-moment legislation that allowed mass mail-in voting) and has their ass in a sling over voter fraud. Every one of them believes the Pennsylvania Supreme Court ruled that whether an observer was 6 feet, 60 feet, 600 feet, or on the moon, that the law that the vote be observed was upheld. I am willing to bet that every witness here except for Leah and myself, are going to testify that they "didn't see anything.""

Greg kept at it, "This is all going to be on national television with a narrative that we just had "the most secure election ever," which we know is false. At the end of the day, the Republican Senators are going to gravely nod and mutter that there were improprieties but that there is nothing they can do, and - boom - they are off the hook, and we are all screwed. I won't be part of that."

We walked into the hearing room, with chairs set up for hundreds of people, the senate hearing table with microphones and blinding lights, and the back part of the room filled with reporters from every news station. Gettysburg took place the night before Thanksgiving, November 25th, 2020, a day I will never forget. When they told me I was going up in the first panel I was super nervous. I noticed not a single witness was sworn in. We were not protected.

Waldron escorted both of us to a side room, where other witnesses were assembling, and took the papers and notes Greg had brought to Mayor Giuliani where they spoke in private. Waldron returned to Greg and said: "Your concerns have been noted, and you can go to sit in the audience if you like."

Greg went into the main conference room and took a seat behind those reserved for witnesses. When the hearing began sometime later, Greg was surprised to be called in the first batch of four witnesses, immediately after I was called.

Looking back, it was a monumental moment. It felt in that instance, that everyone was there to hear us and that after hearing about the corruption the newly energized cavalry would swoop in to save the country. Which is not even close to what happened, of course.

Startled by being called, Greg momentarily considered remaining seated. Senator Mastriano again called out his name and asked if he was present. Greg decided in that moment that it would be more useful to be a witness than to refuse to testify because he was dubious about the circumstances.

Argall and Mastriano indicated that each group would be given 15 minutes to speak, and the first witness, Justin Kweder, a lawyer, took the entire allocation of 15 minutes for himself. As expected, the bulk of the first two witnesses' testimony was that they "couldn't see anything."

LEAH'S MOMENT IN FRONT OF THE LIGHTS

My testimony focused on the results of our Watchdog group's months of investigation prior to the election regarding: the voting machine warehouse supervisor Jim Savage, who was a Bernie Sanders delegate and lobbyist; our concerns about the $2.1 million that the Center for Tech and Civic Life had dumped in Delco; that Delco housed 46% of the state's ballot drop boxes; and that the centralized counting center was in the middle of nowhere, near a loading dock. We had been calling for a seizing of the machines and a full forensic audit since November 4th.

GREG'S APPEARANCE

Greg was restrained but forceful, and extremely factual in his testimony. He spoke of the 47 missing USB sticks, the lack of chain of custody, the forensically destructive process, and the blatant, deliberate obstruction of our view to see the ingestion of ballots in the back room.

After I spoke, Greg noted that the Senators shifted nervously. By the time Greg had completed his testimony, the Senators appeared shell shocked at the profoundly serious allegations of fraud that had been leveled -- with physical evidence available to back them up. No one had expected that.

Greg had retired to the back of the conference room at that point to tend to business calls and noted that many of the liberal news media were packing up their cameras or had already left at the completion of his testimony. Not the story they had come for.

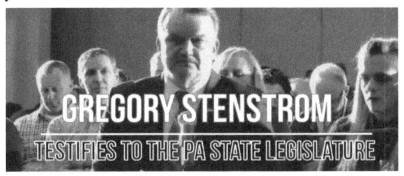

Figure 60 - Gregory Stenstrom testifying at Gettysburg

This supported Greg's earlier assumption that the event was a "show" constructed for the benefit of the PA GOP Senators who were under fire for passing Act 77. The hearing was meant to look like they were doing something about the thousands of reports of election fraud with which their offices had been deluged, notwithstanding the leftist narrative that the election was "the most secure in history." At the completion of the hearing, the PA GOP Senators scrambled out of the room to avoid interviews.

I had to practically tackle PA Senator Mastriano, who's only statement was "I have to go and get on the bus to DC," while avoiding eye contact with Greg who was directly in front of him. We left without speaking to anyone.

It is noteworthy that not a single PA Senator, including Argall or Mastriano, ever contacted either of us afterwards to investigate the allegations. In fact, they went to great lengths to avoid contact with us, nor would any of them engage meaningfully in investigating any of the allegations levied in the Gettysburg hearing. Nor did anyone subpoena a single election official to cross examine.

BETRAYED BY AN ALLY

We felt betrayed and abandoned, but also extremely cynical about Senator Mastriano's behavior. There is a whole string of texts and Facebook messenger conversations between Mastriano and me back and forth from September 2020 until January 5th, 2021. (I kept screen shots.) So, when he stopped talking to me after January 6th it was a complete change in behavior.

Figure 61 - PA Senator Doug Mastriano; Chair of the Investigation that did nothing...

Recently he told his followers that Greg and I had betrayed him, that we started factions in the Party and that he had no idea about our 'issues.' These are face saving lies on his part. This is a man who spent campaign money to pay for buses to Washington, DC on January 6th, 2020, and then stopped talking to his biggest supporters immediately following the infamous outcome of that rally. Which explains why I had the FBI show up at my door for being in DC on January 6th (which I wasn't), but somehow the issue was moot for Mastriano.

It is worth recalling that we testified in Gettysburg at his invitation, then made personal sacrifices to file a lawsuit. Our actions have been nothing if not consistent. Whereas he did an abrupt about face after Gettysburg, pawning me off to an aide, while withdrawing all support for our efforts. Doug Mastriano is currently running to be governor of Pennsylvania. I remain curious about what happened that changed his assessments of the work Greg, and I were doing.

GREG'S COMMENTS ON THE HEARINGS

Every PA GOP Senator there in Gettysburg signed Act 77, allowing mass mail-in ballots. With the exception of only Leah and I, none of the other witnesses actually saw anything fraudulent, because they were too far away, which the PA Supreme Court had already ordered was "ok." They didn't care whether an "observer," which was a different and conflated class from "certified poll watcher," was on the moon or even blocked from observing if they were in the same room. If no one saw anything then nothing happened, and the PA GOP Senators would have been off the hook for Act 77 and checked the box that they soberly "investigated" fraud allegations, right? "Problem solved. Let's move on. Nothing to see here." *That's how you hide and obscure collusion and fraud in an open forum* - and it wasn't my first rodeo assessing "public hearings." The goal of that hearing was not to reveal the truth - it was to bury it. I saw that within a minute of walking in the door. Why would the PA GOP invite CNN, MSNBC, NPR, ABC, CBS, NBC, and every liberal media propagandist they could find? I was told it would be a quiet affair to assemble facts and the truth so the PA GOP majority Senate could act, and hold the Governor and Election Officials accountable, force an audit, and verify the vote before certifying it. Those were worthy-sounding goals.

If you re-watch the videos from that day, watch how the Senators send annoyed and alarmed looks, as they text each other as the hearing went to hell.

The liberal news stations all left 10 minutes after Leah's and my testimony, and just a few minutes into Colonel Phil Waldron's, when they didn't get what they wanted. Again -

the intent and purpose of that hearing by the PA GOP was to *bury* the truth, not reveal it. A big deal was later made by the same PA GOP senators that we were not sworn in (which was intentional) but they omitted the fact that we had submitted sworn affidavits and declarations that were entered into multiple court dockets in PA and the Supreme Court of the United States before the hearing was held. I had also informed Mayor Rudy Giuliani and various GOP executives of my observations before the hearing started and asked these same questions.

Not a single Senator stayed afterwards or followed up. If Leah hadn't tackled Mastriano as he was slipping out a side door, he would have escaped. The PA GOP Senate let their term expire in a whimper without bringing any demands to the floor.

It was all theater.

Mastriano later organized buses for Jan 6th to DC, led dozens of his constituents right up to the Capital steps, and then took a hard stage left turn while they went forward, and he retreated to the rear. I have seen the video. He has said zero in support of those citizen constituents, some of whom were charged, arrested, and have been abandoned by all their elected representatives. I would like to hear Mastriano discuss his lack of meaningful action.

As a separate matter, Mastriano and Ward coordinated a voting machine audit in Fulton County, PA after Philadelphia and York County predictably threw their letters telling them to do so in the garbage. I have read the Fulton report and it states that while the scope of investigation did not allow them to discern fraud, the machines had remote communications hardware and software as well as Microsoft SQL database software loaded which is illegal. Mastriano buried that report - the only report and tangible result I saw that came out of his bluster. I can only draw the conclusion that he has become a servant of the GOP/Democrat Uniparty that fraudulently manufactured the 2020 vote, then covered up their malfeasance.

I have broken myself doing my duty as a citizen to hold people accountable for their criminal actions and the collusion of our representatives, law enforcement, and courts. Leah, myself, and others have been threatened with incarceration by Attorney General Shapiro and were sanctioned and sued at the court's insistence for coming forward with a case they chose to dismiss. We have presented two cases now with hard, physical, irrefutable evidence of massive election fraud in Delco and PA and are defending ourselves in a defamation case with President Trump as a codefendant.

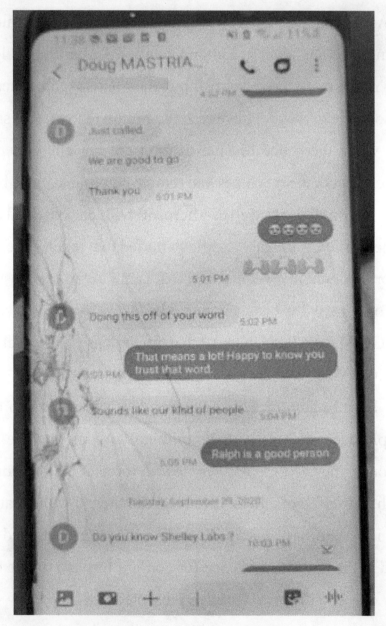

Figure 62 - Text messages btwn Leah and Mastriano 1

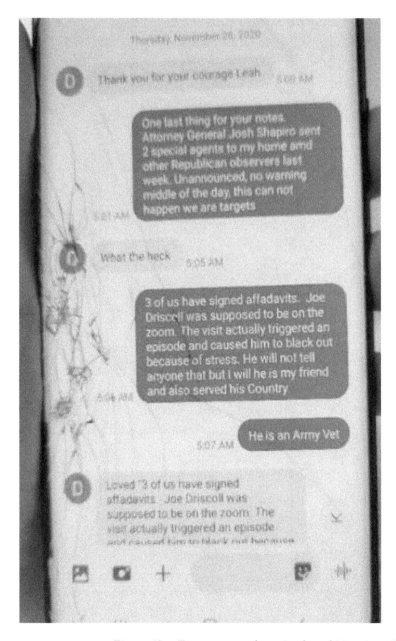

Figure 63 - Text messages btwn Leah and Mastriano 2

10

LEAH HOOPES GETTYSBURG TESTIMONY

My name is Leah Hoopes. I am from Delaware County, Pennsylvania. I was a poll watcher on the day of election, and I was also present at the counting center in Chester, Pennsylvania.

So, first and foremost, thank you to this committee and all those involved, and especially Senator Mastriano, and former Mayor Rudy Giuliani, to our fearless and brave President, thank you for being our shield, and putting us first. I am forever grateful.

It is an honor to be a part of this hearing, and to finally have an opportunity to speak about what took place in Delaware County, Pennsylvania. I feel as an American that is my duty to help protect the integrity of our elections, not just for me, but for every American. There are many who have lost life and limb for my right to vote.

I want to give a brief history of how I got involved in this election. Four years ago, Donald Trump came down an escalator, and I knew that he was here to take back our country. I was born and raised in Delaware County in a conservative home. I was taught from an early age to love thy neighbor, defend your country, and always speak the truth. I took those values throughout my life and applied them in every avenue possible. Which brings me up to the present.

About 18 months ago, I became a volunteer and assisted with a campaign for a Magisterial Judge. In that process, I was approached by my current GOP Chairman, and became an appointed Committeewoman for the Bethel Township Republican Party. In conjunction with my committee position, I also started volunteering for the Trump campaign, registering voters, and assisting with events. During this time, I started a watchdog group and reached out to the Thomas More Society

My associates and I have been focusing our efforts on election integrity. Our greatest efforts have been following closely the newly elected, and completely Democrat-run Delaware County Council, and the Democrat-majority Election Board. This also includes any, and all contractors, support staff, and any key players, involved.

What we found was actually concerning. Not only was private grant money from The Center for Tech and Life being used, but pop-up voter sites were also approved. These pop-up voter sites were placed in heavily Democrat cities, including Chester and Upper Darby, Pennsylvania. In these cases, the grant money from the CTCL was used to pay for electioneering. It was a one-stop shop; walk in, apply, get your ballots, submit, and you are out the door. But where this did not take place was in heavily Republican and Independent areas. Let us also make note that the Voting Machine Warehouse Supervisor is a Bernie Sanders delegate, who is also solely responsible for every scanner, v-card, and all machines - with absolutely zero experience in this area.

So, the real story is the millions of dollars spent to move the Counting Center from the Courthouse in Media, Pennsylvania, where it has been for decades, to the Wharf in Chester, Pennsylvania.

Let me explain you the layout of the Counting Center. It is in the middle of a huge parking lot, which sits back on Seaport Drive, next to loading docks. It has multi-million-dollar connections to the company "Power HRG," and "Subaru Park Soccer Stadium."

The Counting Center was on the first floor. There were multiple places to bring in ballots, in and out of elevators, and many rooms, to which workers had access. I was there for three straight days.

What became of concern, was the back room, which had no observers, no line of sight, or transparency into the process. There was no cooperation. Complete resistance from election night, and every day after. It took until our lawyer got an injunction to get into that back room, in which pre-canvassing was transpiring.

Even with an injunction, which was a joke, we were granted five minutes every two hours and the setup was sitting in a chair, 25-to-50 feet from any physical ballot.

I wish I had enough time today to recreate what I witnessed, and felt, during those moments, but we did not gather here today just for me, and my experience.

What I hope to achieve, for the public to understand, is that we have stuck our necks out, have been intimidated, threatened, bullied, have spent countless hours away from our families, friends, and jobs. We have signed affidavits, under penalty of perjury, which should be enough to know that this is a profoundly serious issue. I am here for one thing only, and that is to speak the truth.

This is not about party. This is about my country. Every American deserves transparency, truth, and to be able to question those in power, without fear of intimidation, bullying or backlash.

I hope this committee takes action, and justice will be swift to anyone involved in fraudulent activity. The nation is angry, disgruntled, tired, beaten up, and ready to defend our Republic. Without election integrity, we are just another banana republic. I thank you again for your time, efforts, and service, and it is an honor to be here, and to be part of a historical moment.

Thank you.

11

GREGORY STENSTROM GETTYSBURG TESTIMONY

My name is Gregory Stenstrom. I'm from Delaware County, Pennsylvania.

"I'm a father, and a family man. I was a former commanding officer/executive officer in the Navy and am a veteran of foreign wars. I'm the CEO of my own private company. I'm a data scientist; a forensic computer scientist; and an expert in security and fraud.

"Leah Hoopes had recruited me for this election. And I thank her for that.

"For the first part of the day I was a poll watcher in the city of Chester, and I was with just another former US Marine officer. And the two of us were the only GOP poll watchers in the city of Chester, which is about 40,000 people. Because of the consolidation for COVID there was seven polls we were allowed to make it to in 22 precincts.

"What we saw there was pretty orderly and exciting – people were excited to vote. One of the things we saw out in the field, was that quite a few people had done mail-in ballots. They hadn't been updated the Delaware County database yet so they would come in and say, "The database is not showing me on the database I'd like to vote." So, one of the processes was to give them a provisional ballot. They would vote provisionally and then later on their vote would be sorted out.

"That didn't happen.

"I observed, and the gentleman who is with me observed, seven different polls where the people were given a regular ballot. So, they cast the vote and put it in. You know we let it happen a few times. We didn't jump all over them, you know, if happened a couple of times we went up. In all cases the election judges were very forthcoming. Very polite, they apologized, and they said they couldn't do it. But that somewhat spurred me to go down to the counting center on Seaport Ave. It's a remote building – not much around it – and I wanted to take a look.

All day long I had been told that there were 10 to 20 GOP poll watchers down there, and everything was well on hand. Out of curiosity, I decided to go down.

I arrived at six o'clock, with four other gentlemen — again, former military and some good citizens from Delaware County. We weren't allowed to get in until 11 o'clock at night and we had to get some legal help get us in.

It took us five hours to get upstairs.

After that, what we saw here is what I really think the crux of this in Delaware County. As an expert in this, I think it's impossible to verify the validity of about 100,000 to 120,000 votes.

Delaware County's got 425,000 registered voters. Approximately 300,000 of them voted – I don't know what the exact number ended up. Mayor Giuliani nailed that number. But of that number, over 100,000 are in question in my mind.

What I saw as a forensics expert was an election process that was forensically destructive in the manner it was conducted, with the envelopes being separated from the ballots and going to the other side of the room.

The problem with that (from being forensically destructive) is when you go to do a recount.

Okay, the machines did a pretty good job of recount, so if I have 120,000 mail-in ballots at one side of the room, and envelopes at the other side of the room, there's still going to come out 102,000 votes for Vice President Biden and 18,000 votes for President Trump.

I don't care how many times you recount those votes. The value is going to come out the same every time.

So, the notion of a recount in a forensically destructive process is it doesn't work very well.

What we saw there was a chain of custody that in all cases was broken. Broken for the mail-in ballots; the drop box ballots; the Election Day USB card flash drives. In all cases, the chain of custody and the procedures that were defined by the Delaware County Board of Elections and election process review – they didn't follow one.

I couldn't even red-line this multi-page document because the entire document would be – they didn't follow any of the procedures.

So, I personally observed USB cards being uploaded to voting machines, by the voting machine warehouse supervisor on multiple occasions. I saw this personally, I brought it to the attention of the deputy sheriff who was stationed there, who is a senior law enforcement officer. And I brought to the attention of the clerk of elections.

I brought to their attention I objected, and I said, "This person is not being observed – he's not part of the process that I can see. And he's walking in with baggies – which we have pictures of and are submitted in our affidavits – and he was sticking these USBs into the machines.

I personally witnessed that happen over 24 times.

We have multiple other witnesses who saw it, including democrat poll watchers. And I was told the next day by the solicitors – well actually not the solicitor but the attorney that we had secured – that they said every election, they leave a couple of USBs in the voting machines, and they're brought back and generally the warehouse manager comes over and puts them in.

In talking to the US Attorney General McSwain, and other law enforcement officers, I found out that was not the case; that generally, more than two is unusual. So, they denied they did it, but as of today 47 USB v cards are missing. And they're nowhere to be found.

I was told, personally, that these 24 to 30 cards that were uploaded weren't there. Those cards I demanded – they didn't update the vote live time, they only updated it about once every two or three hours. I demanded they update the vote so I could see what the result was, and it was 50,000 votes. And I think as a computer scientist and American and a patriot, it doesn't matter who those 50,000 votes were. I'll tell you they were Vice President Biden. But what was shocking to me as an American, as someone who has gone to war, is that could even happen.

Several other things that came up was, on Thursday, it took us three days for them to obey the court order that I secured with Leah's help, and the help of the Thomas Moore society, who we thank – incredibly good patriots; they got us in there. They got the order for us to get in and look at the backup offices – which are locked – for five minutes every two hours.

I was the first one allowed to go in at 1:30 on Thursday, and then again at 3:30 for five minutes. The county solicitor had a stopwatch. On the first time I was not allowed to touch anything, the second time I did.

What I observed in the locked room in the back office was 70,000 unopened mail-in ballots. They were in boxes of 500 stacked in neatly.

The gentleman that came in with me is a Democrat poll watcher. (He's) a forensic pathologist; a very detailed, very resolute man. He took meticulous notes as well, and I verified with him, "Are you seeing what I'm seeing?"

We both agreed – as GOP poll watchers, and a Democrat poll watcher – that we had witnessed 60,000 to 70,000 (ballots). We had a little bit of a disagreement there.

The problem with that was by that time, the mail-in ballots had already been counted. So, 120,000 mail-in ballots had already been counted, posted, and done. So, my question is, where did the 70,000 ballots go? And nobody knows.

We have a picture in here (that I took) of a large number of boxes that were filled with what appeared to be ballots, sitting by the BlueCrest machine. They were there for about three hours and then they disappeared.

I thought it notable when I watched it at first, they were taking the ballots up and down. As I said, I am an expert in fraud. I saw the ballots going up multiple elevators and racks. And I think a lot of well-meaning people, and a lot of honest people there doing that – they were trying to participate in the process. And I would say that 99% of the people there – the way the process was designed – I believe that people thought it was a non-fraudulent process.

I heard that said many times. I said, there's no fraud going on here – I didn't even bring that up – but I think people saw what they wanted to see, and they saw what was intended for them to see.

At one point I called this kabuki theater. I said it was all designed for us to see. It was entertaining; there were cameras on it.

When we finally got in the back room where the votes were being ingested, as a data scientist, I wanted to see where the data is coming in.

And I wanted to know the universe of the votes.

Well, the universe of the votes was only supposed to be 120,000 mail-in ballots. We were told there were 6000 ballots remaining. So, I said okay, we have a universe of 126,000 votes. And when I get back there, the universe wasn't 126,000 votes, the universe was 200,000 votes.

So that's a problem.

I think a couple other things is the BlueCrest sorter machine was only manned by one person. You know, people ask me all the time, 'How do people commit crimes?' I know there's a lot of theories here, and I always look for the simplest thing. People are stuffing – you know, sticking USB sticks in, putting ballots in. Very simple thing; only takes a couple of people. Doesn't take a big conspiracy.

I think people look at things and they use inflammatory words, you know, like fraud and so forth. As a forensic computer scientist my interest is in the data.

Where did it go?

Where did the spoilage go?

How did the data come in and go out the system?

So, I think as a scientist, we need to look at that; we need to audit that.

What was really upsetting to me – the most upsetting – was I had spoken to multiple law enforcement agencies, and literally begged multiple law enforcement agencies, to go in, in order to prove that nothing's happening. You either exonerate yourselves in the process or refute what I'm saying. Please, it's a very simple process. Just go get the forensic evidence from the computers. It's a simple process: you turn the computer off, it's nondestructive, takes moments – maybe half an hour, 20 minutes to do it properly – you collect the evidence. You open the computer. You take a device called a bit blocker. You put it in the hard drive, it's done under the observation of law enforcement officers. They take a forensic image of the drive, put it all back together, it wouldn't have taken more than an hour to image all five machines.

"That was never done, despite my objections, and that was three weeks ago.

Lastly, when they said well, we've got all the forensic records and so forth. We just learned two days ago that virtually all chain of custody logs, records, yellow sheets – everything was gone.

All forensic evidence, all custody sheets in Delaware County are gone.

They had a signing party where they sat down, and poll workers were invited back to recreate those logs, and our understanding as of today, was that they were unsuccessful in getting them all.

So, we have a situation where we have 100,000 ballots to 120,000 ballots, both mail-in and a USB, which are in question.

Now there's no cure for this; there's no remedy for this. As a home charter, we could have a re-election in Delaware County for our own representatives within our own town. But there is no cure for that for the President of the United States. And I don't believe as a citizen, and an observer to this, that anybody could certify that vote in any good conscience.

If the Democrats that have a power of this process, had done things to follow their procedures – which they created almost unilaterally– we'd be in a situation where they could exonerate themselves, and they could say, "Mr. Stenstrom, you've been misinformed. We have evidence here that refutes what you say."

But that's not the case – they can't do that.

I say if you can't certify that vote, and you can't certify 100,000 votes out of 300,000, then you can't certify Delaware County."

12

COGNITIVE WARFARE; THE BATTLE FOR OUR REPUBLIC

In cognitive warfare, the human mind becomes the battlefield. The aim is to change not only what people think, but how they think and act. Waged successfully, it shapes and influences individual and group beliefs and behaviors to favor an aggressor's tactical or strategic objectives. In its extreme form, it has the potential to fracture and fragment an entire society, so that it no longer has the collective will to resist an adversary's intentions. An opponent could conceivably subdue a society without resorting to outright force or coercion.

— Countering cognitive warfare: awareness and resilience; Johns Hopkins University & Imperial College London; 20 May 2021; NATO Review

The Parallel election provided a wealth of opportunities for the ruling class to wage cognitive warfare and send otherwise well-meaning people down unproductive rabbit holes.

Even assuming the truth could occasionally get oxygen, the dominance over the technological battlespace by left-leaning social media platforms and propagandists like Facebook, Twitter, and YouTube quickly silenced it.

The chaos the Uniparty created with tens of millions of mail-in ballots, counting centers, and fraud across multiple fronts, using the same old election fraud cons, while running the new parallel election scam made it impossible for the uninitiated to figure out what had happened. For that matter, as this chapter will outline, the cognitive warfare tactics of flooding the zone with myriad trails that ultimately led nowhere, made it difficult for intelligent professional political people and lawyers to really understand what, specifically, had happened to create Biden's massive, fraudulent win.

In a cognitive warfare environment where Facebook was shaping the ideas of over 2 billion readers, and Twitter was influencing over 330 million – and banning anything contrary to the "safest election in history" narrative, it would have been pointless to develop information in our investigation of election fraud if there was no way to reliably share it. That is why I cofounded www.Patriot.Online. Our user base is relatively small at the time of this publication at 36,000 readers and 900 members (content providers), but growing steadily, and organically. It is where most of the links in this book point to.

THE POLITICIANS DID NOTHING

Let's review how we got here. The politicians that created the mess in Pennsylvania by enacting Act 77 and enabling "no excuse" mail-in ballots, were the prime enablers for fraud. The very architects of no-excuse mail-in ballots, drop boxes, "pop-up" voting centers, and the "keep adding ballots and keep counting until you get the desired result," shamelessly campaigned for "election integrity" after thoroughly undermining it. And large swaths of people bought it.

Doug Mastriano – a key member of the State Government select committee that gave us Act 77, later crafted his entire gubernatorial campaign out of "Fighting for Freedom," and "Walk as Free People," based on words without action. He raised millions of dollars for "election integrity," and his campaign. He promised to press the "fight," but didn't give a single nickel or even acknowledge multiple efforts to sort through the 2020 election fraud. He certainly never returned our calls for political support.

Mastriano had nothing to do with *Doug McLinko v Commonwealth* of Pennsylvania, which was combined by the Courts with a similar lawsuit by seven PA House of Representatives members, culminating in the appellate Commonwealth Court of Pennsylvania finding that "no excuse" mail-in ballots were unconstitutional; yet when that verdict was announced Mastriano was the first to take credit for it. He got lots of media coverage which didn't mention that it wasn't his litigation.

For the record, when a politician tells you he or she is fighting for you, and that he is "sticking it to the man," remember that most are either working for "the man," or are "the man."

PROJECT AMISTAD

Immediately after our Gettysburg testimony, Leah and I were called to Arlington, Virginia to work primarily with Phil Kline's crew from Project Amistad, which is funded by The Thomas More Society. As a group, they had been very supportive of our efforts in Delaware County, and we had remained in regular contact.

Phil was the former Attorney General for Kansas, and had run afoul of pro-abortionists, and specifically Planned Parenthood, during his tenure, and they had gone after him with claw hammers for his pro-life political views and prosecutorial discretion in those matters – and successfully disbarred him.

Rather than blunt his passion for law, justice, and accountability, he took the strategic lead for Project Amistad on sorting out election fraud across the country. Project Amistad's point man in Pennsylvania was attorney Tom King, and Tom and Phil were the ones who facilitated getting John McBlain Esq. down to the Delaware County Wharf Building Counting Center to get us into the counting room on election day evening. They could not know McBlain was a confederate any more than we did at the time.

The reason that Project Amistad requested that we collaborate with their team, was to provide firsthand accounts and information required to file litigation documenting the election violations and fraud that had altered the course of the election.

LITIGATION is the key differentiator between an organization that uses their donors money effectively, and those that are more likely wasting time, or outright grifting. If they are not litigating, or funding litigation, or supporting litigation through public relations, then there can be no meaningful change, or different outcomes. Surely, we have learned this from the left after 50 years of "lawfare."

During our first day in Arlington, we learned that Phil was sharing information with Rudy Giuliani's and Sidney Powell's legal teams, to reduce redundancy. It was not so much an integrated effort, but a mutually cooperative one. The security coordinator for Amistad was Colonel Tony Shaeffer, and he was the point man for marshalling resources and assets. Tony is best known for his involvement in Operation Able Danger as a whistle blower who had alleged that the US Defense Intelligence Agency (DIA) had not communicated critical intelligence that could have prevented the terrorist acts of 9/11, and that there were inefficiencies at the CIA and other intelligence agencies in handling and integrating critical information. Shaeffer was predictably pilloried and called a liar for his efforts, which was also a harpoon into the side of then Congressman Curt Weldon (R-Delaware County, PA), when the DoD Inspector General and Senate Intelligence Committee reported that Able Danger did not identify any 9/11 hijackers before September 11, 2001. So, Tony was "debunked" before "debunking" became a core media term to describe anything the government needed to deny, without having to actually provide any contrary evidence.

Eventually, both Colonel Schaeffer and Congressman Weldon would be vindicated a decade later when evidence emerged that they had been truthful and justified in their allegations, in their testimony and attempts to implement corrective actions to prevent future intelligence failures. Sadly, that wasn't in time to save their careers, or reward them for their courage in testifying.

I met Curt Weldon multiple times after he served his last term in Congress. I hold him in the highest regard. A very senior elected representative once ridiculed Weldon in my presence as "the only honest Congressman to pass through Washington in 30 years, and the poorest" laughing at him behind his back for not being "smart enough" to wet his beak or be another pig at the trough in DC. I held Curt in even higher esteem after that, and was well acquainted with Able Danger, and knew who Tony was when Leah and I were introduced to him. Tony knew where the land mines were, and how to navigate them from the hard lessons learned from Able Danger.

We were briefed on the fact that evidence was emerging that Dominion voting machines had been remotely compromised and flipped, and Leah and I discussed what we had observed, and informed them that Delaware County, PA used Hart Intercivic machines and systems. Powell's camp focused on the Dominion angle more so than the other aspects of election fraud that was perpetrated.

Leah and I told everyone in the strongest terms that we had plenty of physical evidence – and evidence that still needed to be collected with court orders – that we could present, that was easy to understand, and that time was critical. I told the attorneys, who were now attentive, that evidence of Dominion machine remote logins would require router and firewall logs that probably didn't exist, or would be nearly impossible to forensically retrieve if they did, and that given that voting machine certifications were not supposed to allow modems or network connections, that any centrally managed, systemic manipulation of Dominion machines could involve Power Line Communications (PLC) and/or confederates with specialized equipment in the centralized counting centers around the country. Regardless that it was likely true based on the information we had, all of that would take too much time, and potentially years to investigate, replicate and assess, document, and litigate – and could not possibly be leveraged before county and state certification hearings, and January 6th Congressional certification. Most importantly, it would be virtually impossible to convey to even the most diligent and patient prospective judges and juries. We couldn't shake them from their determination to go down the Dominion path as a primary vector to demonstrate election fraud.

It is my opinion that the Dominion method of election fraud of electronically modifying voting machines and tabulation servers using fractional, percentage-based changes to election outcomes remotely, while plausible, and even likely, was part of the "old con" parallel election 1 fraud. It was meant to distract and divert attention away from the more obvious, and easier to prove parallel election 2 wholesale substitution of mail-in ballots and digital vDrive batch vote uploads.

The information provided regarding Dominion seemed too "pat" and "tidy" compared to the more common experience in security breaches and forensics investigations which are more often puzzles. The biggest problem with the Dominion tack was that while it was detectable, it was not necessarily quantifiable, and in order to litigate and decertify and change outcomes we needed quantifiable data that could be presented before a "trier of fact," and pass the scrutiny of a judge and a jury.

Regardless of efficacy of choice of which election fraud vector to investigate – the punishment meted out to anyone who dared to pursue any of them was brutal, and meant to send a message.

Leah and I could not have quietly gone about our efforts that were spoliation-centric, had it not been for Rudy Giuliani, Sydney Powell, Phil Kline, and other brave citizens that took horrible public beatings in the media and in courts. All were sued and sanctioned. Rudy and Sydney were sued for ridiculous multi-billion-dollar amounts, and Rudy was actually disbarred. All for the temerity of asserting the citizenry's lawful rights.

General Michael Flynn was very publicly attacked. He was the subject of false testimony from FBI Special Agents, his son was reportedly threatened unless he agreed to plead "guilty" to making a false statement (which he didn't do), and finally he was financially stricken. Regardless of the fact that General Flynn was exonerated of any wrongdoing, the damage to him, his family, his career, and financial devastation was done – and sent a loud message to any other flag officers or Senior Executive Staff (SES) who might decide not to play well with the Democrats.

Whatever the political persuasion or personal feelings or opinions of these high-level attorneys and officers, it would be prudent to remember that they were not simply the targets of the "Democrats." They were the targets of a Uniparty without checks or balances, and the same things could happen – and have happened to large personalities that dare to buck the status quo of the Uniparty.

Leah and I both engaged multiple attorneys and investigators on the subject of election law versus civil law and were surprised that in many cases we were as familiar, or more familiar with the law than the attorneys. It was during this time that we first learned many of the attorneys were volunteers, or minimally paid, and that while they were experienced and capable in other aspects of the law, they had only a thin academic knowledge of election law and constitutional law, with minimal practical experience.

And how could they have had the tools and experience in challenging a coup d'état? How could they reasonably predict that the Courts in the targeted swing states and pivot counties would be so heavily stacked against them?

Leah and I recommended that the attorneys and investigators focus on violations of civil codes and enumerate violations that would challenge certification. I suspected (and later confirmed) that Delaware County, PA, was not alone in the specific elements of fraud and election violations that we had observed and documented.

It wasn't "sexy" to document broken chains of custody and pour through paper tapes (proof sheets) and return sheets, or subpoena mail-in envelopes to compare to state election role data (SURE in PA). But that is where the fraud was and where the hard physical evidence was that could be most readily litigated, or at least provided to state legislators and Congressmen to make determinations on whether the vote should be certified, in the near term. And that is where it still is.

It's important at this point to again state that neither Leah nor I, nor anyone we met or worked with, was a "Trumper" or exclusively a "GOP" advocate or operative. We were all focused on the fact that we had observed what we believed at that time, and subsequently verified and corroborated beyond any reasonable doubt, was massive election fraud.

What we pressed the Project Amistad team hard about, was that it was probably a losing battle to try and prove outright fraud within the time constraints of election law, especially in the environment of a media narrative of "the most secure and safest election in history," regardless of the fact that we had evidence to the contrary in hand. Further, it was not our intent, nor was it good optics, to assert that we were trying to "overturn" the election. We just wanted the truth of it to be exposed.

What we could prove was that there were so many election law violations, and outright deviations to processes in counting mail-in ballots and accounting for inexplicable electronic vote changes and swings, that <u>it was virtually impossible to certify the vote</u>.

If the counties and states could not reliably and ethically determine who won, and certify the vote, the US Constitution provides for procedures to be implemented by Congress, and if necessary, the Supreme Court, to investigate and delay, if necessary, until the vote could be properly vetted, verified, and certified – and also, later decertified.

Instead, we ended up in discussions on Constitutional Law. The working premise the clutch of Amistad, Powell, Giuliani, and GOP State Attorney Generals initially went with was those states like Pennsylvania, which had blatantly ignored and violated federal election laws and their own individual state election laws and constitutions, had infringed on other states' rights for fair and honest elections.

Most notable was *Texas v Pennsylvania*, filed by Texas State Attorney General Ken Paxton with the Supreme Court of the United States (SCOTUS), which alleged that Georgia, Michigan, Pennsylvania, and Wisconsin violated the United States Constitution by changing, and/or not following, election procedures through non-legislative means in violation of law.

The suit sought to temporarily withhold the certified vote count from the four states prior to the Electoral College vote on December 14, 2020. Our testimony and declarations were included in the *Texas v Pennsylvania* litigation as exhibits, and offered as evidence of election law violations, and fraud.

We were familiar enough with election and civil law, and Constitutional law, that we argued passionately with the attorneys who crafted the original legal theory and petitions, that it was our understanding of the Constitution that States maintained rights to be self-governing bodies, particularly in election of government officials, and that whatever State AG they might convince to file the suit would likely not be heard for lack of standing.

We were familiar with "standing" regarding elections, and most importantly that the practical application of the law differs from the actual wording of the Constitution and federal election law, but (theoretically) meets the intent of the law regarding who can file litigation – and who can't.

The letter of the law says that all citizens have a right to fair and free elections, and theoretically, can individually file litigation for election law violations and observed fraud, as harmed parties. But that could potentially end up with thousands – and even millions – of individual and class action lawsuits with every election, filed by any voting citizen. That can't work as a practical matter, so the body of the law that has developed says that a candidate for an election has standing as a "harmed" party, and a certified "poll watcher" has standing as a qualified "intervenor" on behalf of candidates and the citizenry in general. Leah and I were dubious that one state (Texas) could prevail against any other state (Pennsylvania) in that regard.

The US Supreme Court, in an order dated December 11th, declined to hear the case on the basis that Texas lacked standing under Article III of the Constitution to challenge the results of the election held by another state.

December 11th was a peculiar date because the deadline for state certifications was December 10[th.] So, it was essentially a moot point, <u>and seemingly an intentional swat by the US Supreme Court to President Trump,</u>

Having done our best to get as much information about what we observed to the attorneys and cooperating teams of Kline (Amistad), Giuliani and Powell, we expected that President Trump and this very capable team had everything well in hand, that they would press forward with all necessary litigation, and ultimately prevail in presenting the evidence we had gathered of the massive election fraud we observed in Delaware County, PA. We had learned that the same fraud had occurred throughout the country with blueprint-like similarity, and expected that it would be corrected over the coming months. So, we felt that our duties as citizens were fulfilled, and we could go home and trust that the future of our nation was in capable hands.

Before our departure, Leah and I were invited to attend the press conference at the Republican National Headquarters in the heart of DC, and we were excited to go. The press room/ lobby is surprisingly small and narrow, and when packed with reporters, media, cameras, staff, and hot halogen camera lights, the temperature rapidly went above 100 degrees with humidity so high there was actually a cloud of vapor in the room. We were early and secured a spot directly in front of the podium that Phil, Rudy, and Sidney would speak from. The conference started a half hour late. Phil, Rudy, Sidney, Jenna Ellis, and their respective media handlers marched in line, weaving through the reporters jammed into the little room to the podium.

Leah and I were only 6-to-8 feet from Mayor Giuliani when his black hair dye started streaming down the side of his face in rivulets, mixing with the tan pancake makeup on his face. Both of us saw it at the same time, and looked like crazed beekeepers swatting the sides of our faces trying to signal to anyone behind the podium that Rudy's face was melting. The CNN cameraman who had been slightly behind us, elbowed and body checked us to get in front and started snapping high-definition photos that would be on the news before we left the building.

What snapped into focus during that short, brutal press conference, which punctuated our time in D.C., was that the media would never give the truth a fair hearing. Saul Alinsky's thuggish rule to ridicule and lie about anyone with the courage and honesty to expose the truth prevailed in our media. They didn't want to hear what Mayor Giuliani might say. The room was comprised of mostly youthful media reporters who were seething with contempt and hatred for President Trump, disrespectful, and notably, more than a few reeking of B.O.

When Leah and I arrived back home, we spent the better part of two days calling attorneys listed as GOP / Republican election lawyers in Eastern Pennsylvania down to Maryland and Delaware. I don't remember how many we dialed, but only fourteen attorneys answered our calls. Thirteen, several whom were renowned, would not take our case. All were scared. Deborah Silver, a Georgetown Law graduate, was the 14th attorney to take our call. After a couple of days to mull it over, she took the case, and she has been a fearless advocate ever since, and a brilliant legal mind.

Depending on which cases you count, there were more than 65 lawsuits filed that challenged the votes and certifications across the country – all filed, funded, and coordinated mostly by the core President Trump group of lawyers and their financial benefactors.

Not one court – in any venue - allowed any evidence to be submitted, and most did not even hazard a hearing.

With the primary guns of Powell, Giuliani, Kline, and General Flynn under heavy fire in the courts, media, and taking hits to discuss the truth, the Uniparty and their allies (and money) centralized, coalesced, and focused on attacking anyone who brought up the notion of fraud.

Cognitive warfare and "lawfare" have been waged against any celebrity, journalist, talk show host, and even comedians who have attempted to practice their professions or exercise their 1st Amendment rights.

An increasingly nasty Uniparty political leadership that was fueled into a frenzy by a myopic media, joined in the action.

With our litigation filed and in motion, and the publication of this book, and the Patriot.Online platform and infrastructure fully up and running, we are prepared to engage in counter-cognitive warfare. The Uniparty and adversaries to fair and honest elections have carried the day thus far with deception, misinformation, and disinformation and run roughshod – without evidence - on anyone who has opposed them.

We will correct their lies.

13

CONCEALING, AND REVEALING MASSIVE ELECTION FRAUD

After Leah, Dasha Pruett (GOP candidate for Congress) and I, filed our initial litigation with Attorney Deborah Silver shortly after the November election on December 22, 2020, we expected the case might be dismissed based on other election related cases up to that point being summarily dismissed.

We did, however, expect that we would at least be allowed to have an "evidentiary hearing," which was customary for all such cases. Consultation with several attorneys who had made decades long careers in Delaware County Common

Pleas Courts (in Media, PA) were shocked that Judge Capuzzi had not allowed an evidentiary hearing, and they were unaware of any other cases where that had happened – ever. The most obvious reason being that it is unfathomable how the judge could arrive at the conclusion that there "wasn't a scintilla of evidence" when he refused to entertain or allow any, and because as a matter of law and protocol, such a break in process would leave the case open for reasonable appeal.

Figure 64 - Delaware County, Court of Common Pleas in Media, PA

We were informed that there was no hearing, or any transcript (which we were required to request and file with any appeal), and it was a mystery how Judge Capuzzi had arrived at his conclusion that there was no evidence until Delaware County Solicitor William Martin disclosed in a highly agitated statement to the Board of Elections, in January 2022, on video, that there had indeed, been a hearing that had omitted the petitioners and intervenors (Leah, Greg and Dasha) as plaintiffs, but had included McBlain, Parks, Martin, and Judge Capuzzi, and implied they had unilaterally agreed to dismiss the case and recommend crushing sanctions against the petitioners, and disbarment for Deborah Silver.

Our expectation was that the case might be wrongly dismissed for reasons of "judicial climate," and that we would have to appeal it. Dozens of attorneys explained this dilemma – virtually every attorney we spoke from the eve of the election on November 3rd, 2020, to present day - that modern law and courts are now driven by "judicial climate." This was confusing to us because we presumed – with good reason, as citizens – that the law is just the law – and adjudicated and ruled on as it is written, and as can be supported by precedent, similar cases, to illustrate and be consistent with previous applications of law.

From our perspective, and as we wrote in our complaints, both civil and election law required a chain of custody, proof sheets (tapes), return sheets, and electronic "vDrives" containing the Cast Vote Record (CVR) to be handled, reconciled, and certified in accordance with straight forward procedures defined in the law, most of which began with "Shall."

We learned differently.

"Judicial Climate" is a term that should not be included in the practice and application of law, but now provides a lens and prism through which all law and facts must be viewed through.

We (Leah and Greg) had some experience with litigation, and reasonable expectations of the trajectory we would likely travel. The first being that our case, while it might be dismissed (and appealed), could be used in other litigation that was in motion around the country.

From previous experience investigating and sorting through fraud, Greg fully expected the defendants would likely fabricate or destroy as much evidence as required to both support their fraud, and to hide their criminal actions.

In law, this is called "spoliation" and specifically in civil law, when a defendant wantonly destroys or alters evidence that is required to be maintained that would exonerate them and prove them to be not guilty – then defacto they can only be guilty.

Why would you destroy evidence that would exonerate you unless you were guilty?

We knew there might ultimately be at least two cases, and probably more, with the first being our December 22nd, 2020, case alleging election law violations and election fraud, and a second (separate) spoliation case that would evolve from the destruction of evidence and fraudulent counting of votes.

Had US Attorney William McSwain stood up to US Attorney General William Barr's unlawful – and suspicious – order to "stand down" from securing forensic images of the tabulation machines and BlueCrest sorter, then we could have easily and quickly proven massive election fraud and ended the façade not only in Pennsylvania, but the rest of the country. Since his courage failed him at the most critical moments of his life, and one of the most critical junctures in US history, we would have to make do with developing our own evidence.

We knew they had fabricated the 120,000+ mail-in ballots they counted, and that there were 70,000 uncounted and unopened ballots we had seen in the back rooms that would have to be processed, moved, stored, or destroyed. We suspected they would destroy the outer mail-in envelopes for the fake ballots, and likely all electronic evidence on the voting machines, BlueCrest sorter hard drive, and tabulation machines, and they would also have to re-create the USB vDrives CVR's.

All we had to do was catch them doing it.

And they obliged spectacularly, exceeding even our low expectations of their callousness and desire not to be caught.

As Leah and I discussed and planned, I recalled the 2013 government case against Kermit Gosnell, a physician who operated an abortion clinic in Philadelphia, PA. The government had deviated from the normal protocol of filing a case with just enough evidence to permit the Judge to decide that the case had merit and could proceed forward with whatever civil, criminal, constitutional, family, bankruptcy, election, etc., law processes applied.

Instead, the prosecutor had included graphic, color photos in line with the petition, and in the Exhibits, and had put the bulk of his case and evidence within the body of the filing.

Abortion, and the legal allowances permitting it is probably the most contentious and debated topic in the US, next to perhaps the toxicity of attempts to infringe on the second amendment and gun laws, and as such is vigorously protected.

It is a topic that is most prone to "judicial climate" more so than any other.

The prosecutor knew his odds of getting the case to trial would be lowered by the "judicial climate" and adverse media coverage that would result from a "normal" filing. Hence, the stomach churning and gory graphic photos of bloodied, aborted carcasses of infants strewn about like rotting trash. They were so appalling to even those that supported abortion, that it forced everyone involved to simply focus on the evidence – the facts of the case – and put aside "judicial climate."

Gosnell was convicted of multiple crimes.

Given that most of the litigation and cases arising from the November 2020 election fraud in the country were being dismissed for lack of standing, lack of jurisdiction, laches (timeliness), and "lack of evidence" in the "safest and most secure election in history," Leah and I knew that any subsequent filing by common citizens, like us, could only succeed if we included graphic evidence roughly equivalent to gory, bloody, dead infants to both snap the citizenry out of its complacency, and force even the most politicized and rabidly leftist courts into submission that there was, indeed, "evidence."

As Leah and I researched and prepared, she found a well-researched hard news article by Ralph Cipriani which corroborated what we had seen, and included several photos and the testimony of a whistleblower in Delaware County, PA.

Leah – always a woman of action – called Ralph's number listed in the article immediately, and he picked up. She informed him who we were, and that we had testified in Gettysburg and were preparing a lawsuit, and asked if he would give our contact information to the whistleblower, and coordinate a meeting.

We met the Whistleblower shortly thereafter, and we discussed our mutual findings and observations, and the likelihood that as time and pressure were applied, that election officials would alter and destroy evidence.

It is important at this point to once again reiterate that Leah and I were not "anti" anything or emotionally attached to President Trump or any other candidate. We were focused on the fraud itself, and the only shared emotion was anger that the "ruling class" could so easily pick and choose who should be installed, in whatever office, as they pleased, and that our votes – the citizenry's votes – didn't matter. We wanted an honest election and those that had perverted it, to be held accountable.

The focus for all of us has always been the evidence, and letting it do the talking for us.

For legal reasons, and the fact that our December 2020 case will be appealed to the US Supreme Court, and our recent filing in January 2022 of the spoliation, wanton alteration, and destruction of evidence case, we cannot provide any more detail in this revision of the book.

Suffice it to say, that a Right to Know request was composed demanding the election materials required by law to be maintained for 22 months after an election, combined with other elements specific to our December 2020 "litigation hold" that defined in detail all evidence (in addition to statutory evidence) that would have to be retained for review and discovery until our case(s) had exhausted all appeals.

The whistleblower was able to corroborate many of the allegations of fraud that Leah and I had documented, and capture election officials admitting to election law violations, crimes, fraud, and destroying and altering evidence.

In the movie, "The Wolf of Wallstreet" the US Attorney and Prosecutor explain what "a Grenada" is, the PG version being:

> "Grenada's very interesting because it is a small island nation that was invaded by the United States of America in 1983. It's about 90,000 people."

> "And essentially, it means this case is unlosable."

> "So, you know, we can come in, we can have

> *our stuff hanging out of our pants. Nobody cares."*
>
> *"I'm gonna win."*
>
> *"You, sir. Are what's known as 'a Grenada.'"*
>
> *"You're looking at real prison time."*
>
> *"Money laundering can get you as much as 20 years.*
>
> *"And our case couldn't be stronger if we caught you shoving cash in your mattress."*

In order to ultimately prevail in our efforts to reveal and expose the massive election fraud of November 2020, we would need a "dead baby," "Grenada," total (figurative) head shot, that would be immune from "judicial climate," and keep Judges, juries, legislators, and the citizenry focused on the evidence.

Combined with our stance that the culprits in all of this are NOT ideologically identified "Democrats" or "Republicans," and was in fact a corporate two-headed snake of the DNC and GOP corporate Uniparty, we were confident that we could mitigate and manage emotionally charged actions and responses, and eventually be heard in an honest court of law, or failing that, our State legislature, or the Constitutional last stand of the Congress as the ultimate body of redress for the citizenry.

We would need to be quiet, and figuratively set ourselves back from the celebrity litigators and professional media personalities, several hundred yards in the woods, like a hunter, and patiently wait for the natures of the men and women who facilitated the fraud to take their course.

"Do not cry havoc, when you should but hunt
with modest warrant" – Coriolanus

14

THE PATH FORWARD; FIGHTING GRAND CORRUPTION

Two hundred and forty-six years ago, our Republic's founding fathers anticipated current political events as they are playing out in 2022. History is full of tyrants and failed democracies and republics, and the architects of our Constitution, being learned men, were aware of most of the pitfalls that the Republic they were setting up would face.

They were aware of the potential for grand corruption so insidious and embedded that it could appear to be impenetrable and permanent.

What they required most of all to address such a drastic circumstance was patience and moderation. A citizen must exhaust all administrative remedies and stay on the path of a Constitutionally defined trajectory to effect orderly change.

Leah and I knew this from the start and planned accordingly. It would not suffice to simply state that "law enforcement refused to act." We needed to document this grand corruption with formal correspondence, certified mail, writs of mandamus, litigation, and expose those who are corrupt, and publicly shame those who are too cowardly to ferret them out and do their duty.

It would not be good enough to simply say that our partisan courts and judges are dysfunctional and corrupt, refuse to hear evidence, or fulfill their duties, without evidence of those facts. We had to show this and collect evidence of the courts' deliberate actions to obfuscate the truth – a process that was still ongoing at the first publication of this book.

We had to approach our state legislators concurrent with our litigation before the courts and pursue Freedom Of Information Act (FOIA) and Right To Know (RTK) requests.

We had to engage with grass roots groups and speak weekly to groups as small as a few, and up to 1,000 plus, and educate them on the processes.

We expected that the ruling class conspirators and cheaters would fight back, destroy evidence, attack us personally, refuse to comply with the law, dismiss cases, and delay as long as possible.

We anticipated that law enforcement, the Department of Justice, the judiciary, and state legislators would abrogate their duties to investigate and remedy cases of election fraud, as they have with all other cases, and that we would receive no support.

We are not so callous as to welcome lawsuits against us for giving names to our villains, and pressing our right to have our evidence heard before a trier of fact, but do not fear them, as each lawsuit such as Savage's, provides another venue for exposing the truth.

We have been threatened with incarceration by corrupt officials, and classified as "domestic terrorists" so they can deny us our rights, for having the temerity to press those rights. We will fulfill our duty to expose the illegitimate government that has usurped the beloved Republic, and citizenry, that I served faithfully for over two decades – and am still serving to this day.

The next steps – assuming our multiple cases are delayed or dismissed regardless of evidence included directly in the body of the complaints and exhibits – are private prosecution and demanding a hearing by our State Legislature and the US Congress.

Everything – every remedy – is outlined and described within the body of the Constitution, including the potential and prospect for increasingly kinetic action only AFTER all constitutional and every other available remedy has been explored. It is those that have stolen our nation, and despise our Constitution, and want to "transform" our Republic that foment and need violence. The path forward is using the very laws they knowingly hate, and pervert, to peacefully shine a light on them.

We are determined to see voting integrity restored, no matter how long the battle. We owe it to our children. If that means prompting vigorous debates on the floor of Congress – if we can, we will. We will not stop.

And so, it must proceed today – with lawful litigation and redress before the courts and Congress as permitted by law, and the restoration of fair and honest elections.

If we're lucky, and regain our national sanity and an appetite for moderation and reconciliation, and honest elections, then we will see the great mass of Americans who are not on the far left or the far right, flourishing in a society where the majority rule, but the rights of minorities are respected and maintained.

Whatever happens in our litigation, we have identified how the ruling class and Uniparty took control of our country via our elections, and how they executed fraud on only a small number of pressure points to take over the whole. Once you understand how it is done, it is much more possible to prevent in the future. It is with eternal optimism and love of our country that we move forward to preserve it for our children, future generations, and as a beacon for the world.

15

APPENDIX A: EVIDENCE; SELECTED EXHIBITS

Commonwealth of Pennsylvania

County of Delaware
Watcher's Certificate

This will Certify that **Gregory Stenstrom** residing at 1541 Farmers Lane has been regularly appointed as a **WATCHER** for the Election District of **EDGMONT TOWNSHIP 2nd Precinct** by Thomas H. **KILLION**, Candidate for the office of Senator in the General Assembly 9th District to serve at the General Election, 3rd day of November, 2020.

Witness our hands and official seal, the 5th day of October, 2020.

Laureen T. Hagan
Chief Clerk

Gerald Lawrence
Ashley Lunkenheimer
James J. Byrne, Jr.
County Board of Elections

NOTE – 25 PS 2687
"Each candidate for nomination or election at any election shall be entitled to appoint 2 watchers for each election district in which such candidate is voted for." Furthermore, "only one watcher for each candidate at primaries, or for each party or political body at general, municipal or special elections, shall be present in the polling place at any one time..."

Figure 65 - Exhibit C, Notarized Poll Watcher Certificate

The Delaware County Board of Elections provided Mr. Stenstrom with a notarized certificate of appointment as a poll watcher. These certificates were in many cases more detrimental to observers than if they had not gone to the trouble of being a poll watcher, and instead been one of the thousands of nameless Democrat volunteers who were given unrestricted access.

June 22, 2020 PRE GENERAL ELECTION MEETING OF THE DELAWARE COUNTY ELECTION BOARD

PRESENT: Gerald Lawrence, Chairman
               Jim Byrne
               Ashley Lunkenheimer
               J. Manly Parks, Board Solicitor
Also Present: Laureen Hagan, Bureau of Elections
               Jim Savage, Voting Machine Warehouse

Pledge of Allegiance.

Primary election reflections. Mr. Lawrence shared some observations from the June 2nd primary election experience, including that 140,000 people voted with 75,000 of them voting in-person and the balance voting by mail. Beginning with the 2020 primary election, the state required the use of voting machines utilizing paper ballots to produce permanent paper records. The new systems involved different technology, requiring new procedures to be followed and training for poll workers. Passage of Act 77 in 2019 introduced a notable change by allowing people to vote from home with "no-excuse" mail-in ballots. The record demand for mail-in ballots was very challenging with ballot processing complicated by the covid-19 outbreak and having to rely on using an old state-managed online system that often slowed with so many county election bureaus across Pennsylvania logged on at once. Given the high demand and operating circumstances, Delaware County was unable to keep up with the daily influx of incoming applications despite additional staff using more computer equipment purchased before the election and working long, extended hours verifying applications and mailing out ballots to reduce the backlog. The state must certify that any ballot challenges have been resolved before county election bureaus can begin producing and sending out ballots to voters requesting them. There were significant operating issues identified at poll locations and with the process for returning ballots and materials to Media on election night. Good-faith efforts were made to address problems in real-time as best as possible. Lessons learned will be applied moving forward to be better prepared and resourced for managing anticipated heavy voter turnout for the general election. County departments stepped up in a dedicated all-hands-on-deck effort to do solve problems and serve Delaware County voters to the very best of their collective ability.

Certification of election results. Ms. Hagan explained that three reports make up the County's official certification of election results – cumulative, precinct, and write-in reports. In response to Mr. Byrne's question about whether public comments should be read at this time, Mr. Parks said it would be appropriate to read public comments received relating to the accuracy of the election results before Board members voted on certifying the results. Ms. Lunkenheimer moved a motion to certify the election results and Mr. Byrne seconded. Mr. Byrne acknowledged the hard work put forth but adding mistakes must be owned. He believed the Board didn't do its job well. He recommended assembling a nine-member bipartisan panel to review primary election activities and the Board's actions moving forward. Mr. Lawrence, like Mr. Byrne, believed there was transparency and a free and fair election notwithstanding previously described challenges and reiterated his willingness to listen to all voices in the interest of making improvements. Ms. Lunkenheimer expressed the election was carried out with transparency, a lot of hard work by many and in the spirit of following a bipartisan process in internal meetings. She owned and wanted to learn from past mistakes coupled with a personal commitment to doing better in the future. The motion to certify the election results carried with Ms. Lunkenheimer and Mr. Lawrence voting yes and Mr. Byrne voting no.

State reimbursement for ballot processing. Ms. Hagan discussed certification for state reimbursement in the amount of $81.60 for sending absentee ballots to military service members domestically and overseas. Ms. Lunkenheimer moved a motion to seek state reimbursement for sending ballots as presented and Mr. Byrne seconded. The motion carried by the unanimous vote of the Board.

Ratification of election results. Ms. Hagan requested approval of documents reporting election results to the Pennsylvania Department of State, as required by law. Ms. Lunkenheimer moved a motion to ratify the reports and Mr. Byrne seconded. The motion carried with Ms. Lunkenheimer and Mr. Lawrence voting yes and Mr. Byrne voting no.

Polling place changes. Mr. Lawrence explained Mr. Savage has the duty to assign temporary use of poll locations on an emergency basis when designated locations become unavailable after the last meeting of the Board of Elections and prior to an election.

Mr. Savage presented emergency changes in poll locations for the Board's approval.

1. Ridley 1-3 to move to Woodland Fire Company.

2. Folcroft 1 to move to Folcroft Union Church.

Ms. Lunkenheimer moved to ratify the proposed poll locations and Mr. Byrne seconded. The motion carried with the unanimous vote of the Board.

Public comments. The first public comment was read by Mr. Byrne followed by others read by Ms. Hagan and Mr. Lawrence.

Andy Reilly – Virtual meetings conducted as a result of the pandemic shuts out important public comment and cooperation from the political parties. Consideration should be given to having one representative from each political party to participate live to ensure a smooth and error-free election.

Shane Lair – Expressed concern that Republican poll workers in Aston did not show up nor was any notice provided to the minority party regarding their intentions not to fulfill their duties and (consequently) to abandon voters on election day, necessitating the emergency appointment of poll workers.

Victoria Brown – More staff and equipment is needed to achieve smoother election operations.

Diane Leahan – Suggested having more training sessions so people feel more confident answering questions and working inside the poll.

James Zigelhoffer – Commended the efforts of all who worked under very challenging conditions, created in part by the pandemic and introduction of new voting equipment and processes.

Pam & Hal Allen – Expressed that some primary election voters were confused about whether facemasks must be worn by greeters standing outside a poll location and departed without voting. A voter who believed he registered as an independent and, whose name did not appear in the poll book, was allowed to vote with a regular Republican ballot after the judge of elections

claimed he knew the person voted Republican in past elections. Ms. Hagan was instructed to share the email with Mr. Parks for investigation.

David Director – The primary was a dry run to work out issues with a new voting system leading up to the general election. The voting process became more challenging to manage when the pandemic hit and a change in the law allowed the use of no-excuse mail-in ballots, which created record demand for voting by mail.

Rachel Amdur – Consolidation of more than 400 poll locations was a huge undertaking complicated by the arrival of the pandemic, requiring collaboration across party lines to staff polls in Haverford on election day that wasn't forthcoming from Republicans.

Margaret Patton – Consolidation of poll locations makes it harder and more confusing to vote; ability to vote by mail becomes more important if the coronavirus flares up in the fall.

Christina Iacono –Delaware County will need more printers, mail sorters, and label machines capable of working in tandem with state databases print out ballots; state database must be able to handle the workload without crashing or slowing down.

Mr. Lawrence adjourned the meeting after stating there was no other business.

Figure 66 - Exhibit D, Return Board and Savage Responsibilities

Defendant, Delaware County Return Board was created by the Board of Elections subsequent to recommendations made by Defendant Byrne at a June 22, 2020, pre-general election meeting of the Board of Elections. Defendant Savage also had "the duty to assign temporary use of poll locations on an emergency basis when designated locations become unavailable after the last meeting of the Board of Elections and prior to elections." Defendant Savage was responsible for the storage, security, programming, testing, and delivery of all voting equipment distributed to 428 Delaware County precincts and over three hundred polling locations. The characterization by Defendants attorneys that Savage played a minor, functionary role in the election is incongruent with his assigned responsibilities and control he had over the process, ballots, and USB vDrives.

LEGAL NOTICE

The Delaware County Board of Elections will resume the November 23, 2020 Election Board meeting at 5:15pm on November 24, 2020 in County Council Meeting Room to certify the election results of the 165th Legislative House District.

Due to COVID 19 safety protocols the general public may view the live streamed meeting via othe following link:

https://delcopa.gov/vote/index.html

Residents can email their public comment. Public comments must be submitted with the same information that is requested at a public meeting including the person's name and address. Emails can be sent immediately to: ElectionBoardMembers@co.delaware.pa.us

DELAWARE COUNTY BOARD OF ELECTIONS

Gerald Lawrence
Ashley Lunkenheimer
James J. Byrne, Jr.

Laureen T. Hagan
Chief Clerk

Figure 67 - Exhibit F2, Delaware County Determined the Election Outcome for Pennsylvania

It appears Delaware County was the last county to submit its presidential vote total in the state on November 24, 2020, changing November 3, 2020, election results in numerous races. Prior to Delaware County submitting its vote totals, Donald J. Trump was leading Joseph Biden by 7,515 votes. Delaware County submitted its presidential votes total with a difference of 88,070 between the two presidential candidates, which secured, in its entirety, Biden's 80,000+ vote margin, that hade presciently been almost exactly predicted by PA Attorney General candidate Josh Shapiro and former PA Governor Rendell weeks prior to the election.

Media (https://www.media.pa.gov) > State (http://www.media.pa.gov/Pages/State.aspx) > Details

Department Of State Certifies Presidential Election Results

11/24/2020

Harrisburg, PA – Following certifications of the presidential vote submitted by all 67 counties late Monday, Secretary of State Kathy Boockvar today certified the results of the November 3 election in Pennsylvania for president and vice president of the United States.

Shortly thereafter, as required by federal law, Governor Tom Wolf signed the Certificate of Ascertainment for the slate of electors for Joseph R. Biden as president and Kamala D. Harris as vice president of the United States. The certificate was submitted to the Archivist of the United States.

The Certificate of Ascertainment included the following vote totals:

Electors for Democratic Party candidates Joseph R. Biden and Kamala D. Harris – 3,458,229
Electors for Republican Party candidates Donald J. Trump and Michael R. Pence – 3,377,674
Electors for Libertarian Party candidates Jo Jorgensen and Jeremy Spike Cohen – 79,380
"Today's certification is a testament to the incredible efforts of our local and state election officials, who worked tirelessly to ensure Pennsylvania had a free, fair and accurate process that reflects the will of the voters," said Gov. Wolf.

"We are tremendously grateful to all 67 counties who have been working extremely long hours to ensure that every qualified voter's vote is counted safely and securely. The county election officials and the poll workers are the true heroes of our democracy, enabling us to vote in record numbers, amid challenging circumstances, so that every eligible voter's voice could be heard," Sec. Boockvar said.

MEDIACONTACT: Wanda Murren, (717) 783-1621

Figure 68 - Exhibit F1, PA Certification Presidential Election Results

Pennsylvania certified the presidential election on November 24, 2020, receiving Delco's certification that evening, with Joseph Biden having 80,555 more votes than Donald Trump

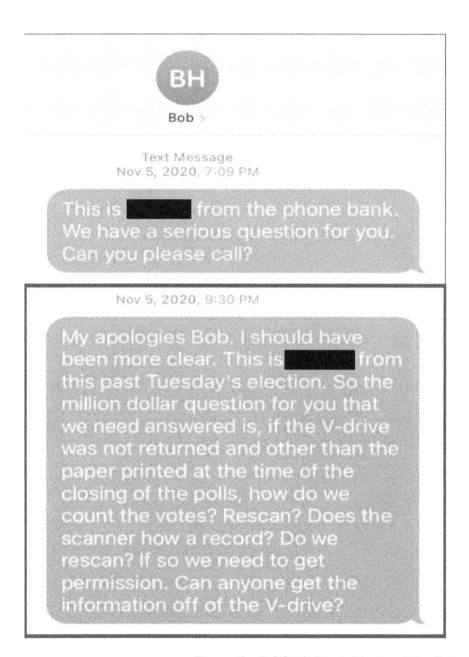

Figure 69 - Exhibit G Part 1, Missing vDrive Texts

Text message exhibits between Stacy Heisey-Terrell, Hart Intercivic technician and Whistleblower to recreate missing USB vDrives with Cast Vote Records (CVR's). The Delaware County Chairman (Lawrence) of the Board of Elections (BOE) stated that none were missing when the BOE certified the 2020 Delco presidential and general election.

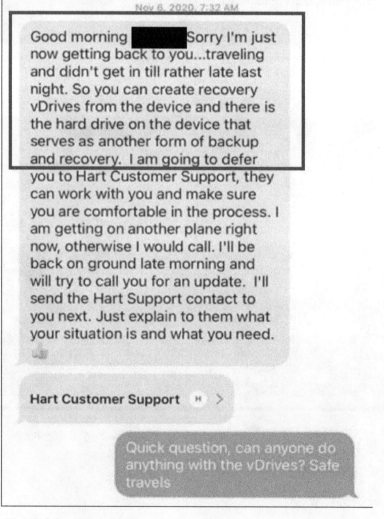

Nov 6, 2020, 7:32 AM

Good morning ▮▮▮▮▮Sorry I'm just now getting back to you...traveling and didn't get in till rather late last night. So you can create recovery vDrives from the device and there is the hard drive on the device that serves as another form of backup and recovery. I am going to defer you to Hart Customer Support, they can work with you and make sure you are comfortable in the process. I am getting on another plane right now, otherwise I would call. I'll be back on ground late morning and will try to call you for an update. I'll send the Hart Support contact to you next. Just explain to them what your situation is and what you need.

Hart Customer Support

Quick question, can anyone do anything with the vDrives? Safe travels

Figure 70 - Exhibit G Part 2, Missing vDrive Text

Nov 6, 2020, 6:22 PM

Thank you for all of your help this morning Bob 💀 While the whole world is waiting on PA to submit our numbers we lost 48 vDrives!! Well, that is how many got lost in the shuffle. 3 of them never got returned for sure. So in the end we did end up having to create recovery vDrives today. Thank you again 💀 You saved PA!!!! Hope your on the ground long enough to get some rest.

GREAT news, I am sooo relieved the recovery vDrive process went so well. I'm sure there were some anxious moments for the warehouse team but I hope you didn't fall victim to ugly blowback from it! Finally made it home this afternoon, long week but I believe it was a good week! Look forward to catching up soon, hope you can relax a bit and enjoy the weekend 😊

Figure 71 - Exhibit G Part 3, Missing vDrive Texts

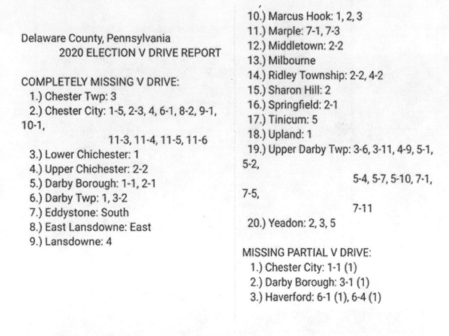

Delaware County, Pennsylvania
2020 ELECTION V DRIVE REPORT

COMPLETELY MISSING V DRIVE:
1.) Chester Twp: 3
2.) Chester City: 1-5, 2-3, 4, 6-1, 8-2, 9-1, 10-1,
                11-3, 11-4, 11-5, 11-6
3.) Lower Chichester: 1
4.) Upper Chichester: 2-2
5.) Darby Borough: 1-1, 2-1
6.) Darby Twp: 1, 3-2
7.) Eddystone: South
8.) East Lansdowne: East
9.) Lansdowne: 4

10.) Marcus Hook: 1, 2, 3
11.) Marple: 7-1, 7-3
12.) Middletown: 2-2
13.) Milbourne
14.) Ridley Township: 2-2, 4-2
15.) Sharon Hill: 2
16.) Springfield: 2-1
17.) Tinicum: 5
18.) Upland: 1
19.) Upper Darby Twp: 3-6, 3-11, 4-9, 5-1, 5-2,
                5-4, 5-7, 5-10, 7-1, 7-5,
                7-11
20.) Yeadon: 2, 3, 5

MISSING PARTIAL V DRIVE:
1.) Chester City: 1-1 (1)
2.) Darby Borough: 3-1 (1)
3.) Haverford: 6-1 (1), 6-4 (1)

Figure 72 - List of Missing vDrives

Stenstrom and Hoopes were provided multiple corroborating lists of missing USB vDrives, that had in turn been provided to Delaware County Watchdogs by election workers during the November 2020 election week. The list was reportedly compiled with the full knowledge of BOE Chairman Lawrence, DelCo Solicitor Martin, BOE Solicitor Parks, and multiple other Board of Elections and Bureau of Elections officials and employees.

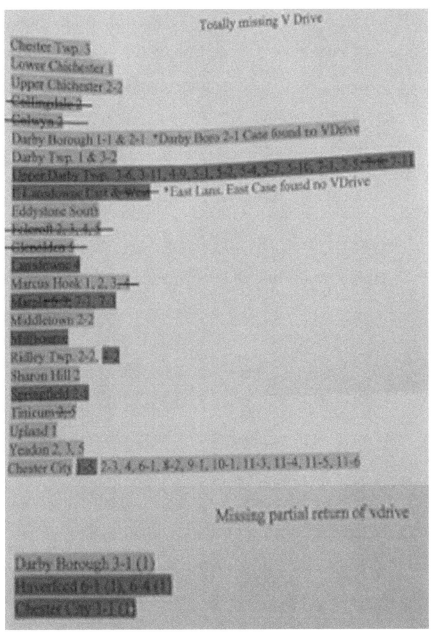

Figure 73 - List of Missing vDrives by Precinct (Paper Printou

The evidence that there were more than 47(+) missing vDrives is overwhelming. Corroborating texts, affidavits, witness testimony, printed memorandums distributed to poll workers, inability of the BOE to synchronize return sheets, proof sheets (paper tapes), and tabulation, were all proof of irregularities that only valid USB vDrives could resolve. While the Chairman of the Board of Elections (who was also a Biden elector) denied there were missing vDrives at the vote certification hearing, and BOE and Delco "statespersons" repeatedly denied there were missing vDrives, BOE defense attorneys admitted that Jim Savage did, in fact, upload "a" (singular) vDrive, and further characterized it as both a single vote (singular) and ballots (plural). An individual USB vDrive normally holds hundreds or thousands of votes.

In addition to hard, physical evidence that the whereabouts of tens of thousands of votes still remains in question, which is enough evidence by itself to challenge the certification of the vote, the Whistleblower caught multiple election officials admitting in video and audio that the 47+ vDrives were, in fact, missing, and later refabricated, and they could not reconcile the vote.

OPEN RECORDS OFFICE
County of Delaware
201 W. Front Street, Room 206
Media, PA 19063
(610) 891-4260 – Office
(610) 891-8759 - Fax

OPEN RECORDS REQUEST FORM

Name of Requester

Howard	Ann	
(Please print)	Last	First	MI

Signature: _____ Date: 5/21/2021

Mailing Address: 26100 American Dr. Suite 607
Street/P.O. Box

Southfield	MI	48034
City	State	Zip Code

Telephone Number: 248-356-6162   FAX Number: 248-356-6163

Email Address: amh1968@protonmail.com

> Please identify each of the documents that are subject to this request. You must identify these documents with **sufficient specificity** so we may ascertain whether we have these documents and how to locate them.
> I request the final certified return sheets from the November 3, 2020 general election. There is one return sheet from every precinct in Delaware County. Each return sheet includes the paper tapes from the voting machines, these paper tapes are also requested. If there are any additional notes written on the back of the return sheet, as well as any attached notes that are related to each return sheet. I request all 428 certified return sheets from all of Delaware County.

Please check one of the following boxes:

☐ I am only requesting access to the documents identified above.
☐ I am only requesting a copy of the documents identified above.
☑ I am requesting access to the documents identified above **and** a copy of those documents.

If you are requesting a copy of the documents identified above, please check one of the following boxes:

☑ I want a paper copy of the documents

☐ Other format (please specify). _____

Figure 74 - Exhibit H, Right To Know Request for Election data

On May 21, 2021, a request for November 3, 2020, election data and information were submitted to Delaware County under Pennsylvania's Right to Know Law (RTKL). See 65 P.S. Ann. §§ 67.101-67.3104.

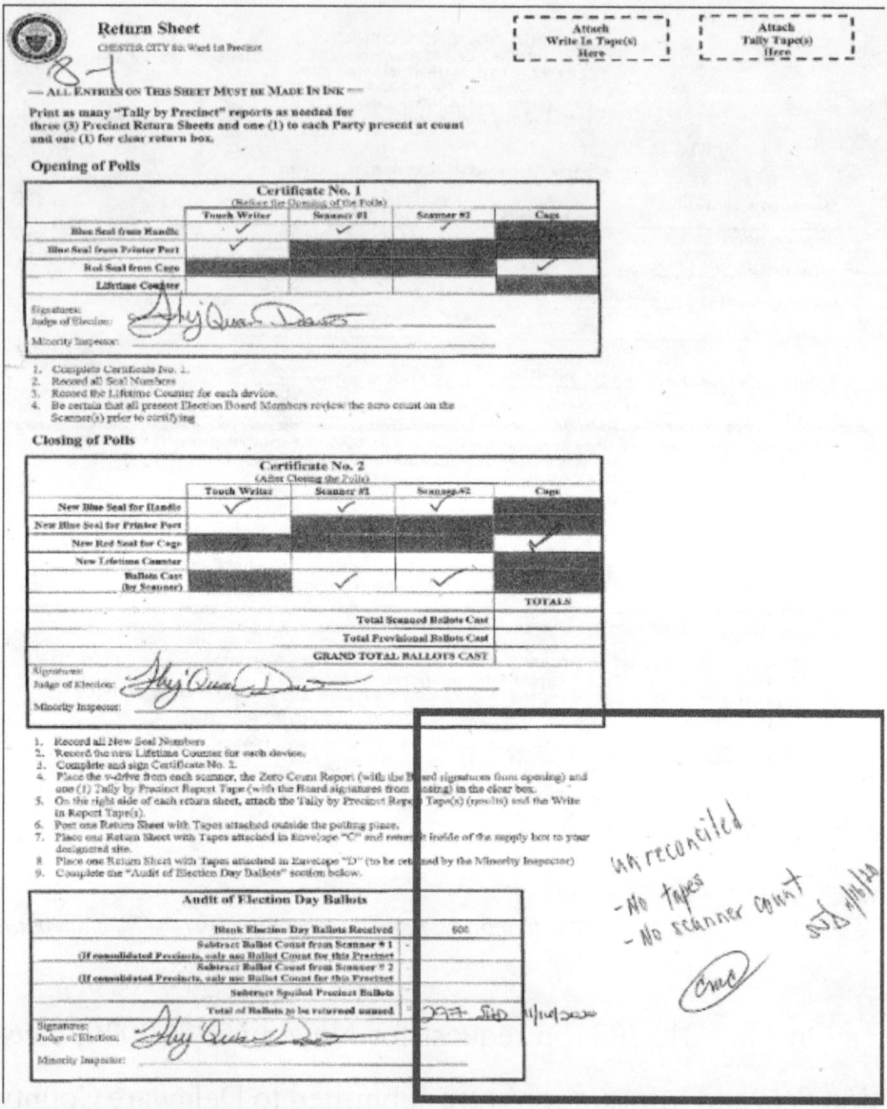

Figure 75 - Exhibit H, Right To Know Request for Election data

The Return Sheet depicted above from Chester City 8th Ward 1st Precinct (8-1) was typical of the reconstructed (<u>fabricated</u>) election data provided by the BOE in response to the

RTK request. There are supposed to be numeric values in boxes where there are check marks (✓), there is a signature for the Majority Judge of Elections (JOE) with no countersignature for the Minority JOE, and it is dated 11/16/2020 with initials that do not match the JOE, 600 starting ballots, and a count of 297 returned ballots, which would indicate that they used 303 ballots for 303 voters. Handwritten notes state "Unreconciled," "No tapes," "No scanner count."

Now let's look at the "official results" reported by Delaware County, PA for the same precinct. The BOE recorded only 226 election day walk-in votes, and an un-auditable 82 mail-in votes for 310 total votes (94% for Biden) out of 728 registered voters. There were zero (0) provisional ballots recorded for 8-1. **There are no other records to reasonably determine what the actual vote was, and none of the data that is available can be reconciled or matched.**

This is only one example of hundreds of similar fabrications.

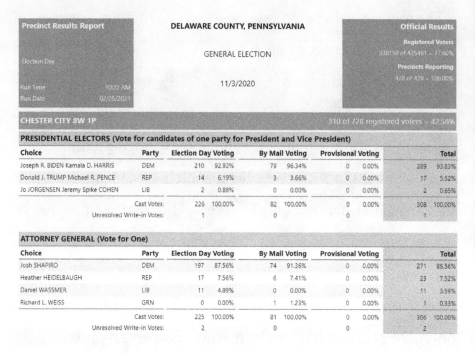

Figure 76 - Chester City Precinct 8-1 "Official Results" 2020 General Election

WHAT IS A RETURN SHEET?

A Pennsylvania Return Sheet contains the following information: instructions that require "all entries on this sheet must be made in ink" opening poll chain of custody, blue seal numbers from the handle of each scanner, blue seal numbers from the printer port of the printer port, red seal numbers from the cage, lifetime counter data, signature of Judge of Election, signature of Minority Inspector, instruction to complete certificate number one, requirement to record all seal numbers, record the lifetime counter for each device, show that all present Election Board Members reviewed the zero count on the scanner prior to certifying, closing of polls, new blue seal number for handle on touch writer, new blue seal numbers on handle of scanners, new blue seal numbers on printer port, new red seal numbers for cage, new lifetime counter, ballots cast by scanner, total scanned ballots, total provisional ballots cast, grand total ballots cast, signature of Judge of Elections, signature of Minority Inspector, instructions to record all new seal numbers, record the new lifetime counter for each device, complete and sign certificate number two, place the vDrive from each scanner, the zero count report with the Board signatures from opening, and one tally by precinct report tape with the Board signatures from closing in the clear box, attach the tally by precinct report tape(s) (results)and the write in report tape(s) on the right side of each Return Sheet, post one Return Sheet with tapes attached outside of the polling place, place one Return Sheet with tapes attached in envelope C, and return it inside of the supply box to your designated site, place one Return Sheet with tapes attached in envelope D to be maintained by the minority inspector. Complete the audit of election ballots section, record the blank Election Day Ballots Received, subtract Ballot Count from Scanner One, subtract ballot Count from Scanner Two, Subtract Spoiled Ballot Precinct Ballots, Record Total of ballots to be returned unused, signature of Judge of Election, signature of Minority Inspector.

NO PROCEDURES FOLLOWED

A summary of the above is that a Return Sheet encompasses the universe of everything that happened at a polling location, and when placed with all election materials in the sealed canvas bag it is the ground truth of election results.

The Return Sheet, and the Proof Sheet (paper tape), and the vDrive containing the Cast Vote Record (CVR), and the number of cast ballots and unused ballots must all match up. In Delaware County, PA, this was NOT the case, and election officials compensated by fabricating results.

November 18, 2020

Delaware County Board of Election
201 West Front Street
Media PA, 19063

Dear Members of the Delaware County Board of Elections:

Re: Report of the Delaware County Return Board for the General Election, November 2020

Pursuant to the Post-Election General Reconciliation Project dated November 2016 from the Commonwealth of Pennsylvania, the undersigned Delaware County Return Board met from Friday, November 6 through Monday, November 16, 2020, from 8:30 AM to 3:00 PM every day.

The Return Board consisted of 18 Tabulators, including 9 Democrats and 9 Republicans. The below report is a summary of our findings and recommendations. Also attached is a spreadsheet that elaborates on the specific tasks undertaken pursuant to 25 P.S. § 3154(b)(c)(d); 25 P.S. § 3031.17 and paragraph 10 of the Directive Concerning the Use, Implementation and Operation of the Electronic Voting Systems by County Board of Elections, Election Code, 25 P.S. § 3031.17 et al., dated 6/09/2011.

All work was performed in teams of two (one Republican and one Democrat) and all individual work was signed off by team members that performed the task(s). These documents have been organized for storage at the Voting Machine Warehouse for the statutorily required timeframe, except for the voted ballots used in the hand recount. These ballots were sealed in ballot bags and returned to Media by a member of Delaware County Sheriff's Department.

We met with the representatives of 202 Delaware County Precinct Election Boards to comply with the Election Code, from Friday November 13 through Monday November 16, 2020. The individual precinct representatives were most helpful in assisting in our efforts. It should be noted that a majority of the precinct Election Board members remarked that the training materials were often lacking in clear instruction as to

Figure 77 - Exhibit J Page 1, Report of Delco Return Board

On and after November 3, 2020, the Delaware County Return Board was missing necessary November 3, 2020, election data, materials, results, and equipment which was needed to reconcile all Delaware County precincts and certify the November 3, 2020, election.

the opening and closing of the polls and the preparation of the Return Sheets. The Return Board is available to discuss specific areas of concerns and will await the Board of Elections directions to assist the County in preparing appropriate training materials for the Election Board members going forward.

The Return Board wishes to acknowledge the guidance and help of the Voting Machine Warehouse Supervisor, Jim Savage, and his staff during the Return Board's daily work.

Initially, as part of our duties, we reviewed the list of voters (Yellow Book) and compared same to the County Public Count, Return Sheets, and noted the differentials. We determined that most inconsistencies in the Yellow Book numbers were human error, except for a small number of precincts and those precincts were referred to the Delaware County District Attorney.

As part of our interviews with the 202 precinct Election Board representatives, we discussed the unused paper ballots, a majority of which, were available for our review. We noted on their Return Sheets any extra ballots that the precinct received during the day from the Bureau of Elections as well as those produced by the precinct Touch Writers. As part of the process, we analyzed ballots issued, the number of spoiled ballots, and the number of ballots cast. Finally, we insured that provisional ballots were not included in the scanner tallies or the Yellow Books.

We were able to reconcile the above numbers in a majority of the precincts that sent representatives to help assist the Return Board in its audits. It was determined that out of a total of 428 Delaware County precincts, we needed to meet with 220 individual precincts, the remainder of which were able to be reconciled with the provided/returned documentation. Of the 220 precincts, 94 precincts were Reconciled; 29 precincts had minor Discrepancies with Explanations and 79 precincts could not be Reconciled. Additionally, 18 precincts did not respond to the County's multiple emails and phone calls, requesting their cooperation during the four days that we designated as interview dates (November 13, 14, 15, and 16).

It is important to note that there was no indication of fraud in the data or during the interviews throughout our assignment. We point out that each and every Unreconciled or Discrepancies with Explanation Return

Figure 78 - Exhibit J Page 2, Report of Delco Return Board

Sheets were the result of training issues. The election workers were consistent in wanting "to do it right" but did not know how. It is assumed that these training issues have been noted and will be corrected going forward.

Next, as part of our duties, we reviewed the Return Sheets from the 220 precincts identified as needing additional information and noted the missing scanner tapes. In those precincts where the tapes were missing, it can be explained by lack of training, lack of properly attaching them to the Return Sheets, human error, or a lack of Return Sheets in the precinct Election Officers' "White Box."

The Return Board recommends that the County eliminate the combination of scanners that permitted voters to submit marked ballots into any scanner at voting locations where there were two or more precincts. The precinct Election Boards did not know how to correctly co-mingle the final scanner print outs from multiple precincts, hence the inability to reconcile unused ballots or had no information in the Audit section on the Return Sheets. Attempts were undertaken to help the precinct Election Boards, during the interviews, to calculate the final scanner numbers for the Return Sheets and we were successful in a majority of the questioned precincts. The scanner printout numbers were compared to the removable storage media used by the County to count votes cast at each precinct and were found to be Reconciled.

Finally, the Return Board undertook a statistical hand recount of ballots from a number of randomly selected precincts that totaled over 2,300 ballots cast. This count was done by hand and compared to the electronic tabulation numbers generated by the County V-drives from the scanners. The hand count tabulation was consistent with the votes reported from the machines by the County.

The Return Board would like to thank the County Board of Elections for the trust that you have given us to perform this important Post-Election General Reconciliation Audit. We stand ready to assist you again in Spring 2021 Primary and if any of our analysis or recommendation needs further explanation, please contact us if necessary.

Figure 79 - Exhibit J Page 3, Report of Delco Return Board

<u>**Conclusion/ Recommendations**</u>

1. The Election Day Guide, the Alphabetized envelopes and the Return Sheets must be redone with the assistance of experienced Judges of Elections (JOE).

2. Training for opening, closing and preparing Return Sheets.

3. Eliminate co-mingling of scanners in locations with multiple precincts.

4. Better efforts made to ensure JOE's can contact the Bureau of Elections during the day. JOE's had multiple questions that could have been solved but were unable to contact anyone.

5. Completely revise the Poll Workers' Election Day Guide.

6. Revise Return Sheets at the bottom – "Audit" – need to include:

   A. Extra ballots printed on Touch Writers.

   B. Extra ballots received on election day from the Bureau of Elections.

7. Better explanation of the purpose of the "List of Voters" and the need for accuracy. Errors were noted throughout, as well as cross-outs and voters signing the book versus poll worker (the Clerk).

8. Return sheets need to be distributed in the "White Box."

9. The White Boxes must be left in-tack for Return Board review when questions arise.

10. Unused ballots must be returned in the box that they were delivered in and placed in the sealed cages delivered to the Voting Machine Warehouse.

11. Precinct Election Boards must count unused ballots after the polls close, not back the numbers in by subtracting the voted and spoiled ballots from the total received.

12. Precinct Election Boards complained that precinct property owners/supervisors would not open the buildings/polling locations to poll workers until 6 AM. It takes over 1 hour and 15 minutes to set up one precinct and some Judges had 2 precincts.

13. Need a short and specific checklist for the closing of polls from 8 PM to dropping materials off at the County Government locations.

Figure 80 - Exhibit J Page 4, Report of Delco Return Board

14. The Security Seals that are required to be installed after polls are closed, need specific instructions as to their placement.

15. Specific Provisional Ballot video training would help.

16. The online training quiz needs to explain why the answer by the poll worker was determined to be incorrect. "What is the right answer/proper procedure?"

17. The precinct Election Boards have requested hands-on training on how to produce required reports from scanners and Touch Writers.

18. The human errors can be greatly eliminated by additional training and revising the Return Sheets/Alphabetical envelopes and the Election Day Guide.

Figure 81 - Exhibit J Page 5, Report of Delco Return Board

Their report is an unconscionable sidestep of responsibility and implausible explanations. They blame over 220 precincts missing "proof sheets," which are the machine tapes with the voting records, and blank return sheets – essentially admitting losing more than half of all votes in Delaware County on "lack of training," and recommended certifying a "vote" that is almost entirely fabricated out of air.

They want the public to believe that they could lose and fabricate hundreds of Return Sheets, lose, or destroy hundreds of Proof Sheets (paper tapes), but that they did not lose, destroy, or fabricate 47+ vDrives containing tens of thousands of votes.

Again, even without the Whistleblower video and audio exhibits where election officials knowingly and laughingly admit to fabricating the vote, and that it was impossible to reconcile, and that tens of thousands of votes were missing along with the 47+ missing vDrives – the election officials admit in official documents that the election was a fugazi. The fact that not a single Return Board or election official would sign official documents might help with plausible deniability and a Bart Simpson "I didn't do it" criminal defense, but from an election code, civil code, and constitutional perspective, they broke every possible law.

Note that the official documents were NOT signed by any official.

Return Board Members

Karen Reeves	Mary Jo Headley
Donna Rode	Jennifer Booker
Norma Locke	Kenneth Haughton
Jean Davidson	James A. Ziegelhoffer
S. J. Dennis	Regina Scheerer
Marilyn Heider	Cathy Craddock
Tom Gallagher	Maureen T. Moore
Louis Govinden	Pasquale Cipolloni
Doug Degenhardt	Gretchen Bell

NO SIGNATURES

Figure 82 - Exhibit J Page 6, Report of Delco Return Board

339

the opening and closing of the polls and the preparation of the Return Sheets. The Return Board is available to discuss specific areas of concerns and will await the Board of Elections directions to assist the County in preparing appropriate training materials for the Election Board members going forward.

The Return Board wishes to acknowledge the guidance and help of the Voting Machine Warehouse Supervisor, Jim Savage, and his staff during the Return Board's daily work.

Initially, as part of our duties, we reviewed the list of voters (Yellow Book) and compared same to the County Public Count, Return Sheets, and noted the differentials. We determined that most inconsistencies in the Yellow Book numbers were human error, except for a small number of precincts and those precincts were referred to the Delaware County District Attorney.

As part of our interviews with the 202 precinct Election Board representatives, we discussed the unused paper ballots, a majority of which, were available for our review. We noted on their Return Sheets any extra ballots that the precinct received during the day from the Bureau of Elections as well as those produced by the precinct Touch Writers. As part of the process, we analyzed ballots issued, the number of spoiled ballots and the number of ballots cast. Finally, we insured that provisional ballots were not included in the scanned tallies or the Yellow Books.

We were able to reconcile the above numbers in a majority of the precincts that sent representatives to help assist the Return Board in its audits. It was determined that out of a total of 428 Delaware County precincts, we needed to meet with 220 individual precincts, the remainder of which were able to be reconciled with the provided/returned documentation. Of the 220 precincts, 94 precincts were Reconciled; 29 precincts had minor Discrepancies with Explanations and 79 precincts could not be Reconciled. Additionally, 18 precincts did not respond to the County's multiple emails and phone calls, requesting their cooperation during the four days that we designated as interview dates (November 13, 14, 15, and 16).

It is important to note that there was no indication of fraud in the data or during the interviews throughout our assignment. We point out that each and every Unreconciled or Discrepancies with Explanation Return

Figure 83 - Exhibit K, Referral to District Attorney

On or about November 3, 2020, the Delaware County Return Board (and individual members including various Defendants) discovered numerous election law violations, and/or incidents of election fraud, and referred these to the District Attorney for investigation. In fact, only a small number of precincts were actually referred and there was no evidence that anything was actually investigated. [Exhibit K].

ATTORNEY GENERAL JOSH SHAPIRO ANNOUNCES CRIMINAL CHARGES FOR INTERFERENCE IN SPECIAL ELECTION IN 197TH LEGISLATIVE DISTRICT

OCTOBER 30, 2017 | TOPIC: CRIMINAL   SHARE

Charges, Including Fraud by Four Election Officers, Filed Today

PHILADELPHIA — Attorney General Josh Shapiro, joined by Philadelphia District Attorney Kelley B. Hodge, today announced criminal charges against four Philadelphia election workers for violating the Pennsylvania Election Code during a March special election for a state House seat in Philadelphia.

"Pennsylvania law clearly states that fraud by election officers is not permissible and this behavior – such as certifying false results – is fraud," Attorney General Shapiro said. "We're watching, and we have no tolerance for any interference in free and fair elections here in Pennsylvania."

Figure 84 - Exhibit L, PA AG Shapiro Definition Election Fraud

According to PA Attorney General candidate Josh Shapiro, "Pennsylvania law clearly states that fraud by election officers is not permissible and this behavior such as certifying false results is fraud."

Both PA Attorney General Shapiro and DelCo DA Jack Stollsteimer failed to act, investigate, or charge Delaware County election officials despite referrals for investigation.

Shapiro was referred to investigate the missing vDrives and mail-in ballots by US Attorney McSwain – but Shapiro denied that.

Shapiro predicted that President Trump "could not win," and would lose by 80,000 votes,

Before Delaware County, PA was last in the State to submit their falsely certified vote results, President Trump was ahead by almost 8,000 votes.

After Delaware County submitted their results, Trump was behind by a little over 80,000 votes.

PA AG Shapiro – who was on the ballot with Biden, and also a Biden elector, never investigated and continues to insist the there was "no fraud."

On or about May 21, 2021, Delaware county employees (including various Defendants) began to conspire as to how to respond on behalf of Delaware County to the May 21, 2021, Right to Know Request knowing that numerous election laws had been violated and massive election fraud and other irregularities had occurred during the November 3, 2020 election, and these individuals began planning how they were going to conceal the November 2020 violations of the election code and the fraud in the process of responding to the Right to Know Request.

On or about April 29, 2021, James A. Ziegelhoffer, also known as "Ziggy", disclosed to the Whistleblower that the Return Sheets and Proof Sheets (paper tapes) from the November 3, 2020, election were not stored with the election data, equipment, and materials on the main, and second floor with the remaining November 3, 2020, election data, materials, and equipment in the Voting Machine Warehouse in Delaware County as required by Pennsylvania law, or in accordance with the BOE's own directives and procedures. [Exhibit O (BELOW)].

Figure 85 - Exhibit O Pg 1, Hidden Return Sheets and Tapes

Return Sheets, Proof Sheets (paper tapes) for Delaware County, PA were stored in the Voting Machine Warehouse basement, some in canvas bags used for precinct polling locations, carboard boxes, and manilla envelopes.

Figure 86 - Exhibit O Inset 1, Unreconciled Return Sheets

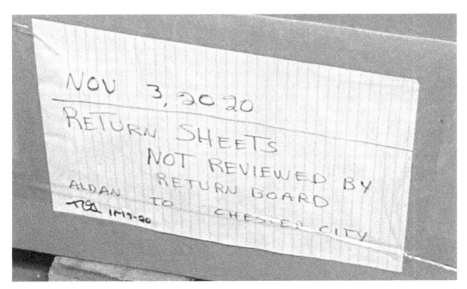

Figure 87 - Exhibit O Inset 2, Return Sheets Not Reviewed

Figure 88 - Exhibit O Page 2, Hidden Election Returns

Figure 89 - Exhibit O Page 3, More Hidden Election Materials

Figure 90 - Exhibit O Page 4, Locked Basement of Warehouse

Figure 91 - Exhibit O Page 5, Hidden Return Discrepancies

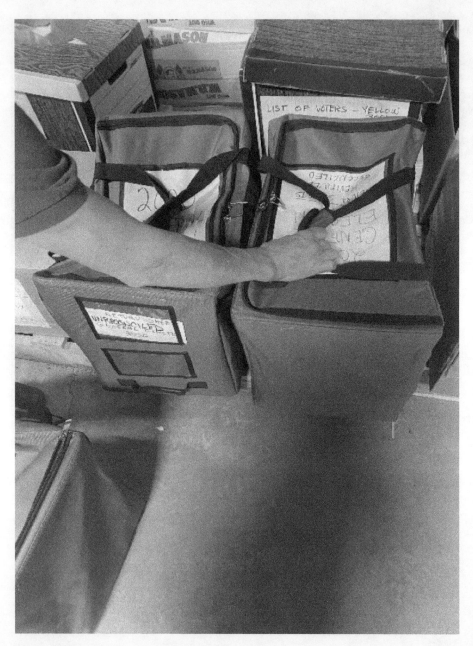

Figure 92 - Exhibit O Page 6, Hidden Yellow Sheets

Figure 93 - Exhibit O Page 7, Hidden Cabinets

DETAILS INCLUDED IN MOTON, HOOPES AND STENSTROM LITIGATION REGARDING FRAUDULENT CERTIFICATION OF 2020 ELECTION IN DELAWARE COUNTY, PA

The Delaware County November 3, 2020, election was certified without the necessary election data, materials, and equipment required to reconcile the election results.

Specifically, out of 428 precincts, 15 precincts did not have Return Sheets at the time of certification. [Exhibit N].

Specifically, out of 428 precincts, 16 precincts submitted blank Return Sheets at the time of certification. [Attached hereto as Exhibit N].

Delaware County's response to the May 21, 2021, Right to Know (RTK) Request, revealed that 213 precincts had return sheets that were missing information, yet Delaware County certified the November 3, 2020, election.

The May 21, 2021, Right to Know (RTK) Request revealed 213 precincts had return sheets that were missing information. [Attached hereto as Exhibit N]. Despite this deficiency, Delaware County certified the November 3, 2020, election.

On or about November 24, 2020, Delaware county certified the November 3, 2020, election with over half (244) of the precincts missing necessary election data to determine accurate election results (15+16+213=244) according to Delaware County's Response to the May 21, 2021, Right to Know Request. [Exhibit N].

On June 28, 2021, Delaware County responded to the May 21, 2021, Right to Know Request and provided data it used to certify the November 3, 2020, election.

The information and data produced does not align with or match the November 3, 2020, election data the County referred to in its November 18, 2020, letter to the Election Board regarding certification of the November 3, 2020, election.

RTK TABULATION SUMMARY

The election results, return sheets, proof sheets, etc., requested in the Right To Know (RTK) were fully tabulated and indexed by our attorneys against the official reported results, and compared with the Return Board report.

These comparisons provide undeniable evidence that entire precincts and <u>tens of thousands of votes were fabricated</u> by election officials, fraudulently certified, and resulted in multiple candidates who did not win being fraudulently and illegitimately installed in office.

We have provided several screen captures of sections of the RTK tabulation report that show precincts from Chester City where Stenstrom was assigned as a certified poll watcher.

Specifically, while a bit difficult to discern within the constraints of a book and paper, there were no election materials at all – no Return Sheets, No Proof Sheets, No data, for:

- Chester City 5th Ward 2nd Precinct – 281 Registered Voters

- Chester City 8th Ward 1st Precinct – 728 Registered Voters

- Chester City 10th Ward 1st Precinct – 624 Registered Voters

- Chester City 11th Ward 5th Precinct – 811 Registered Voters

The "official," "certified," results for these four precincts alone compromised 2,444 citizens for whom the BOE allowed a third party to unilaterally decided how they would cast their votes.

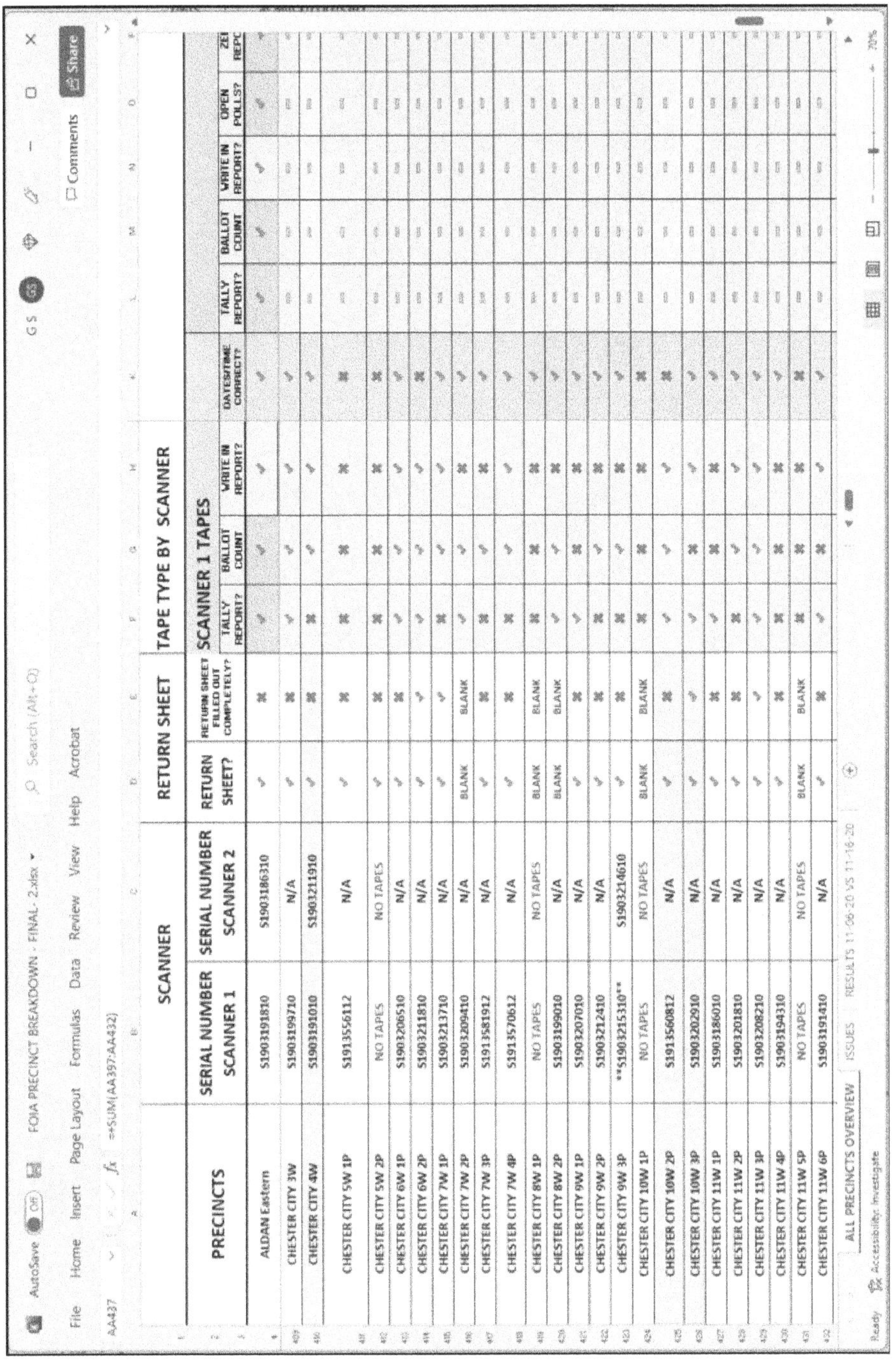

Figure 94 - Screenshot 1 of Chester City RTK Tabulation

PRECINCTS	SCANNER		RETURN SHEET		
	SERIAL NUMBER SCANNER 1	SERIAL NUMBER SCANNER 2	RETURN SHEET?	RETURN SHEET FILLED OUT COMPLETELY?	TALLY REPORT?
ALDAN Eastern	S1903191810	S1903186310	✓	✗	✓
CHESTER CITY 1W 5P	S1913558412	N/A	BLANK	BLANK	✗
CHESTER CITY 1W 6P	S1903180910	N/A	BLANK	✓	✗
CHESTER CITY 1W 7P	S1903202310	N/A	✓	✓	✓
CHESTER CITY 1W 8P	S1913574812	N/A	✓	✗	✗
CHESTER CITY 2W 1P	S1903210410	N/A	✓	✗	✗
CHESTER CITY 2W 2P	S1913570812	S1903207210	✓	✓	✗
CHESTER CITY 2W 3P	S1903177510	N/A	✓	✗	✓
CHESTER CITY 2W 4P	S1913571612	N/A	✓	✗	✓
CHESTER CITY 3W	S1903199710	N/A	✓	✗	✓
CHESTER CITY 4W	S1903191010	S1903211910	✓	✗	✗
CHESTER CITY 5W 1P	S1913556112	N/A	✓	✗	✗
CHESTER CITY 5W 2P	NO TAPES	NO TAPES	✓	✗	✗
CHESTER CITY 6W 1P	S1903206510	N/A	✓	✗	✓
CHESTER CITY 6W 2P	S1903211810	N/A	✓	✗	✓
CHESTER CITY 7W 1P	S1903213710	N/A	✓	✓	✗
CHESTER CITY 7W 2P	S1903209410	N/A	BLANK	BLANK	✓
CHESTER CITY 7W 3P	S1913581912	N/A	✓	✗	✗
CHESTER CITY 7W 4P	S1913570612	N/A	✓	✗	✗
CHESTER CITY 8W 1P	NO TAPES	NO TAPES	BLANK	BLANK	✗
CHESTER CITY 8W 2P	S1903199010	N/A	BLANK	BLANK	✓
CHESTER CITY 9W 1P	S1903207010	N/A	✓	✗	✓
CHESTER CITY 9W 2P	S1903212410	N/A	✓	✓	✗
CHESTER CITY 9W 3P	**S1903215310***	S1903214610	✓	✗	✗
CHESTER CITY 10W 1P	NO TAPES	NO TAPES	BLANK	BLANK	✗
CHESTER CITY 10W 2P	S1913560812	N/A	✓	✓	✓
CHESTER CITY 10W 3P	S1903202910	N/A	✓	✓	✓
CHESTER CITY 11W 1P	S1903186010	N/A	✓	✗	✗
CHESTER CITY 11W 2P	S1903201810	N/A	✓	✓	✓
CHESTER CITY 11W 3P	S1903208210	N/A	✓	✗	✓
CHESTER CITY 11W 4P	S1903194310	N/A	✓	✗	✗
CHESTER CITY 11W 5P	NO TAPES	NO TAPES	BLANK	BLANK	✗
CHESTER CITY 11W 6P	S1903191410	N/A	✓	✗	✓

Figure 95 - Screenshot 1 of Chester City RTK Tabulation

E BY SCANNER

SCANNER 2 TAPES						DO RESULTS MATCH TALLY TAPE?
TALLY REPORT?	BALLOT COUNT	WRITE IN REPORT?	OPEN POLLS?	ZERO REPORT?	DATES/TIME CORRECT?	
✓	✓	✓	✓	✓	✓	✓
						✓
✗	✓	✓	✓	✗	✓	
						✗
						✓
						✓
						✓
						✓
						✓
						✓
						✓
						✓
						✓
						✗
						✓

Figure 96 - Screenshot 3 of Part of Chester City RTK Tabulation

Precinct Results Report

Election Day

Run Time 10:22 AM
Run Date 02/25/2021

DELAWARE COUNTY, PENNSYLVANIA

GENERAL ELECTION

11/3/2020

Official Results

Registered Voters
330150 of 425461 = 77.60%

Precincts Reporting
428 of 428 = 100.00%

CHESTER CITY 5W 2P 161 of 281 registered voters = 57.30%

PRESIDENTIAL ELECTORS (Vote for candidates of one party for President and Vice President)

Choice	Party	Election Day Voting		By Mail Voting		Provisional Voting		Total	
Joseph R. BIDEN Kamala D. HARRIS	DEM	101	89.38%	33	94.29%	12	100.00%	146	91.25%
Donald J. TRUMP Michael R. PENCE	REP	10	8.85%	2	5.71%	0	0.00%	12	7.50%
Jo JORGENSEN Jeremy Spike COHEN	LIB	2	1.77%	0	0.00%	0	0.00%	2	1.25%
Cast Votes:		113	100.00%	35	100.00%	12	100.00%	160	100.00%
Unresolved Write-in Votes:		0		1		0		1	

ATTORNEY GENERAL (Vote for One)

Choice	Party	Election Day Voting		By Mail Voting		Provisional Voting		Total	
Josh SHAPIRO	DEM	95	84.07%	32	94.12%	10	90.91%	137	86.71%
Heather HEIDELBAUGH	REP	12	10.62%	2	5.88%	1	9.09%	15	9.49%
Daniel WASSMER	LIB	3	2.65%	0	0.00%	0	0.00%	3	1.90%
Richard L. WEISS	GRN	3	2.65%	0	0.00%	0	0.00%	3	1.90%
Cast Votes:		113	100.00%	34	100.00%	11	100.00%	158	100.00%
Unresolved Write-in Votes:		0		0		0		0	

Figure 97 - Official Results for Chester City 5W 2P

Precinct Results Report | **DELAWARE COUNTY, PENNSYLVANIA** | **Official Results**

GENERAL ELECTION

11/3/2020

Election Day

Run Time	10:22 AM	
Run Date	02/25/2021	

Registered Voters
330150 of 425461 = 77.60%

Precincts Reporting
428 of 428 = 100.00%

CHESTER CITY 8W 1P   310 of 728 registered voters = 42.58%

PRESIDENTIAL ELECTORS (Vote for candidates of one party for President and Vice President)

Choice	Party	Election Day Voting		By Mail Voting		Provisional Voting		Total	
Joseph R. BIDEN Kamala D. HARRIS	DEM	210	92.92%	79	96.34%	0	0.00%	289	93.83%
Donald J. TRUMP Michael R. PENCE	REP	14	6.19%	3	3.66%	0	0.00%	17	5.52%
Jo JORGENSEN Jeremy Spike COHEN	LIB	2	0.88%	0	0.00%	0	0.00%	2	0.65%
Cast Votes:		226	100.00%	82	100.00%	0	0.00%	308	100.00%
Unresolved Write-in Votes:		1		0		0		1	

ATTORNEY GENERAL (Vote for One)

Choice	Party	Election Day Voting		By Mail Voting		Provisional Voting		Total	
Josh SHAPIRO	DEM	197	87.56%	74	91.36%	0	0.00%	271	88.56%
Heather HEIDELBAUGH	REP	17	7.56%	6	7.41%	0	0.00%	23	7.52%
Daniel WASSMER	LIB	11	4.89%	0	0.00%	0	0.00%	11	3.59%
Richard L. WEISS	GRN	0	0.00%	1	1.23%	0	0.00%	1	0.33%
Cast Votes:		225	100.00%	81	100.00%	0	0.00%	306	100.00%
Unresolved Write-in Votes:		2		0		0		2	

Figure 98 - Official Results for Chester City 8W 1P

Precinct Results Report

Election Day

Run Time 10:22 AM
Run Date 02/25/2021

DELAWARE COUNTY, PENNSYLVANIA

GENERAL ELECTION

11/3/2020

Official Results

Registered Voters
330150 of 425461 = 77.60%

Precincts Reporting
428 of 428 = 100.00%

CHESTER CITY 10W 1P

398 of 624 registered voters = 63.78%

PRESIDENTIAL ELECTORS (Vote for candidates of one party for President and Vice President)

Choice	Party	Election Day Voting		By Mail Voting		Provisional Voting		Total	
Joseph R. BIDEN Kamala D. HARRIS	DEM	269	97.46%	114	98.28%	4	100.00%	387	97.73%
Donald J. TRUMP Michael R. PENCE	REP	7	2.54%	2	1.72%	0	0.00%	9	2.27%
Jo JORGENSEN Jeremy Spike COHEN	LIB	0	0.00%	0	0.00%	0	0.00%	0	0.00%
Cast Votes:		276	100.00%	116	100.00%	4	100.00%	396	100.00%
Unresolved Write-in Votes:		1		1		0		2	

ATTORNEY GENERAL (Vote for One)

Choice	Party	Election Day Voting		By Mail Voting		Provisional Voting		Total	
Josh SHAPIRO	DEM	249	95.40%	112	98.25%	4	100.00%	365	96.31%
Heather HEIDELBAUGH	REP	4	1.53%	2	1.75%	0	0.00%	6	1.58%
Daniel WASSMER	LIB	5	1.92%	0	0.00%	0	0.00%	5	1.32%
Richard L. WEISS	GRN	3	1.15%	0	0.00%	0	0.00%	3	0.79%
Cast Votes:		261	100.00%	114	100.00%	4	100.00%	379	100.00%
Unresolved Write-in Votes:		1		0		0		1	

Figure 99 - Official Results for Chester City 10W 1P

Precinct Results Report

DELAWARE COUNTY, PENNSYLVANIA

GENERAL ELECTION

11/3/2020

Election Day

Run Time 10:22 AM
Run Date 02/25/2021

Official Results

Registered Voters
330150 of 425461 = 77.60%

Precincts Reporting
428 of 428 = 100.00%

CHESTER CITY 11W 5P

423 of 811 registered voters = 52.16%

PRESIDENTIAL ELECTORS (Vote for candidates of one party for President and Vice President)

Choice	Party	Election Day Voting		By Mail Voting		Provisional Voting		Total	
Joseph R. BIDEN Kamala D. HARRIS	DEM	266	92.68%	109	98.20%	20	80.00%	395	93.38%
Donald J. TRUMP Michael R. PENCE	REP	20	6.97%	1	0.90%	4	16.00%	25	5.91%
Jo JORGENSEN Jeremy Spike COHEN	LIB	1	0.35%	1	0.90%	1	4.00%	3	0.71%
Cast Votes:		287	100.00%	111	100.00%	25	100.00%	423	100.00%
Unresolved Write-in Votes:		0		0		0		0	

ATTORNEY GENERAL (Vote for One)

Choice	Party	Election Day Voting		By Mail Voting		Provisional Voting		Total	
Josh SHAPIRO	DEM	261	91.26%	103	92.79%	19	79.17%	383	90.97%
Heather HEIDELBAUGH	REP	21	7.34%	4	3.60%	3	12.50%	28	6.65%
Daniel WASSMER	LIB	2	0.70%	1	0.90%	0	0.00%	3	0.71%
Richard L. WEISS	GRN	2	0.70%	3	2.70%	2	8.33%	7	1.66%
Cast Votes:		286	100.00%	111	100.00%	24	100.00%	421	100.00%
Unresolved Write-in Votes:		0		0		0		0	

Figure 100 - Official Results for Chester City 11W 5P

361

Figure 101 - Exhibit P, Return Sheets Not Reviewed by Board

On or about April 29, 2021, Defendant James A. Ziegelhoffer escorted the Whistleblower to the basement of the Voting Machine Warehouse and showed her where the Return Sheets and election tapes were hidden along with the November 3, 2020, election materials stored in a cardboard box labeled "Return Sheets not Reviewed by Return Board November 3, 2020, Election". [Exhibit P].

Ziegelhoffer stated that during the interviews, <u>the Return Board provided the election workers with election data and prompted them to create new Return Sheets for the November 3, 2020, election as part of the certification process</u>. [Attached hereto as Exhibit R].

The combination of hard physical evidence with the Whistleblowers corroborative testimony and videos of election officials admitting to committing election fraud and other felonies, the Return Sheets, Proof Sheets, Blue Books, Yellow Books, and other election material evidence provided with the RTK materials clearly show that results were fabricated and forged.

The following pages will provide additional Exhibits supporting these allegations.

GLENOLDEN 1P

Election Header

GENERAL ELECTION

Election Date: 11/3/2020

DELAWARE COUNTY,
PENNSYLVANIA

Glenolden 1, 2, 3, 4, 5, 6

Election Day Voting

Verity Scan

S/N: S1903206810

Version: 2.3.1

Ballot Counter: 27
Lifetime Counter: 59

Tally Report By Precinct

Date & Time Printed:

11/03/2020   8:45 PM

Qty Pcts/Splits Included   6

PRESIDENTIAL
ELECTORS
(Vote for candidates of
one party for President
and Vice President)

Joseph R. BIDEN Kamala D. HARRIS	2
Donald J. TRUMP Michael R. PENCE	5
Jo JORGENSEN Jeremy Spike COHEN	0
Write-ins	0
Undervotes	0
Overvotes	0

ATTORNEY GENERAL
(Vote for One)

Josh SHAPIRO	2
Heather HEIDELBAUGH	5
Daniel WASSMER	0
Richard L. WEISS	0
Write-ins	0
Undervotes	0

Figure 102 - Exhibit R DelCo PA Glenholden 1P - 1

364

AUDITOR GENERAL
(Vote for One)

Nina AHMAD	2
Timothy DEFOOR	5
Jennifer MOORE	0
Olivia FAISON	0
Write-ins	0
Undervotes	0
Overvotes	0

STATE TREASURER
(Vote for One)

Joe TORSELLA	3
Stacy L. GARRITY	4
Joe SOLOSKI	0
Timothy RUNKLE	0
Write-ins	0
Undervotes	0
Overvotes	0

REPRESENTATIVE IN
CONGRESS
5TH DISTRICT
(Vote for One)

Mary Gay SCANLON	2
Dasha PRUETT	5
Write-ins	0
Undervotes	0
Overvotes	0

REPRESENTATIVE IN
THE
GENERAL ASSEMBLY
162ND DISTRICT
(Vote for One)

Dave DELLOSO	2
Pete GAGLIO	5
Write-ins	0
Undervotes	0
Overvotes	0

Figure 103 - Exhibit R: Delco PA Glenholden 1P - 2

Exhibit R is actually the voting machine tape, or officially, the "PROOF SHEET" for the precinct, and is a record of all ballots scanned by the voting machine. What the tape says for Precinct Glenholden 1P is that (only) 27 ballots were scanned for this election cycle, and (only) 59 ballots have been scanned for the machine since it was initialized one, two, three, or more elections, ago. Given that there are 804 registered voters for Glenholden 1P, and the Delaware County Board of Elections "official" voting results they loaded on their website, reported the week of the November 2020 election, fraudulently certified, and that Chairman Laurence stated he referred to District Attorney Stollsteimer for <u>investigation was for 405 registered voters who CAST votes in person, versus 29 recorded on the tape</u>. The RETURN SHEET for Glenholden 1P, that Ziegelhoffer and Gallagher admit to wholly fabricating out of air, showed 335 CAST votes, 70 less than was reported as the "official" certified results. For illustrative purposes, let's use the "official" report that was "certified" and look at the top of the ticket. Biden was given 156 election day illegitimate votes, and President Trump was given 246 illegitimate votes for a 39% to 61% lead for President Trump. Now factor in the Mail-in ballots, which show 178 total ballot count in the "official" certified results, of which Biden was given 122 and

President Trump was given 56 for a 69% to 31% margin. The provisional vote was 13 for Biden and 4 for President Trump. All, for a grand total of 601 registered voters reportedly casting ballots for a 75% voter turnout. The end result in Glenholden 1P is 291 for Biden and 306 for President Trump and 49% to 51% margin. The undercard is results were similar for PA Attorney General Shapiro who lost to Heather Heidelbaugh on election day by 156 votes to 238 and a 39% to 59% margin, and then after mail-in ballots, the vote flips and Shapiro is on top 296 to 286 for a 49% to 48% margin. The machine tape shows 5 votes for Heidelbaugh to 2 votes for Shapiro.

Precinct Results Report

DELAWARE COUNTY, PENNSYLVANIA

GENERAL ELECTION

11/3/2020

Election Day

Run Time 10:22 AM
Run Date 02/25/2021

Official Results

Registered Voters
330150 of 425461 = 77.60%

Precincts Reporting
428 of 428 = 100.00%

GLENOLDEN 1P

601 of 804 registered voters = 74.75%

PRESIDENTIAL ELECTORS (Vote for candidates of one party for President and Vice President)

Choice	Party	Election Day Voting		By Mail Voting		Provisional Voting		Total	
Joseph R. BIDEN Kamala D. HARRIS	DEM	156	38.52%	122	68.54%	13	76.47%	291	48.50%
Donald J. TRUMP Michael R. PENCE	REP	246	60.74%	56	31.46%	4	23.53%	306	51.00%
Jo JORGENSEN Jeremy Spike COHEN	LIB	3	0.74%	0	0.00%	0	0.00%	3	0.50%
Cast Votes:		405	100.00%	178	100.00%	17	100.00%	600	100.00%
Unresolved Write-in Votes:		0		0		0		0	

ATTORNEY GENERAL (Vote for One)

Choice	Party	Election Day Voting		By Mail Voting		Provisional Voting		Total	
Josh SHAPIRO	DEM	156	38.52%	119	66.85%	11	68.75%	286	47.75%
Heather HEIDELBAUGH	REP	238	58.77%	53	29.78%	5	31.25%	296	49.42%
Daniel WASSMER	LIB	7	1.73%	2	1.12%	0	0.00%	9	1.50%
Richard L. WEISS	GRN	4	0.99%	4	2.25%	0	0.00%	8	1.34%
Cast Votes:		405	100.00%	178	100.00%	16	100.00%	599	100.00%
Unresolved Write-in Votes:		0		0		0		0	

Figure 104 - Official Results for Glenholden 1P Part 1

AUDITOR GENERAL (Vote for One)

Choice	Party	Election Day Voting		By Mail Voting		Provisional Voting			Total	
Nina AHMAD	DEM	145	35.98%	108	61.36%	12	75.00%		265	44.54%
Timothy DEFOOR	REP	239	59.31%	60	34.09%	4	25.00%		303	50.92%
Jennifer MOORE	LIB	14	3.47%	3	1.70%	0	0.00%		17	2.86%
Olivia FAISON	GRN	5	1.24%	5	2.84%	0	0.00%		10	1.68%
	Cast Votes:	403	100.00%	176	100.00%	16	100.00%		595	100.00%
	Unresolved Write-in Votes:	0		0		0			0	

STATE TREASURER (Vote for One)

Choice	Party	Election Day Voting		By Mail Voting		Provisional Voting			Total	
Joe TORSELLA	DEM	149	36.88%	109	61.93%	11	68.75%		269	45.13%
Stacy L. GARRITY	REP	246	60.89%	62	35.23%	5	31.25%		313	52.52%
Joe SOLOSKI	LIB	9	2.23%	0	0.00%	0	0.00%		9	1.51%
Timothy RUNKLE	GRN	0	0.00%	5	2.84%	0	0.00%		5	0.84%
	Cast Votes:	404	100.00%	176	100.00%	16	100.00%		596	100.00%
	Unresolved Write-in Votes:	0		0		0			0	

Figure 105 - Official Results for Glenholden 1P Part 2

REPRESENTATIVE IN CONGRESS 5TH DISTRICT (Vote for One)

Choice	Party	Election Day Voting		By Mail Voting		Provisional Voting			Total	
Mary Gay SCANLON	DEM	174	43.07%	124	69.66%	11	68.75%		309	51.67%
Dasha PRUETT	REP	230	56.93%	54	30.34%	5	31.25%		289	48.33%
	Cast Votes:	404	100.00%	178	100.00%	16	100.00%		598	100.00%
	Unresolved Write-in Votes:	0		0		0			0	

REPRESENTATIVE IN THE GENERAL ASSEMBLY 162ND DISTRICT (Vote for One)

Choice	Party	Election Day Voting		By Mail Voting		Provisional Voting			Total	
Dave DELLOSO	DEM	150	37.31%	122	68.93%	10	66.67%		282	47.47%
Pete GAGLIO	REP	252	62.69%	55	31.07%	5	33.33%		312	52.53%
	Cast Votes:	402	100.00%	177	100.00%	15	100.00%		594	100.00%
	Unresolved Write-in Votes:	2		0		0			2	

Figure 106 - Official Results for Glenholden 1P Part 3

369

GLENOLDEN 2P

PRESIDENTIAL ELECTORS (Vote for candidates of one party for President and Vice President)	
Joseph R. BIDEN Kamala D. HARRIS	0
Donald J. TRUMP Michael R. PENCE	0
Jo JORGENSEN Jeremy Spike COHEN	0
Write-ins	0
Undervotes	0
Overvotes	0

ATTORNEY GENERAL (Vote for One)	
Josh SHAPIRO	0
Heather HEIDELBAUGH	0
Daniel WASSMER	0
Richard L. WEISS	0
Write-ins	0
Undervotes	0
Overvotes	0

AUDITOR GENERAL (Vote for One)	
Nina AHMAD	0
Timothy DEFOOR	0
Jennifer MOORE	0
Olivia FAISON	0
Write-ins	0
Undervotes	0
Overvotes	0

STATE TREASURER (Vote for One)	
Joe TORSELLA	0
Stacy L. GARRITY	0
Joe SOLOSKI	0
Timothy RUNKLE	0
Write-ins	0
Undervotes	0
Overvotes	0

Figure 107 - Exhibit R; Delaware County PA Glenholden 2P

The Tape (Proof Sheet) for Glenholden 2P shows ZERO cast votes. Yet in the official count, we see 391 ballots reported in the official, certified vote, out of 483 registered voters, an 81% turn out, and a 57% to 42% Biden "win" over President Trump, and a flip from 264 Election Day CAST ballots and a 53% to 45% margin that had President Trump beating Biden.

These numbers are merely illustrative, because in fact they are made up out of air, and a complete fugazi produced by Ziegelhoffer and Gallagher, by their own admissions, and as supported by the wildly incongruent results between the tapes (proof sheets), election day return sheets that were fabricated well after the election, and the "official" certified count.

So, where did the "official" count come from, and why in most cases are the amount of CAST ballots so much higher than the fabricated return sheets?

Precinct Results Report

DELAWARE COUNTY, PENNSYLVANIA

GENERAL ELECTION

11/3/2020

Election Day		
Run Time	1022 AM	
Run Date	02/25/2021	

Official Results

Registered Voters
330150 of 425461 = 77.60%

Precincts Reporting
428 of 428 = 100.00%

GLENOLDEN 2P

391 of 483 registered voters = 80.95%

PRESIDENTIAL ELECTORS (Vote for candidates of one party for President and Vice President)

Choice	Party	Election Day Voting		By Mail Voting		Provisional Voting		Total	
Joseph R. BIDEN Kamala D. HARRIS	DEM	120	45.45%	99	83.90%	3	37.50%	222	56.92%
Donald J. TRUMP Michael R. PENCE	REP	141	53.41%	16	13.56%	5	62.50%	162	41.54%
Jo JORGENSEN Jeremy Spike COHEN	LIB	3	1.14%	3	2.54%	0	0.00%	6	1.54%
Cast Votes:		264	100.00%	118	100.00%	8	100.00%	390	100.00%
Unresolved Write-in Votes:		0		1		0		1	

ATTORNEY GENERAL (Vote for One)

Choice	Party	Election Day Voting		By Mail Voting		Provisional Voting		Total	
Josh SHAPIRO	DEM	119	45.59%	90	77.59%	4	50.00%	213	55.32%
Heather HEIDELBAUGH	REP	130	49.81%	17	14.66%	4	50.00%	151	39.22%
Daniel WASSMER	LIB	9	3.45%	7	6.03%	0	0.00%	16	4.16%
Richard L. WEISS	GRN	3	1.15%	2	1.72%	0	0.00%	5	1.30%
Cast Votes:		261	100.00%	116	100.00%	8	100.00%	385	100.00%
Unresolved Write-in Votes:		0		0		0		0	

Figure 108 - Official Results for Glenholden 2P

The "election day" ballots are collected on the voting machine vDrives, which were supposed to be brought to the Wharf Counting Center on the eve of the election in the sealed ballot bags so Poll Watchers can see them opened and verify the Chain of Custody.

Instead, hundreds of loose vDrives showed up in a large Tupperware plastic tub to be shoved into the voting tabulation machines, up until approximately 1:00AM, when the voting was stopped by the Delaware County Solicitor, William Martin, and his appointed outside counsel for the Board of Elections, Manly Parks, from the Philadelphia law firm Duane Morris, and the observers were directed to leave the building.

Leah and I were informed from multiple sources that a large number of the vDrives were not accounted for at the Government Center where the ballot bags were disassembled before the vDrives, Proof Sheets (tapes) and Return Sheets were transported to the Wharf Counting Center in the aforementioned Tupperware tubs. The preliminary list we were provided showed 47 missing vDrive sticks listed by precincts by Bureau of Election officials.

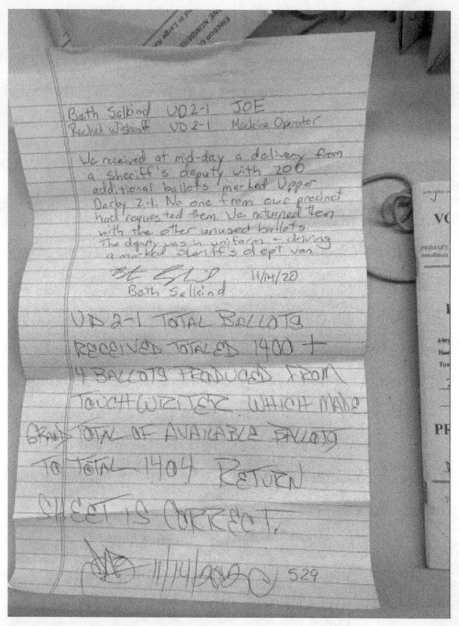

Figure 109 - Exhibit S, Return Sheet Notes Retrieved from Trash

Ziegelhoffer disclosed to the Whistleblower that the Return Sheets from the November 3, 2020, election contained various notes written on the front and back of the sheets detailing missing election evidence needed to reconcile the November 3, 2020, election.

The Whistleblower observed numerous Delaware County employees, including Gallagher and Ziegelhoffer destroying election data/evidence. The whistleblower was able to retrieve a note from the trash regarding Upper Darby 2. The note written on a yellow piece of paper, stated that additional and unrequested ballots were delivered to the precinct by a Sheriff. [Exhibit S]

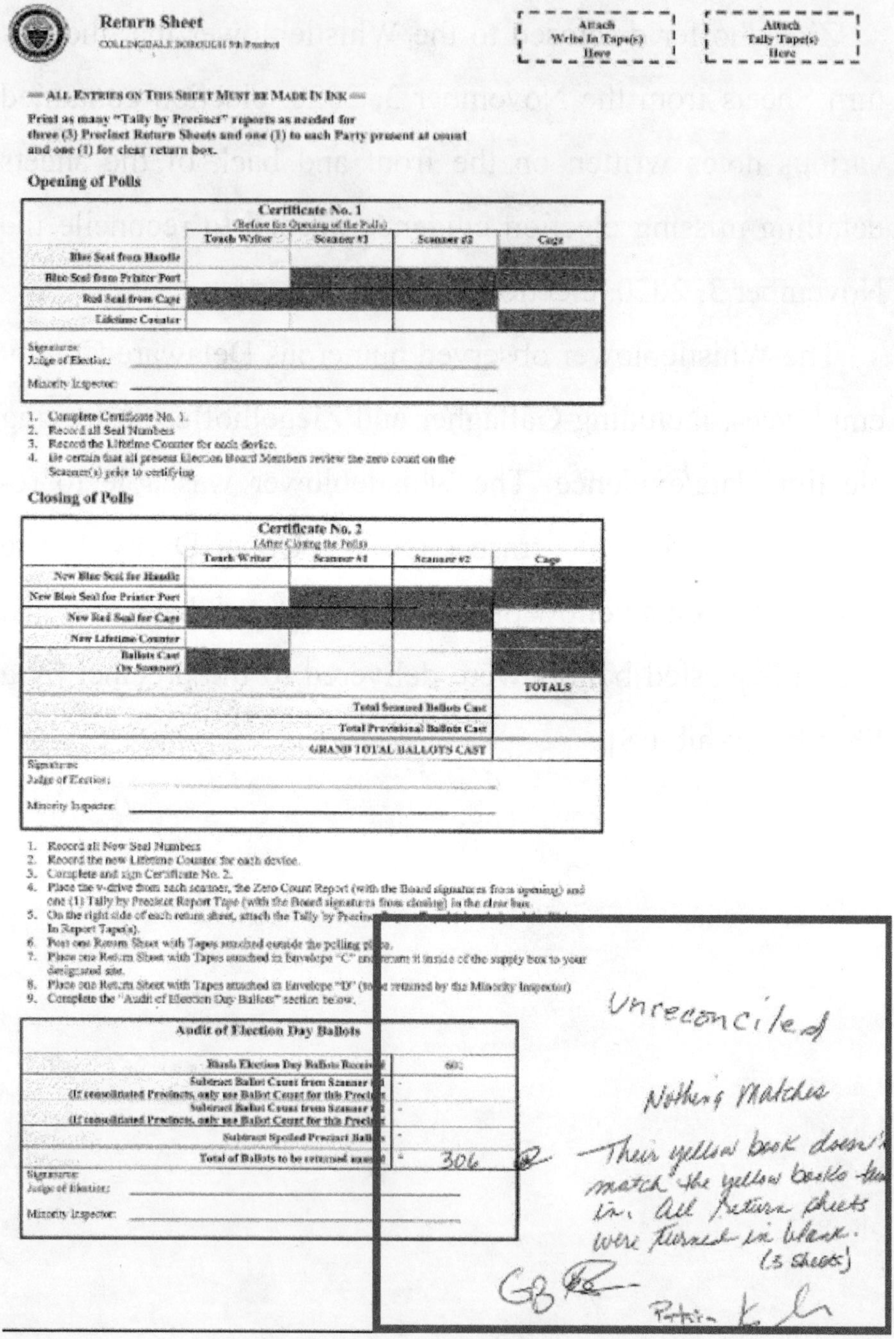

Return Sheet
COLLINGDALE BOROUGH 5th Precinct

┌ ─ ─ ─ ─ ─ ┐ ┌ ─ ─ ─ ─ ─ ┐
│ Attach   │ │ Attach   │
│ Write In Tape(s) │ │ Tally Tape(s) │
│ Here   │ │ Here   │
└ ─ ─ ─ ─ ─ ┘ └ ─ ─ ─ ─ ─ ┘

═══ ALL ENTRIES ON THIS SHEET MUST BE MADE IN INK ═══

Print as many "Tally by Precinct" reports as needed for
three (3) Precinct Return Sheets and one (1) to each Party present at count
and one (1) for clear return box.

Opening of Polls

	Touch Writer	Scanner #1	Scanner #2	Cage
Certificate No. 1 (Before the Opening of the Polls)				
Blue Seal from Handle				
Blue Seal from Printer Port				
Red Seal from Cage				
Lifetime Counter				

Signature:
Judge of Election: _____

Minority Inspector: _____

1. Complete Certificate No. 1.
2. Record all Seal Numbers
3. Record the Lifetime Counter for each device.
4. Be certain that all present Election Board Members review the zero count on the Scanner(s) prior to certifying

Closing of Polls

	Touch Writer	Scanner #1	Scanner #2	Cage
Certificate No. 2 (After Closing the Polls)				
New Blue Seal for Handle				
New Blue Seal for Printer Port				
New Red Seal for Cage				
New Lifetime Counter				
Ballots Cast (by Scanner)				
				TOTALS
Total Scanned Ballots Cast				
Total Provisional Ballots Cast				
GRAND TOTAL BALLOTS CAST				

Signature:
Judge of Election: _____

Minority Inspector: _____

1. Record all New Seal Numbers
2. Record the new Lifetime Counter for each device.
3. Complete and sign Certificate No. 2.
4. Place the v-drive from each scanner, the Zero Count Report (with the Board signatures from opening) and one (1) Tally by Precinct Report Tape (with the Board signatures from closing) in the clear box.
5. On the right side of each return sheet, attach the Tally by Precinct ⬚⬚⬚⬚⬚ In Report Tape(s).
6. Post one Return Sheet with Tapes attached outside the polling place.
7. Place one Return Sheet with Tapes attached in Envelope "C" on ⬚⬚⬚⬚ it inside of the supply box to your designated site.
8. Place one Return Sheet with Tapes attached in Envelope "D" (to be returned by the Minority Inspector)
9. Complete the "Audit of Election Day Ballots" section below.

Audit of Election Day Ballots	
Blank Election Day Ballots Received	601
Subtract Ballot Count from Scanner #1 (If consolidated Precincts, only use Ballot Count for this Precinct)	-
Subtract Ballot Count from Scanner #2 (If consolidated Precincts, only use Ballot Count for this Precinct)	-
Subtract Spoiled Precinct Ballots	
Total of Ballots to be returned unused	306

Signature:
Judge of Election: _____

Minority Inspector: _____

(handwritten annotations):
Unreconciled

Nothing matches

Their yellow book doesn't match the yellow books they're in. All return sheets were turned in blank. (3 sheets)

Figure 110 - Exhibit T –Return Sheet Collingdale 5P

The Return Sheet from Collingdale 5th Precinct contained a note which stated that the election data did not match, and the ballots were not requested. The Right to Know Request specifically asked for all notes front, back, and attached, on and to return sheets. Delaware County employees, including but not limited to Ziegelhoffer, Savage, Gallagher, and Allen, obscured, secreted, hid, and destroyed notes, both attached to, and written on, return sheets. [Exhibit T]

Precinct Results Report

Election Day

Run Time 10:22 AM
Run Date 02/25/2021

DELAWARE COUNTY, PENNSYLVANIA

GENERAL ELECTION

11/3/2020

Official Results

Registered Voters
330150 of 425461 = 77.60%

Precincts Reporting
428 of 428 = 100.00%

COLLINGDALE 5P

434 of 695 registered voters = 62.45%

PRESIDENTIAL ELECTORS (Vote for candidates of one party for President and Vice President)

Choice	Party	Election Day Voting		By Mail Voting		Provisional Voting		Total	
Joseph R. BIDEN Kamala D. HARRIS	DEM	143	59.34%	149	81.87%	9	90.00%	301	69.52%
Donald J. TRUMP Michael R. PENCE	REP	95	39.42%	33	18.13%	1	10.00%	129	29.79%
Jo JORGENSEN Jeremy Spike COHEN	LIB	3	1.24%	0	0.00%	0	0.00%	3	0.69%
Cast Votes:		241	100.00%	182	100.00%	10	100.00%	433	100.00%
Unresolved Write-in Votes:		1		0		0		1	

ATTORNEY GENERAL (Vote for One)

Choice	Party	Election Day Voting		By Mail Voting		Provisional Voting		Total	
Josh SHAPIRO	DEM	142	59.41%	154	84.62%	7	87.50%	303	70.63%
Heather HEIDELBAUGH	REP	89	37.24%	28	15.33%	0	0.00%	117	27.27%
Daniel WASSMER	LIB	3	1.26%	0	0.00%	1	12.50%	4	0.93%
Richard L. WEISS	GRN	5	2.09%	0	0.00%	0	0.00%	5	1.17%
Cast Votes:		239	100.00%	182	100.00%	8	100.00%	429	100.00%
Unresolved Write-in Votes:		1		0		0		1	

Figure 111 - Official Results Collingdale 5P

Figure 112 - Exhibit U 1, Boxes of Hidden Evidence

Notes were written on the return sheets, some notes were obscured, some not copied, and some appended or attached notes were not produced. Evidence reflects that the production in response to the right to know request was inaccurate and demonstrates deletion, alteration, manipulation, and in some cases outright destruction of the requested information.

On or about June 3, 2021, Ziegelhoffer discussed and conspired with Defendant, Attorney Thomas Gallagher, as to how to fulfill and respond to the May 21, 2021, Right to Know Request and worked in unison sorting through November 3, 2020, election data, tapes, and return sheets and conspired as to how they would fulfill and respond.

The pair tried to create a Right to Know Response that was consistent with the November 3, 2020, reported election results for Delaware County and hide or mask the fraud and election law violations committed in Delaware County by election official for the November 3, 2020, election.

Specifically, Gallagher and Ziegelhoffer destroyed November 3, 2020, election data to hide, secrete, obscure, and prevent discovery of election fraud, irregularities, or unreconcilable precinct results from the November 3, 2020, election.

Ziegelhoffer presented a large cardboard box marked "miscellaneous tapes" and reminded Gallagher that the tapes in the box marked "miscellaneous tapes" pertained to the precincts that were called in for interviews before the Delaware County Return Board. [Exhibit U].

Figure 113 - Exhibit U 2, Hidden Proof Sheets (scanner tapes)

SELECTED VIDEOS

In addition to video exhibits in case links, the annotated and subtitled videos below provide corroboration of evidence. https://cloud.patriot.online/s/So2eyPBddsJzwoE?

- Audit Video Clip HD.mp4

- Destroying Video Clip HD.mp4

- Felony Video Clip HD.mp4

- Election Fraud 2020 Delaware County Investigation HD Version for Meda.mp4

16

APPENDIX B: FOIA AND RTK RECOMMENDATIONS

The Freedom of Information Act (FOIA) is a federal law that gives the public the right to make requests for federal agency records. Agencies may withhold information according to nine exemptions contained in the statute. <u>The FOIA applies only to federal agencies</u>. It does not apply to records held by Congress, the courts, or by state or local government agencies. Each state has its own public access laws that should be consulted for access to state and local records.

- I request the final certified return sheets from the November 3, 2020, general election.

- There is one return sheet from every____(precinct, ward, parish, etc.)___ in ___(name of your County) ____County.

- Each return sheet includes the paper tapes (otherwise known as "Proof Sheets") from all the voting machines used in each ____(precinct, ward, parish, etc.)____, and these paper tapes ("proof sheets) are also requested.

- If there are any additional notes written on the back of the return sheet, as well as any attached noted that are related to each return sheet.

- I request all certified return sheets from all from all of Delaware County.

- Request access and a copy of all documents

- I want a paper copy of the documents

- I want an electronic copy of all documents if available

17

APPENDIX C: REQUESTING EMAILS

When requesting emails in FOIA or equivalent State Acts like Pennsylvania's Right To Know (RTK), it is important to request electronic copies and specifically request that message headers are included.

A message header of an email contains its pedigree, and all information required to determine if all other associated emails have been included in response to my RTK FOIA request.

As an example, please examine the full email message headers below from a sample email thread sent, and responded to, between parties:

EMAIL HEADER 1 EXAMPLE (SENT)

Return-Path: <XXXX@XXXX.com>

Delivered-To: <XXXX@XXXX.gov>

Received: from atl4dovecotp02pod7 ([10.30.34.254])

by atl4dovecot09pod7.mgt.hosting.qts.netsol.com with
LMTP id KAvUB2ohzGCRpgAAG8TFow

for < XXXX@XXXX.com >; Fri, 18 Jun 2021
00:30:34 -0400

Received: from atl4dcmail02pod7.mgt.hosting.qts.
netsol.com ([10.30.34.254])

by atl4dovecotp02pod7 with LMTP id yBXAB2ohzG-
BAmwAAxaz/ig

; Fri, 18 Jun 2021 00:30:34 -0400

Received: from atl4mhib06.registeredsite.com (atl4m-
hib06.myregisteredsite.com [209.17.115.141])

by atl4dcmail02pod7.mgt.hosting.qts.netsol.com (Post-
fix) with ESMTP id 0B13E300989A0

for < XXXX@XXXX.com>; Fri, 18 Jun 2021
00:30:34 -0400 (EDT)

Received: from innernet.net (outbound.innernet.net
[206.251.24.105])

by atl4mhib06.registeredsite.com (8.14.4/8.14.4) with
ESMTP id 15I4UWYF014484

for < XXXX@XXXX.com >; Fri, 18 Jun 2021
00:30:33 -0400

Received: from [192.168.2.113] (unverified
[192.173.186.220]) by EMAIL2.inet.local

(Vircom SMTPRS 6.5.33.22837/7170.7.4.) with ES-
MTP id <C0526698372@EMAIL2.inet.local> for <
XXXX@XXXX.com >;

Fri, 18 Jun 2021 00:30:29 -0400

X-Modus-ReverseDNS: Error=0x0000232A

X-Modus-BlackList: 192.173.186.220=OK; XXXX@
XXXX.com =OK

X-Modus-RBL: 192.173.186.220=OK

X-Modus-Trusted: 192.173.186.220=NO

X-Modus-Spam-Version: 6.5.33.22837/7170.7.4.

X-Modus-Audit: FALSE;0;0;0

To: XXXX@XXXX.com

From: < XXXX@XXXX.gov>

Subject: items sent?

Message-ID: <1471f829-5f0b-6be1-89d2-8116bbbf-
b50c@innernet.net>

Date: Fri, 18 Jun 2021 00:30:20 -0400

User-Agent: Mozilla/5.0 (Windows NT 10.0; Win64; x64; rv:78.0) Gecko/20100101

Thunderbird/78.11.0

MIME-Version: 1.0

Content-Type: text/html; charset=utf-8

Content-Language: en-US

Content-Transfer-Encoding: 8bit

X-SpamScore: 2.101

X-MailHub-Apparently-To: XXXX@XXXX.com

Jun 18 11:01am

EMAIL HEADER 2 EXAMPLE (RESPONSE)

Jun 18 11:03am

Return-Receipt-To: < XXXX@XXXX.com >

From: < XXXX@XXXX.com>

To: < XXXX@XXXX.gov>

Cc: < XXXX@XXXX.com >

References: <1471f829-5f0b-6be1-89d2-8116bbbf-b50c@innernet.net>

In-Reply-To: <1471f829-5f0b-6be1-89d2-8116bbbf-b50c@innernet.net>

Subject: RE: items sent?

Date: Fri, 18 Jun 2021 10:33:28 -0400

Organization: XXXX

Message-ID:
<!&!AAAAAAAAAAuAAAAAAAAAJ7SK-dvCHqZBoesxfRGxshUBAMO2jhD3dRHOt-M0AqgC7tuYAAAAAAA4AABAAAAB/NEvLz-tCPTpX/nb0gdMzKAQAAAAA=@XXXX.com>

MIME-Version: 1.0

Content-Type: multipart/mixed;

boundary="----=_NextPart_000_0CE3_01D7642D.673B89A0"

X-Mailer: Microsoft Outlook 16.0

Thread-Index: AQK35gswg1MoSC43wym8eovE9T-nerAHJ0WCp

Content-Language: en-us

Disposition-Notification-To: < XXXX@XXXX.com >

Jun 18 11:03am

Note the Reference to the original message: 1471f829-5f0b-6be1-89d2-8116bbbfb50c@innernet.net   Jun   18 11:04am. This is a unique ID that is difficult to modify and obfuscate in bulk. If there is a reference to an email that is not provided in response to a FOIA or RTK request, noncompliance will be apparent during review.

18

APPENDIX D: DELAWARE COUNTY LITIGATION HOLD

*B*elow *is the body of the litigation hold demand sub-mitted to the Delaware County, PA BOE. They responded on November 18th, 2021, the same day of our first appeal before the Commonwealth Court of Pennsylvania that all evidence specified had been retained. This was after they were already aware that they had, wantonly destroyed much of the evidence required by law to be maintained and demanded in the litigation hold.*

We hope that the Board of Elections has taken steps to preserve data since it had an obligation to preserve relevant evidence in connection with the 2020 General Election as required by the Pennsylvania Election Code and federal law.

No procedures should have been implemented to alter any active, deleted, or fragmented data.

Moreover, no electronic data should have been disposed of or destroyed.

We further trust that the Board of Elections will continue to preserve such electronic data, paper files and tangible items throughout this litigation.

Intervening Petitioners suspect that the paper mail-in and absentee ballots counted in this 2020 Election include illegal fraudulent ballots. Intervening Petitioners believe that an independent forensic examination will reveal that fraudulent ballots were counted which were not sent by registered voters of Delaware County in the 2020 General Election.

Hence, it is of the utmost importance that the Board of Elections not have destroyed or failed to preserve the actual ballots, <u>and the envelopes connected to those ballots</u>, which were counted in Delaware County.

There is a myriad of other physical evidence that the Board of Elections is obligated to preserve, including but not limited to:

- USB-vDrives

- Original return receipts prepared and attached to the bag containing USB-vDrives

- Internal voting machine drives, cartridges, and end receipts from each precinct of Delaware County.

- Voting machines and computers used to tabulate and count the votes.

- Event logs showing when the USB-vDrives were inserted into computers used to tabulate and count the votes.

- Security footage from any video surveillance at the Wharf Office Building of the Board of Elections in Chester, Pennsylvania. This video footage should not be altered in any way, to remove any time and/or date stamp on the video surveillance footage.

This request for evidence preservation includes all of the above and more - the Board of Elections is required by the Pennsylvania Election Code to preserve everything, without limitation, connected with the 2020 General Election.

19

APPENDIX E: HAVA STATEMENT OF COMPLAINT

(FOR OFFICIAL USE ONLY)

COMMONWEALTH OF PENNSYLVANIA
DEPARTMENT OF STATE
Harrisburg

STATEMENT OF COMPLAINT – VIOLATIONS OF TITLE III
OF THE HELP AMERICA VOTE ACT OF 2002
(PUBLIC LAW 107-252, 42 U.S.C. § 15301 *ET SEQ.*)

Under section 402(a)(2) of the Help America Vote Act of 2002 (HAVA) (42 U.S.C. § 15512(a)(2)) and section 1206.2(a) of the Pennsylvania Election Code (25 P.S. § 3046.2(a)), any person who believes that a violation of any provision of Title III of HAVA (42 U.S.C. §§ 15481-15501) has occurred, is occurring, or is about to occur, may file a complaint with the Department of State, Bureau of Commissions, Elections and Legislation. Complaints made against a local or county official or employee will be processed and considered by the Department of State under section 1206.2(b) of the Election Code (25 P.S. § 3046.2(b)). Complaints made against the Department of State will be processed and considered by the Commonwealth's Office of General Counsel under section 1206.2(c) of the Election Code (25 P.S. § 3046.2(c)).

In order for the Department of State or the Office of General Counsel to initiate complaint proceedings under section 402(a) of HAVA and section 1206.2 of the Election Code to consider possible violations of Title III of HAVA, a complainant must complete all applicable parts of this complaint form. Complaints should be typewritten or clearly printed in black or blue ink. Please state the facts briefly and clearly, and be sure to submit any documents you have to support your complaint.

YOU MUST SIGN THIS FORM, COMPLETE THE PRESCRIBED AFFIDAVIT BEFORE A LICENSED NOTARY PUBLIC OR OTHER PERSONS AUTHORIZED UNDER PENNSYLVANIA LAW TO ADMINISTER OATHS, AND RETURN THE FORM, *WITH TWO COPIES*, TO THE DEPARTMENT OF STATE, BUREAU OF COMMISSIONS, ELECTIONS AND LEGISLATION, 210 North Office Building, Harrisburg, PA 17120.

THIS FORM MUST BE SIGNED UNDER OATH, NOTARIZED, AND FILLED OUT COMPLETELY IN ORDER TO BE PROCESSED. TO ASSURE PROMPT PROCESSING OF THE COMPLAINT, PLEASE FILE THE ORIGINAL AND *TWO COPIES* OF THE COMPLAINT WITH THE BUREAU OF COMMISSIONS, ELECTIONS AND LEGISLATION

TYPE OF COMPLAINT (PLEASE CHECK ONE):

☐ ALLEGATIONS MADE AGAINST COUNTY OR LOCAL OFFICIAL (S) OR EMPLOYEE (S)

☐ ALLEGATIONS MADE AGAINST THE DEPARTMENT OF STATE

A. COMPLAINT INFORMATION

LAST NAME	FIRST NAME	MIDDLE INITIAL
STREET ADDRESS (Number and Name)		
CITY	COUNTY	STATE	ZIP CODE
TEL. (Include Area Code) (HOME)	(WORK)	

B. COMPLAINANT'S ATTORNEY, IF ANY

LAST NAME	FIRST NAME	MIDDLE INTIAL
STREET ADDRESS (Number and Name)		
CITY	COUNTY	STATE	ZIP CODE
TEL. (Include Area Code)	FIRM NAME	

C. NAME AND ADDRESS OF WITNESS, IF ANY

LAST NAME	FIRST NAME	MIDDLE INITIAL
STREET ADDRESS (Number and Name)		
CITY	COUNTY	STATE	ZIP CODE
TEL. (Include Area Code)	If needed, is this witness willing to support your complaint by appearing at a hearing? ☐YES ☐NO

D. NAME AND ADDRESS OF SECOND WITNESS, IF ANY

LAST NAME	FIRST NAME	MIDDLE INTIAL
STREET ADDRESS (Number and Name)		
CITY	COUNTY	STATE	ZIP CODE
TEL. (Include Area Code)	If needed, is this witness willing to support your complaint by appearing at a hearing? ☐YES ☐NO

NOTE: If additional witnesses are available, list names, addresses, and other pertinent data in a manner similar to above on 8½" x 11" paper.

Figure 114 - HAVA Statement of Complaint - Violation Title III

INFORMATION REGARDING SUBJECT OF COMPLAINT

E. ENTITY INVOLVED (E.G., DEPARTMENT OF STATE, COUNTY BOARD OF ELECTIONS

LAST NAME	FIRST NAME	MIDDLE INITIAL
STREET ADDRESS (Number and Name)		
CITY	COUNTY	STATE	ZIP CODE
TEL. (Include Area Code)	PROPRIETOR	

F. INDIVIDUAL INVOLVED, IF ANY

LAST NAME	FIRST NAME	MIDDLE INITIAL
STREET ADDRESS (Number and Name)		
CITY	COUNTY	STATE	ZIP CODE
TEL. (Include Area Code)	LICENSE, REGISTRATION, CERTIFICATION, COMMISSION TYPE AND NUMBER IF KNOWN

G. DESCRIPTION OF COMPLAINT:

Please describe your complaint in detail below. Please describe the nature and circumstances of the violation(s) of Title III of the Help America Vote Act of 2002 that you allege has occurred, is occurring, or is about to occur. Please provide dates. *Attach copies of documents that are related to your complaint.* If you need more space, please continue on page __ of this form and/or use additional 8 ½ x 11" sheets of paper if necessary.

A. RESOLUTION

How would you like this complaint to be resolved?

If additional space is needed, please attach 8 ½ x 11" sheets.

HAVA-T3CF   2

B. AFFIDAVIT OF COMPLAINANT

I, _____, having been duly sworn according to law, state under penalty of perjury that the facts stated in this Complaint are true and correct to the best of my knowledge, information and belief.

_____
Complainant Signature

SWORN AND SUBSCRIBED BEFORE ME THIS

_____ DAY OF _____, _____, at

_____, Pennsylvania

_____
Notary Public

My commission expires _____

RETURN COMPLETED FORM,
WITH TWO COPIES, TO:

Department of State
Bureau of Commissions, Elections and Legislation
210 North Office Building
Harrisburg, PA 17120
(717) 787-5280

20

APPENDIX F: CASE LINKS AND MEDIA LINKS

The dockets for the cases associated with the Delaware County 2020 General Election that Leah Hoopes and Gregory Stenstrom engaged in are listed in County Dockets in original form but can be cryptic to the lay reader.

We have consolidated (and will continue to update) the filings on Patriot.Online and on associated websites.

- CV-2022-000032 Moton, Hoopes, Stenstrom vs Boockvar, Kathy et al (Jan 2022)

  https://cloud.patriot.online/s/PyGcBrtoMcQDqSQ

- Case ID: 211002495 Savage vs Trump, Giuliani, Ellis, Stenstrom, Hoopes, Kline, et al. (Oct 2021) https://cloud.patriot.online/s/3r5x6iC35H96ZPM

- CV-2020-007523 Pruett, Hoopes, Stenstrom vs Delaware County Board of Elections (Dec 2020) https://cloud.patriot.online/s/qyYfPZTHDJ5N9gR

- **Delaware County, PA Election Fraud Resource Page** https://www.patriot.online/election_resources.html

- **Patriot.Online** https://www.Patriot.Online

TABLE OF FIGURES

INDEX

CPSIA information can be obtained
at www.ICGtesting.com
Printed in the USA
BVHW040617220223
658536BV00005B/30/J

9 781958 682289